GREG DAVENPORT'S

Advanced
Outdoor Navigation

GREG DAVENPORT'S

Advanced Outdoor Navigation

BASICS AND BEYOND

FALCONGUIDE®

GUILFORD, CONNECTICUT
HELENA, MONTANA

AN IMPRINT OF THE GLOBE PEQUOT PRESS

Library of Congress Cataloging-in-Publication Data
Davenport, Gregory J.
    Greg Davenport's advanced outdoor navigation: basics and beyond/
    Greg Davenport. —1st ed.
        p. cm.
    Includes index.
    ISBN 0-7627-3706-9
    1. Orienteering—Equipment and supplies. 2. Navigation—Equipment and supplies. 3. Outdoor recreation—Equipment and supplies. I. Title.
GV200.4.D38 2006
796.58—dc22

                                                    2005023211

Manufactured in the United States of America
First Edition/First Printing

To buy books in quantity for corporate use
or incentives, call **(800) 962–0973, ext. 4551,**
or e-mail **premiums@GlobePequot.com.**

When was the last time you listened to the thunder of a running brook or watched a deer cross your path? How long has it been since you enjoyed the whistling wind or the melody of singing birds? When was the last time you took a hike? If you can't remember such things, this book is dedicated to you! It's time for you to get up and experience what you're missing. I am hopeful this book will be the catalyst that allows you to *enjoy nature with confidence!*

Contents

SECTION I

Preparing for the Backcountry

The backcountry calls to something in all of us. From arid desert to steaming jungle, from snow-covered mountain peaks and glaciers to raging rivers and tortuous coastlines, the backcountry offers escape from everyday life into a worldwide playground. But as any kid who has fallen off the slide or jungle gym knows, the playground can be a dangerous place. Planning for the best—but being prepared for the worst—can help ensure that your backcountry trek is everything you want it to be. Modern navigation equipment can help guide you safely through the wilderness, but even the best equipment can fail, and a fall or other injury could prevent you from traveling until rescue arrives. Preparation is the key to safe backcountry travel—so *know before you go.* This section provides some important background on the history of navigation, the purpose of this book, and the techniques and skills you'll need to survive in the wilderness.

CHAPTER 1

Introduction & History of Navigation

The ability to use primitive and modern tools of navigation is key to a safe trip into the backcountry.

In 2001 a search-and-rescue team performed a successful mission—finding the injured and lost subject and directing the United States Coast Guard (USCG) to the pickup point. The team of ten volunteers, who had used a Global Positioning System (GPS) receiver to navigate in, felt great pride as the helicopter turned and left the location. Imagine how quickly their pride and sense of safety vanished when the GPS batteries went dead. The team had made a potentially fatal error. Not one member knew enough about using a map and compass to navigate back to safety. They swallowed their pride and radioed the Coast Guard rescue helicopter, asking for assistance. After a long wait the helicopter returned and hovered over their base camp—providing a sound vector that helped the team navigate out. This true story emphasizes the importance of basic navigation skills. Take the time to learn them *before* jumping to the wonderful world of technology.

Navigation Overview

Since early times, travelers have been trying to find ways of identifying locations and methods of getting from one location to another. Perhaps the process began by remembering landmarks and passing this information on to others. Over time someone probably used a crude map, drawn in the dirt, showing a village next to a shear cliff on the other side of a river or something similar. Early mariners used the coastline and stars to navigate. Polaris (the North Star) and constellations like Cassiopeia and Orion's Belt helped them stay on course.

Beyond the crude maps and constellations, the next milestone in navigation occurred with the introduction of the magnetic compass and the sextant. The compass's needle provided a northerly heading, and the sextant helped mariners determine their latitude. In 1761 the chronometer (shipboard timepiece) was developed, which lost or gained about a second a day (very accurate for the time). The chronometer allowed the sailor to predict longitude. The magnetic compass, sextant, and chronometer revolutionized navigation, providing both land travelers and mariners much-needed accuracy for long journeys away from coastlines and known locations. For centuries this was what travelers used.

In the early twentieth century several radio-based navigation systems were developed. High-frequency radio waves helped provide an accurate position but could only be picked up in a small, localized area. Low-frequency radio waves covered larger areas but proved much less accurate. Recognizing the shortcomings of these ground-based radio signals was the first step in the development of the Global Positioning System (GPS). The GPS uses high-frequency transmissions that allow satellites, base stations, and GPS receivers to pinpoint multiple locations over a large area.

Purpose of This Book

This book is designed to provide you with the tools you need to handle anything Mother Nature throws at you—and thoroughly enjoy yourself in the process.

The Wilderness Survival chapter provides the most essential tools—the ones that can help you find your way in unfamiliar territory or help you stay alive till others find you should things go wrong. After all, you might know how to use a map and compass—even have a functioning GPS receiver—but they won't keep you warm if you break a leg and have to wait till daybreak for rescue. Proper preparation for all treks includes reviewing your route, inventorying your gear, practicing your skills, and packing an emergency survival kit—whether you're heading deep into the backcountry or exploring your geographical backyard.

The following sections will help you build crucial skills and techniques. You'll become familiar with the most common types of maps and charts and learn how to read them; you'll learn how to determine your location and cardinal direction with a compass—and without one; and you'll learn how to use the heavens as your guide (just in case your batteries fail). Armed with these basics, you'll be ready to move from navigation to travel, including how to pack and carry a backpack, basic hiking techniques, and a six-point route-finding checklist—even navigation at night if you absolutely must.

For the more adventurous trekker, Section Five covers the specialized skills and techniques required to navigate the earth's rougher neighborhoods, including necessary safety gear, all about knots, and travel over rock surfaces as well as snow and ice. Care and use of a GPS receiver rounds out this volume. GPS is a valuable navigation tool—just make sure you know how to find your way without a unit should the need arise.

Navigation has come a long way. The skills used more than 200 years ago, however, are the same skills you need today. The purpose of this book is to review the basic and advanced navigations skills that promote safe wilderness journeys in both easy and rough terrain. As you read the text, pull out your map and compass and follow along. Take the time to perform the exercises at the end of each chapter. Most important, learn these skills BEFORE venturing into the unknown. Be prepared!

Wilderness Survival

Where does wilderness survival fit into a book on advanced navigation? Knowing what to do if something goes wrong is crucial—whether you're planning a short day hike in a local park or a backpacking venture of several days over rough, unfamiliar terrain. The following skills and techniques will make sure you're prepared for whatever comes your way.

Survival is based on three elements: knowledge, equipment, and how badly a person wants to stay alive. In a perfect world, these three elements are synergistic and build upon one another. In a world filled with unknowns, however, it's the "will to survive" that motivates people to triumph over what appears to be insurmountable odds.

Survival is a logical process. Although every survival situation is unique, a survivor's needs are the same, regardless of the climate, terrain, or the person's health. Understanding these needs—and meeting them in order of importance for the given situation—plays a crucial role in decreasing stress and increasing a survivor's odds of success. To help in this process, I have developed a simple three-step approach to global wilderness survival. The algorithm can be applied in all situations. In fact, the only thing that differs from one scenario to another is the order in which a survivor meets his or her needs and the methods used to meet them.

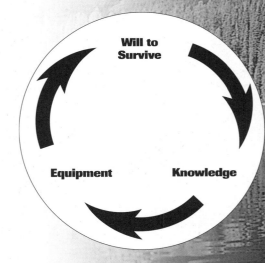

Three elements of survival.

The Three-Step Approach to Wilderness Survival

The three steps of survival are simple. If followed these steps will greatly increase your odds of success, regardless of your circumstances.

1. **Stop and recognize** the situation for what it is.

2. **Identify and prioritize** your five survival essentials for the situation you are in.

3. **Improvise** to meet your needs (using man-made and natural resources).

Greg Davenport's three-step approach to wilderness survival.

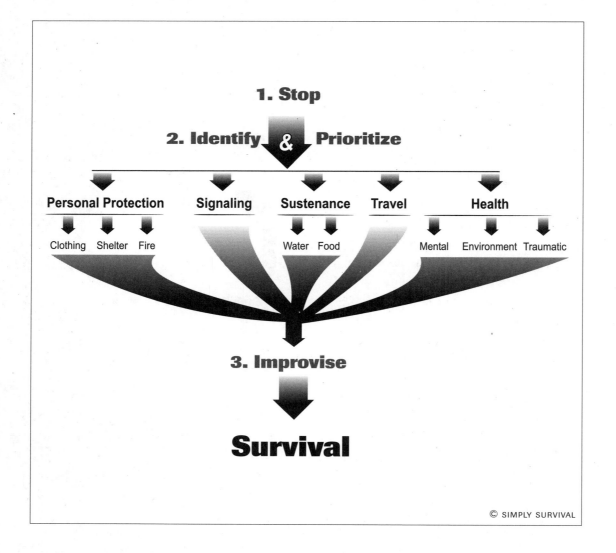

■ Step 1: Stop and Recognize the Situation for What It Is

Early recognition of your predicament is very important to survival and early rescue. It allows you time to meet your needs and keeps you close to the area of probable search-and-rescue attempts. Don't become the wandering lost soul who spends the day trying to find a familiar rock or tree. This common scenario often leads to a cold and frustrating night for both you and the search-and-rescue teams. You'll waste valuable time that could have been better spent building a shelter or putting out a signal.

■ Step 2: Identify and Prioritize Your Five Survival Essentials

Once you've recognized the situation for what it is, it's time to identify your five survival essentials and prioritize them in order of importance for your given situation (which item needs to be done first, second, third, etc.). The five survival essentials are:

1. Personal protection (clothing, shelter, fire)

2. Signaling (man-made and improvised)

3. Sustenance (identifying and procuring water and food)

4. Travel (with and without a map and compass)

5. Health (mental, traumatic, and environmental injuries)

Although these needs are a constant, your situation and the environment will dictate their exact order and the method used to meet them. To better understand the five survival essentials, each is explained in greater detail here (the order of explanation is not necessarily the order in which they will be met).

Survival Essential 1: Personal Protection (Clothing, Shelter, Fire)

Clothing, shelter, and fire are the three elements of personal protection. Each helps protect *you* from the effects of the prevailing climate. Clothing is your first line of personal protection, shelter the second, and fire the third. In most instances, they should be met in this order.

Clothing—the first line of personal protection. Give your clothes the same consideration as you would when selecting an emergency bivy bag. How well will they protect you from the elements in both good and bad times? Will they keep you warm or cool? Will they fend off wind and moisture? Will they allow enough ventilation to reduce wetness from sweat? To help me select and care for my clothes I use the **COLDER** acronym.

C— Keep them **CLEAN**. Dirty clothes lose the ability to insulate.

O— Avoid **OVERHEATING**. Wet clothes (from sweat) lose the ability to insulate.

L— Wear them **LOOSE** and **LAYERED**. Layered clothes allow you to remove and add layers as conditions and work load change. Think in terms of three layers.

- **Inner layer.** This layer wicks the moisture away from your skin (polyester and polypropylene are good materials for this). Don't use cotton, which loses almost all of its insulating quality when wet.
- **Middle layer.** This layer insulates (wool and fleece are two good insulating materials).
- **Outer layer.** This layer protects you from the wind and rain (Gore-Tex is an example of a good outer layer).

D— Keep **DRY**. Wet clothes (from rain, snow, streams, etc.) lose the ability to insulate.

E— **EXAMINE** clothes daily for damage.

R— **REPAIR** as necessary. After all, you don't have a dresser drawer full of clothes to change into.

Shelter—the second line of personal protection. Often people will spend the day trying to light a fire and won't even start thinking about a shelter until dusk has arrived. This can prove to be a fatal error. A well-constructed thermal shelter might take three hours to build, but it will provide you warmth throughout the night. On the flip side, gathering enough wood and maintaining a fire through a long, cold night is difficult. In addition, you'll need to spend the night awake in order to monitor and feed the insatiable flames. Instead, a good thermal shelter and enough wood to start a fire during the coldest hours of the morning will serve you much better. It can make the difference between a cold night out or a warm one.

The environment, available materials, and time will dictate which type of shelter you build. However, all should meet certain safety and construction criteria. Select a shelter site that is close to your construction

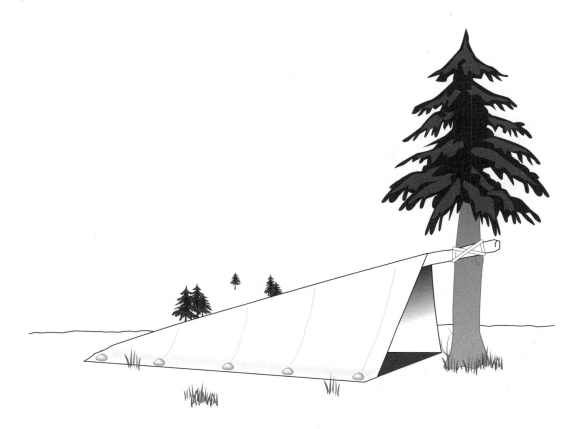

materials, signaling and recovery site, and water. Make sure it is large enough for both you and your equipment and is in an area free of potential safety hazards, including avalanche slopes, dry riverbeds, unstable rock formations, animal trails, and dead trees and upper branches that might fall. Basic shelter designs should incorporate a shingled roof (bottom to top) with an angle of 45 to 60 degrees and, if enclosed, a ventilation hole. Thermal shelters need a roof that is at least 8 inches deep. Snow shelters should only be used when the inside temperatures can be kept below thirty-two degrees Fahrenheit. In higher temperatures the snow will melt, you'll get wet, and your chances of hypothermia will greatly increase.

Shelter is the second line of personal protection.

Fire—the third line of personal protection. In most survival scenarios if you take care of your clothing and build an appropriate shelter, a fire is not necessary. However, a fire can provide many benefits, including a heat source for purifying water, cooking, and warding off hypothermia; a smoke signal by day and fire signal by night; and a light that allows you to work when it is dark. Building a fire requires a successful combination of heat, oxygen, and fuel. All three must be present for the fire's success.

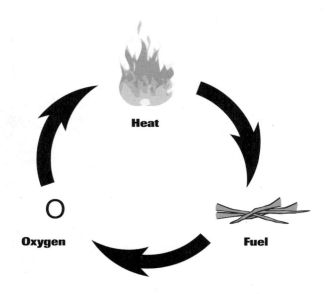

The fire triad.

- **Heat—required to start the fire.** Heat source options include matches, lighters, and artificial flint (sparker). NATO-issued survival matches and lighters like the Colibri Quantum are ideal for wet and windy conditions. Matches and lighters, however, eventually run out and often fail when you need them most. An artificial flint, on the other hand, will virtually never run out and in experienced hands (practice, practice, practice) will rarely fail. Commercial sparkers like the S.O.S Strike Force or the BlastMatch are great options.

- **Oxygen—needed for fuel to burn.** Without oxygen you will not be able to light a fire or sustain one that is burning. When starting a fire, using a platform and brace will allow oxygen to circulate around and through the tinder and kindling (covered below). A platform is any dry material (bark, green branches, or rocks not from a riverbed) that keeps the tinder off the ground. A brace might be a wrist-diameter branch or similar item that is set next to or across the platform. Leaning kindling against the brace and directly over lit tinder promotes good oxygen flow within the fire. Too much oxygen, however, will smother the flame. If the flames begin to dwindle, your brace might be too big—allowing more oxygen than needed to sustain the flames. To correct this problem, find a new brace (smaller diameter) or safely push the kindling down closer to the flames.

- **Fuel—needed to start and maintain the fire.** Some individuals start a fire using gas or diesel fuel. Not only is this dangerous, but it often doesn't work. The gas lights easily, produces a large flame, and then dwindles before the large fuel catches fire. Larger stages of fuel require a hot, sustainable fire to burn. The key word is *sustainable*. Fuel needs to be in multiple-size stages, allowing you to build up the fire from a small flame to a large, sustainable heat source. The best way to accomplish this is to separate your fuel into three sizes—tinder, kindling, and fuel.

■ **Tinder—anything that will light from a spark.** Always carry man-made tinder! It can be used to start the first couple of fires in a survival situation. In wet conditions you can use your initial fire to dry out wet natural tinder for use later. The most common forms of man-made tinder are petroleum-based, solid compressed tinder tabs and compressed fuel tablets. Examples include Tinder-Quick tabs, WetFire tinder tablets, and Esbit fuel tablets. Natural tinder includes bark; scrapings; and grass, ferns, and lichen. All tinder needs to be broken down to allow oxygen circulation and create edges that can catch a spark. This can be done by working the tinder between your hands or by using a knife, held at 90 degrees to the material, to make scrapings. Most natural tinder and tinder improvised from man-made sources (like toilet paper) will need to be dry.

■ **Kindling—anything that will light from a small flame.** Most fire kindling is derived from twigs and wood shavings that range in size from pencil lead to pencil diameter. Small bundles of dry grass, cardboard, and oil- or gasoline-soaked rags are other great options. Kindling is placed against the brace and directly over the tinder flame—gapping the bridge between the tinder and larger fire-sustaining fuel.

■ **Fuel—anything that will sustain the fire.** Most fuel is thumb size or bigger and burns slowly once lit. Sources include the large end of dead branches, broken-down stumps, dead and dry shrubs, dried animal dung, finely split green wood, and bundles of dry grass.

If you decide to build a fire, don't prepare to fail. There is nothing worse then returning with an armload of wood only to find that your fire has gone out. As a rule, gather and prepare enough fuel to light three knee-high fires before actually lighting it. Having three times the needed amount of fuel allows you to return to a smaller stage if your fire starts to have problems and provides enough of the larger material to maintain the fire while you gather more fuel. When breaking fuel down, prepare the kindling and tinder (in that order) last. Doing it this way decreases the amount of moisture your tinder and kindling collect during the preparation process. In addition, keep all fuel off moist surfaces—and don't forget to gather a platform and brace along with your fuel.

Once you have gathered enough wood and it is broken into the various stages, place the tinder on the dry platform, next to the brace, and light it. Using the brace, fan out a handful of kindling directly above the flame. Don't waste time by adding just one stick at a time—use a good handful. Wait until the flames wick through the kindling before adding a perpendicular handful across the first. Continue doing this until you have a medium-size sustainable fire. Finally, perform the same steps using the larger stage fuel until it is well lit and the fire is self-supporting. If at any time you have a problem maintaining the fire, remember that it requires three elements to succeed. The problem is due to a failure of one of the three components—heat, oxygen, or fuel. The key to maintaining the flame is to determine which of the three is failing and then rectify the problem.

Survival Essential 2: Signaling (Man-Made and Improvised)

If your car breaks down, you raise the hood and turn on the flashers. Doing this alerts others of your predicament and often results in someone stopping to help. In the wilderness you'll need to do the same—create a signal that alerts others of your dilemma. Don't wait until a potential rescuer has passed you by. If your situation involves a stranded vehicle, stay close to it. The vehicle provides a great signal and is filled with myriad items you can use to meet your needs. However, overhead cover may obscure the car from view, and a better signal site may be necessary. In such cases, look for the ideal signaling site—a large clearing that is free of shadows and close to your shelter.

Signals are designed with two purposes in mind: to attract rescue and to pinpoint your location. Signals that attract rescue include aerial and parachute flares. These devices clear the tree line, cover a large sighting area, and catch the eye with their movement and color. Once rescue is heading in your direction, you can pinpoint your location with handheld red signal flares, orange smoke signals, signal mirrors, kites, strobe lights, whistles, or ground-to-air signals.

Since many signals can be used only once, review operational directions in advance—and don't ignite them until you see or hear a potential

rescuer heading in your direction. Ground-to-air signals, flags, and kites should be put out early and routinely checked to make sure they are in place. Signal mirrors and whistles should be used every ten to fifteen minutes—blowing the whistle and scanning the horizon with the mirror. After all, you don't know who might be out there.

In many instances you'll need to improvise a signal. If you do, at night consider using a large fire; during the day use smoke (bough-covered fire, tire fire, etc.) and improvised flags and ground-to-air signals. The ideal size for a ground-to-air signal is 18 feet long by 3 feet wide. You can increase its visibility by giving it contrast, sharp angles, movement, and shadows.

Signal mirror as seen from a rescue helicopter.

Survival Essential 3: Sustenance (Water and Food)

Water—more important than food. Water is perhaps one of the most often overlooked necessities. The body needs two to three quarts of water during an average day; during strenuous activity it can require two to three times that amount. Without water, it won't be long before even the simplest of tasks become impossible, and you'll likely perish within three to five days. When planning a trip, bring enough water to meet your needs, and plan a route of travel that crosses many water sources. Sources include rivers, ponds, lakes, and streams. Water also may be found underground close to natural vegetation or bends in dry riverbeds and procured from precipitation such as snow, rain, and dew. Avoid drinking blood, seawater, and urine—all will do more to upset your fluid balance than add to it.

To prevent illness caused by protozoa, bacteria, and viruses, water procured from Mother Nature should be purified whenever possible before drinking. The most often used methods for purifying water include boiling, chemical treatments, and commercial filtration devices. The Environmental Protection Agency (EPA) Office of Water advocates using a vigorous boil for one minute as the preferred method of purifying water. Although not as effective on cryptosporidia, chemical treatments such as iodine and chlorine can also be used. If using iodine tablets, follow the directions on the bottle. For chlorine, the amount used depends on the percentage of chlorine in the solution, as shown in Table 2-1.

Table 2-1: Chlorine Treatment Schedule

Available Chlorine	Drops per Quart of Clear Water
1 %	10 drops
4–6 %	2 drops
7–10 %	1 drop
Unknown	10 drops

If the water is cloudy or colored, double the normal amount of chlorine required for the percentage used. Add the chlorine, wait three minutes, and, with the cap loose, shake the container (allowing some water to weep out through the seams). Seal the cap, and wait twenty-five to thirty minutes; loosen the cap, and shake the container again. At this point the water is ready to drink. If you don't mind the weight, commercial purification devices are a nice luxury. However, make sure the device *purifies*—removes protozoa, bacteria, and viruses. A filter removes only protozoa, and a microfilter removes only protozoa and bacteria. Make sure to read the directions before departing on your trip, and keep the device clean throughout the trip.

Food—a nice luxury. Should you find yourself in a survival situation, it's best to have eaten well beforehand. A well-fed person has greater energy and a heightened morale. The ideal diet contains around 3,500 to 5,000 calories a day with 50 to 70 percent carbohydrates, 20 to 30 percent proteins, and 20 to 30 percent fats. Since you'll be carrying your food, consider dry foods like pasta, rice, and freeze-dried meals. If food supplies run out and your other needs have been met, consider procuring a meal from Mother Nature. Perhaps you'll find an edible plant, bug, or mollusk to assuage your hunger. Or you might catch an edible fish with an improvised hook and line. Wouldn't that be nice? Or maybe you'll build the perfect trap and snare a bird or small rodent that is the ideal size for the spit that sits over the fire you built. If these examples appeal to you, take the time to learn about indigenous plants, fish, and wildlife in the area you'll be traveling in. Learn what's edible, how to procure it, and the best methods of preparing it to eat.

Survival Essential 4: Travel

Navigation is an art and can provide a lot of fun outdoor adventure. However, as a survivor, you should stay put unless certain criteria are met. On land you should consider travel only when one of the following is met:

- You cannot meet your needs (shelter, fire, water, food, and signaling) in your present location.
- You've put out a signal, met your needs, and, after several days of waiting, rescue doesn't appear to be imminent.
- You know your location and have the navigation skills to get from point A to point B.

Hopefully you established an emergency heading before beginning your adventure. An emergency heading is one that takes you to a well-traveled road, regardless of where you might be during your short trip. On longer trips this heading might need daily adjustment. If in a survival situation and you decide to travel, leave a note detailing the date, heading, and final destination.

At sea the same rules apply. Unless the vessel is burning or sinking or poses another threat—stay close to it. If you must travel, consider a heading that takes you toward shipping lanes, land, or rain (you'll need drinkable water).

■ **Shipping lanes.** Most ships travel between continents on an east-west route.
■ **Land.** Large continents have long east and west shores.
■ **Rain.** Winds pick up vapor when traveling over water; therefore, following the wind should ultimately lead to rain.

Hopefully you'll have an idea of your general location. Knowing how to use this information and get from one point to another is covered throughout this book.

Survival Essential 5: Health (Mental, Traumatic, Environmental)

Mental health—the key to survival. When you quit trying, you start dying. The will to survive is the crux to overcoming the obstacles a survivor faces. What motivates you? Is it your family, fear of failure, your religious beliefs? How can you use this motivation to keep you going when all you want to do is lie down and die? The answer is inside each of us, and the ability to draw upon it is a personal one. Whatever it takes, don't give up. You never know when rescue will arrive.

Traumatic injuries—prevent them when you can; treat them when you can't. Anyone who ventures into the outdoors should attend a basic first-aid and CPR class. The ability to identify injuries and treat them properly is key to avoiding a worsening condition. Basic steps include protecting the airway, controlling bleeds, preventing shock, and immobilizing all musculoskeletal injuries.

Environmental injuries—must be prevented. Prevention is the key to environment-related health problems. Avoid injuries from heat and cold by using proper personal-protection techniques (clothing, shelter, and fire). Be aware of poisonous plants, insects, snakes, and wildlife prior to entering a specific area, and know what to do if contact should occur.

■ Step 3: Improvise to Meet Your Needs Using Man-Made and Natural Resources

A water faucet, refrigerator, heater, and nice bed are not present in Mother Nature's den. However, resources to meet your needs and provide some comforts are. After the five survival essentials have been identified and prioritized, you'll need to establish the best method of meeting each need. Since it's unlikely that you'll have all the necessary resources in your gear, you'll need to improvise—using what you have and what Mother Nature can supply. Sometimes this task is easy; at other times it may stretch your imagination to its limits. Use the following five-step approach to help in the decision process:

1. Determine your need (e.g., shelter, signal, heat).

2. Inventory available man-made and natural materials.

3. Consider the options for how you might meet your need (e.g., tree-well shelter, snow cave).

4. Pick the option that best utilizes your time, energy, and materials.

5. Proceed with the plan, ensuring that the final product is safe and durable.

The only limiting factor is your imagination! Don't let it prevent you from creating a masterpiece that keeps you comfortable while waiting for rescue or meets your daily needs while traveling out to safety.

Survival Kits

As a bare minimum, a survival kit should carry the ten essentials listed in Table 2-2. I advise, however, that you carry much more. Take the time to review the survival essential categories, and consider the potential problems when putting your kit together. Try to create a kit that will meet your needs under all situations. Put together several kits: a large one for your pack, a medium-size one for your CamelBak, and a small one that you always have on your person.

Table 2-2: Survival Essentials

Survival Kit Essentials	Survival Essential Category
Map	Navigation
Compass	Navigation
Knife	Improvising, fire, etc.
Water and food	Sustenance
Rain gear and proper clothing for warmth	Personal Protection (clothing)
Headlamp or flashlight	Health (avoid traumatic injuries at night)
First-aid supplies	Health (environmental and traumatic injuries)
Matches or spark source	Personal Protection (fire)
Tinder	Personal Protection (fire)
Sunglasses and sunscreen	Health (environmental injuries)

■ The Semiessentials

Other items you might consider include a tent or shelter material, parachute cord for improvising, signaling devices (signal mirror, ground-to-air panel, flares, etc.), water purifying system, snare wire and fishing gear, wristwatch, note paper and a pencil, toilet paper, and a plastic bag.

■ Final Thoughts on a Survival Kit

I carry my survival gear using a complete yet scattered design. My pack is filled with items that will meet both my everyday and emergency needs. In addition, I carry a smaller yet fairly complete kit in my CamelBak (which goes everywhere with me, including the top of my pack during long trips) and a smaller yet comprehensive kit in the cargo pocket of my pants. When carrying my pack, I have safety gear. If I take my pack off and walk around camp with just the CamelBak on, I am covered. Finally, if I find myself separated from my pack and CamelBak, the kit in my cargo pocket covers me. A list of my smaller cargo pocket kit is provided in Table 2-3. Take a look, and see how it might work for you.

Table 2-3: **The Ultimate Survival Kit**

Survival Category	Items and Potential Uses
Personal Protection	Needle (sewing, splinter removal); dental floss (floss teeth, sewing, gear repair); duct tape (clothing repair, gear repair, medical tape, signaling, note paper); knife (cutting applications, metal match striker, screwdriver, digging, skinning); parachute cord (lashing shelters/tools, gear repair, inner strands for sewing, snares); Vaseline/cotton tinder (tinder, lip balm, moisten dry skin); metal match (fire starter, nighttime signal device); candle (match saver/fire starter, light source); matches (fire starter).
Signaling	Mirror (ground/air signal, ground/ground signal); whistle (audible signal); survey tape (ground signal, trail marker, note paper, gear repair); coins (pay phone, ground/air signal, fishing lure); Sharpie (note-taking, writing messages).
Sustenance	Condoms (compact water bladder, a nonlubricated condom can hold up to a gallon of water when placed inside a bandana or similar item); water purification tablets (water purification); water purification container (air-, watertight container); tubing (water bladder hose, slingshot, snare device, tourniquet); safety pin (secure tubing to clothing, clothing repair, gear repair, splinter removal, secure arm sling); twist ties (secure top of water bladder, keep small gear organized); aluminum foil (water scoop for condom, fire base on wet ground, wind block for small fires, cooking, signaling); snare wire (snares, gear repair); fishing line (fishing, gear repair, sewing, shelter lashing, all cordage applications); fishing hooks (fishing, sewing, gear repair); fishing sinkers (fishing); fishing float (fishing, trail marker).
Travel	Button compass.
Medical	Medical tape (secure dressings, gear repair, clothing repair, all tape applications); Band-Aids (small-wound dressings); antibiotic cream (small-wound care, chapped lip/skin balm); moleskin (blister prevention/repair); alcohol preps (disinfect skin/needles); Ziploc bag for picture of loved ones (relieve stress, motivation to succeed).
Miscellaneous	Ziploc bags (keep small essentials dry/organized); pouch (to carry survival gear); three-step approach card (guidance for a survival scenario).

Before You Go

Part of the pretrip planning process is letting a reliable friend know your itinerary. This includes route of travel, anticipated campsites and dates, who's going with you, check-in times, and whom to notify should you fail to check in. Unless you do this, how will anyone know you are lost or hurt and in need of rescue?

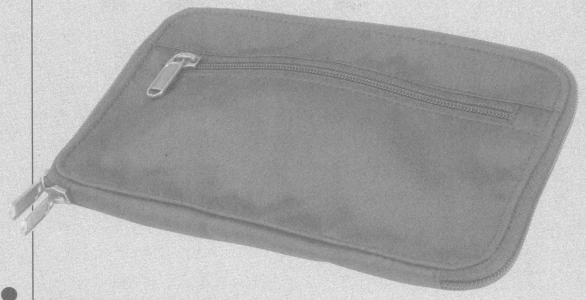

Chapter Exercises

Review the five survival essentials.

Take a look at my three-step approach to survival and the five survival essentials. Think about past experiences and how this approach might apply. Think about how you might use it to meet your needs on future trips.

Make a survival kit.

Take the time to review your survival needs and put together a personal survival kit that will fit into a cargo pocket. When putting your kit together, consider the five survival essentials and your improvising needs.

The old, reliable
map and compass.

SECTION II

Maps, Charts, & Compasses

You know the sun rises in the east and sets in the west, which also gives you an idea of where north and south are. You're following a well-maintained trail, so if you start at one end you should end up at the other, and you can't miss that huge oak tree on the return trip. But what if a sudden rainsquall or fog obscures the sun? What if you wander off-trail to climb a ridge—and can't find the trail again?

Trusting to your sense of direction, memory, or the whims of nature alone is asking for trouble. Instead, reach into your navigation toolbox for your compass and the appropriate map (or chart, if you're on the water) for the area you're traveling. Knowing how to use these tools means you'll always know where you are, regardless of weather conditions or memory lapses.

This section provides details on the nomenclature of maps, charts, and compasses. For details on how to use these tools, refer to Sections III and IV.

CHAPTER 3

All About Maps & Charts

Have you ever taken a road trip and had trouble finding your intended destination? Did you stop at a convenience store for directions? "Hmmm, let me see . . . go to the third light next to Jim's place and take a left . . . go down the road until you see a pig farm and turn right," and so on and so on. How many times have you had a friend meet you in town so that you could follow the person home? If only you had an oriented road map and knew the cross streets close to your destination. Perhaps there wouldn't be so much tension in the car. Wilderness travel isn't much different—once you learn how to read a map, it becomes a very useful tool.

Maps and charts are flat, two-dimensional representations of the earth's three-dimensional surface. As a rule, maps are used for land navigation and provide a great deal of information for a small area. Charts are used for air and sea navigation, covering a large area with much less detail. Understanding the design and nomenclature of a particular map and chart is key to interpreting its information to the world around you.

Chart and Map Projections

Maps and charts for land, sea, and air come from a variety of projections that balance distortion related to convenience. Most coastal charts, inshore charts, and maps use the Mercator, Transverse Mercator, or Gnomeric projection.

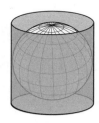 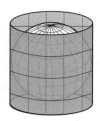 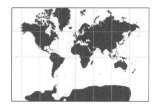

*Mercator
projection.*

■ Mercator Projection

The Mercator projection was created by wrapping a cylinder around a
globe (so that its surface touches the equator), projecting the globe's image
onto the cylinder's inner wall, and cutting the cylinder up one side and
then laying it out flat. When this is done, the meridians of longitude are
projected onto the cylinder as equally spaced straight lines (perpendicular
to the equator), and the parallels of latitude are projected onto the cylinder as straight lines (parallel to the equator) but not necessarily equidis-
tant. In reality, longitude lines get closer together the farther north or
south they are from the equator, and latitude lines maintain equidistance
(1 degree of latitude always equals 60 nautical miles) throughout the projection. For large-scale maps or charts of 1:80,000 or larger (covering a
small area) the Mercator distortion is minimal. However, as the scale
becomes smaller (covering a larger area), the distortion increases propor-
tionately. Displaying latitude and longitude as straight lines can create significant distortion in a small-scale map. Maps or charts that use a
Mercator projection are best suited for areas where only short distances
are covered. In addition, since the distance between 1 degree of latitude is
a constant (60 nautical miles), the vertical scale (meridian of longitude)
should be used for measuring distances.

■ Transverse Mercator Projection

The Transverse Mercator projection was created by wrapping a cylinder
around a globe (so that its surface touches the north and south poles),
projecting the globe's image onto the cylinder's inner wall, and cutting the
cylinder up one side and then laying it out flat. When this is done, the

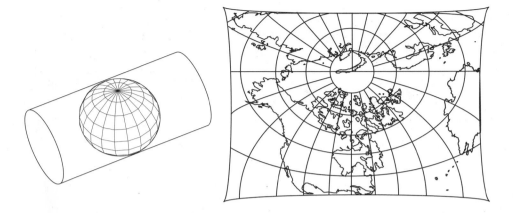

meridians of longitude and the parallels of latitude are projected onto the cylinder as complex curves. On a Transverse Mercator, the central north-south longitude line, which is straight, is the line of true scale. This projection is best suited for trips covering a long north-south area with a narrow east-west border. The farther you are from the central longitude line, the greater the map's or chart's distortion.

Transverse Mercator projection.

■ Gnomeric Projection

For land and the coastline, you're unlikely to see anything other than Mercator or Transverse Mercator maps or charts. However, the distortion created in these projections makes them suboptimal when a large distance

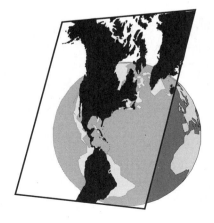

Gnomeric projection.

Gnomeric

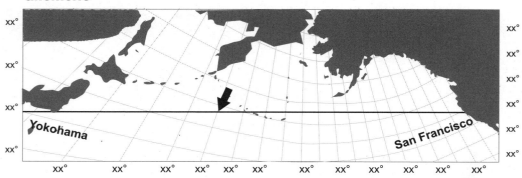

Mercator

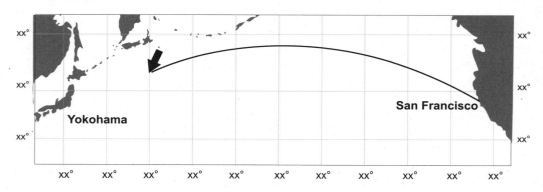

Converting a rhumb line to a great circle.

is covered. In such instances, the Gnomeric projection is a better choice. A Gnomeric projection is created by projecting a globe's surface onto a flat surface. In a Gnomeric projection, lines of longitude are straight and lines of latitude are curved.

This projection accounts for the earth's curve and when used with a Mercator chart (which doesn't account for the curve) helps establish the navigation details necessary for long trips. Drawing a straight line between two points on a Gnomeric projection allows the navigator to establish which lines of latitude and longitude are crossed during the trek. This information is then transferred to a Mercator chart to determine the appropriate course to travel between the two points, which is constantly changing and much shorter than a straight line. This course is called the great circle route.

On long journeys, a significant distances savings occurs when the rhumb line (straight line on a Mercator chart) is converted to a great circle route. This is especially true with east-west passages in higher latitudes. When traveling on a north-south passage, the rhumb line and great circle routes are identical.

Types of Charts and Maps

If traveling on land, you will most likely use large-scale topical maps. When traveling by air or sea, you'll use smaller nautical or aeronautic charts. The exact size of a map or chart is determined by its ratio relationship, also known as its representation fraction. For example, maps or charts with a scale of 1:50,000 have been created so that one unit (any unit of measurement) on the map represents 50,000 units in actual terrain. Maps with a scale of 1:24,000 are considered large-scale maps, since they provide much more detail over a small area. Maps with a scale of 1:250,000 are considered small-scale maps; they provide much less detail

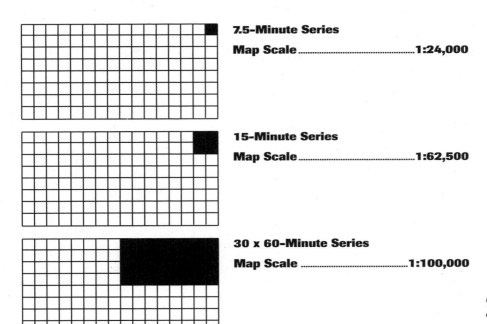

7.5-Minute Series
Map Scale................................**1:24,000**

15-Minute Series
Map Scale................................**1:62,500**

30 x 60-Minute Series
Map Scale **1:100,000**

*Charts and maps
come in many
sizes.*

over a large area. In other words, large-scale maps cover less area and provide much more detail than a small-scale map.

The easiest way to identify a map's or chart's relative size (large or small scale) is to understand that the bigger the second number, the smaller the scale. Think of it as a fraction—1:24,000 is equal to 1/24,000, which is a bigger fraction than 1:100,000, which is equal to 1/100,000.

In addition to scale, maps often list the amount of latitude and longitude area covered. For example, a 7.5-minute series map covers 7.5 minutes of latitude and 7.5 minutes of longitude (discussed later).

■ Aeronautical Charts

Aeronautical charts primarily show information on land elevation, hazards, and navigational aids. In the United States these charts are published by the Federal Aviation Administration's (FAA) National Aeronautical Charting Office (NACO). Basic types of aeronautical charts are detailed below.

Large-Scale Aeronautical Charts

The Visual Flight Rule (VFR) Terminal Area Chart is a large-scale aeronautical chart that uses a 1:250,000 representation fraction, where 1 inch equals 3.43 nautical miles (4.0 statute miles). These large-scale charts provide greater detail in areas that are prone to a high volume of air traffic.

Medium-Scale Aeronautical Charts

Sectional charts are medium-size aeronautical charts that use a 1:500,000 representation fraction, where 1 inch equals 6.86 nautical miles (8.0 statute miles). The sectional chart is the most commonly used aeronautical chart for visual navigation.

Small-Scale Aeronautical Charts

World aeronautical charts are small-size aeronautical charts that use a 1:1,000,000 representation fraction, where 1 inch equals 13.7 nautical miles (16.0 statute miles). This chart is often used for longer trip planning.

■ Nautical Charts

With the exception of the shoreline, nautical charts provide limited information about the land. They primarily show information on water depth, hazards, and navigational aids. Charts covering coastal waters and the

Great Lakes can be purchased from the National Oceanic and Atmospheric Administration (NOAA). Charts that cover inland waterways, lakes, and rivers are covered by the Army Corps of Engineers. Basic types of nautical charts are detailed below.

Very Large–Scale Nautical Charts

Harbor charts are very large–scale nautical charts that use a representation fraction of anything under 1:50,000. These extremely detailed charts cover a small area. Kayakers who travel in harbors, anchorage areas, and small inland waterways often use these charts.

Large-Scale Nautical Charts

Coastal charts are large-scale nautical charts that use a representation fraction of 1:50,000 to 1:150,000. Vessels that navigate large bays and harbors and large inland waterways use these charts.

Medium-Scale Nautical Charts

General charts are medium-scale nautical charts that use a representation fraction of 1:150,000 to 1:600,000. These charts are used by vessels that navigate beyond the reefs but within sight of land or navigational aids.

Small-Scale Nautical Charts

Sailing charts are small-scale nautical charts that use a representation fraction of 1:600,000 and up. Sailing charts cover a big surface area; therefore, details are limited to larger features. Vessels covering large areas of water use these charts.

■ Topographic Maps

Topographic maps show information on land terrain (contour, water, forests, etc.) and man-made features (buildings, roads, towers, etc.). In the United States the best known maps come from the United States Geological Survey (USGS) and can be purchased directly from them or most outdoor stores.

Large-Scale Topographic Maps

Large-scale topographic maps use a representation fraction of 1:24,000 (7.5-minute series), where 1 inch equals 0.3946 statute mile (0.610 km). These highly detailed maps are the map of choice for most backpackers.

Medium-Scale Topographic Maps

Medium-scale topographic maps use a representation fraction of 1:62,500 (15-minute series), where 1 inch equals 0.9864 statute mile (1.588 km). These maps are used for planning long backpacking trips.

Small-Scale Topographic Maps

Small-scale topographic maps use a representation fraction of 1:100,000 (30 x 60–minute series), where 1 inch equals 1.578 statute miles (2.54 km). These maps are used for planning long-distance travel by vehicle or on foot.

Chart and Map Nomenclature

Charts and maps provide a wealth of useful information both within the body and the surrounding margins. This information is very useful when planning a trip or evaluating your progress. The focus of this section is on chart and map nomenclature related to land and coastal navigation.

■ General Information

The chart or map is filled with information about how it was created and how it can be used. Understanding these details makes it easier to move from one map to another or when using the map in conjunction with a GPS unit. Following is some of the information you might find.

Publishing Information

Most charts and maps list the issuing agency and other organization that contributed information, along with the date they were published. You may think the publishing date is a trivial matter, but it isn't. Knowing the date is important when evaluating the relevance of such man-made features as water sources, clear-cuts, roads, and buildings. Roads may be overgrown and new ones built; clear-cuts may now have 20-foot-tall trees; buildings may no longer be present.

Title Information

The title block may contain the chart's or map's name or number, location (country, state, etc.), projection type, and information about adjoining charts or maps.

Ratio and Distance Information

This information includes such measurements as the chart or maps series size, ratio scale, and bar scale for measuring distances.

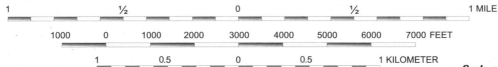

Scale 1:24,000

Scale and distance measurements shown on a 7.5-minute series USGS map.

▇ Coordinate Systems

Coordinate systems allow us to identify a location using intersecting lines. Coordinate systems are not map designs. These systems include angular coordinates (latitude and longitude) and rectangular coordinates (UTM, UPS, MGRS, USPLSS, SPCS).

Angular Coordinates (Latitude/Longitude)

Parallels of latitude and meridians of longitude are imaginary lines that encircle the globe, creating a crisscross grid system that helps you identify your location.

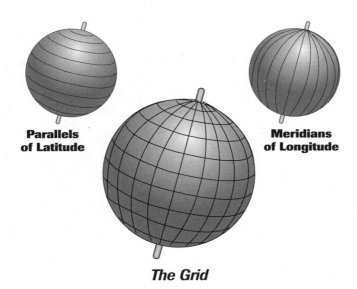

**Parallels
of Latitude**

**Meridians
of Longitude**

The Grid

An angular coordinate system.

Latitude lines run east-west and are numbered from 0 to 90 degrees north and south of the equator. The equator is given the 0° latitude designation (divide between north and south) and, like rungs of a ladder, these lines progress until they reach the North and South Poles (90° North latitude and 90° South latitude, respectively). These lines run parallel to one another and are used to measure north and south distances. Latitude is often noted at the extreme ends of the horizontal map edges.

Latitude and longitude line progression.

Longitude lines run north-south and are numbered from 0 to 180 degrees east and west of Greenwich, England. The 0° longitude line is known as the Prime Meridian. The 0° meridian becomes the 180th East or West meridian once it intersects the extreme north and south sections of

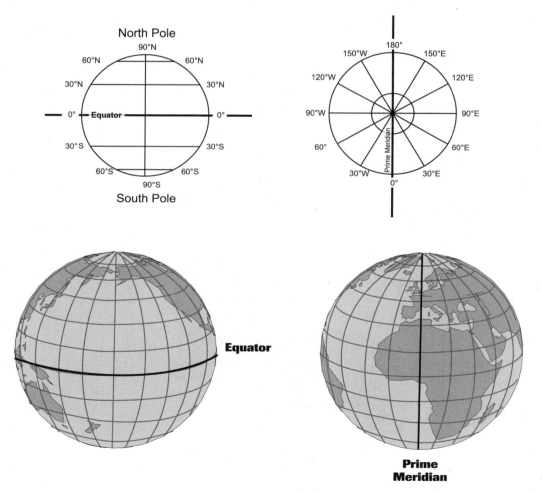

the globe. This line (180th) is also known as the International Date Line. When it is 12:00 at the Prime Meridian (Greenwich Mean Time), it is 24:00 at the International Date Line. The earth rotates 15 degrees an hour, 180 degrees in twelve hours, and 360 degrees in twenty-four hours. Crossing the International Date Line also changes the date. Unlike latitude lines, longitude lines are not parallel to one another and therefore cannot be used for measuring distances. Longitude is often noted at the extreme ends of the vertical map edges. Most maps will display a large plus sign (+) to indicate locations where latitude and longitude lines cross.

Angular coordinate lines (latitude and longitude) are measured in degrees (°), minutes ('), and seconds ("). There are 60 seconds in 1 minute and 60 minutes in 1 degree. One minute of 1 degree of all latitudes is equal to 1 nautical mile (approximately 1.15 statute mile) or 1,852 meters regardless of your location. One degree of all latitudes is equal to 60 nautical miles (69 statute miles). However, since longitude lines are not parallel (converging at the North and South Poles), the distance between 1 minute of longitude decreases as you move up or down the longitude line (greatest at the equator and zero at the poles). Therefore, it is OK to use a degree or minute of latitude to measure distances but not a degree or minute of longitude (which is constantly changing).

Unlike latitude lines, longitude lines get closer together north or south of the equator.

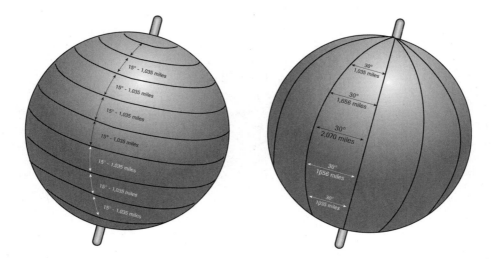

It's important to distinguish north from south when defining latitude, and east from west for longitude. For example, a latitude of 45° 30' 30" north of the equator would read as 45 degrees, 30 minutes, and 30 seconds North. The same coordinate position south of the equator would read 45 degrees, 30 minutes, and 30 seconds South latitude. A latitude line will never be more than 90 degrees north or south. A longitude of 120° 30' 30" east of the Prime Meridian would read as 120 degrees, 30 minutes, and 30 seconds East longitude. The same coordinate position west of the Prime Meridian would read 120 degrees, 30 minutes, and 30 seconds West longitude. A longitude line will never be more than 180 degrees east or west. Whenever giving latitude and longitude coordinates, always read the latitude first.

In some instances you will come across latitude and longitude measurements where decimals are used in place of minutes and seconds. Or perhaps you will want to change the coordinates to a decimal. Knowing that there are 60 seconds in a minute and 60 minutes in a degree is the key to this conversion, as illustrated in Table 3–1.

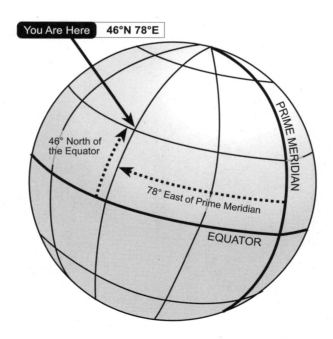

Reading latitude and longitude.

Table 3-1: Converting Units of Angular Measurement

Decimal Seconds to Decimal Degrees

Decimal Seconds	Decimal Minutes	Decimal Degrees
23° 27' 30.0"	23° 27' 30/60 = 23° 27.5'	23° 27.5/60' = 23.4583°

Decimal Degrees to Decimal Seconds

Decimal Degrees	Decimal Minutes	Decimal Seconds
23.4583°	23°.4583 x 60 = 23° 27.5'	23° 27' .5 x 60 = 23° 27' 30.0"

Rectangular Coordinates (UTM)

Although there are several types of rectangular coordinate systems, the **Universal Transverse Mercator (UTM) system** is the most often used. The UTM grid system utilizes a rectangular framework that links its coordinate system to a measurement of distance. Using a Transverse Mercator projection, the UTM system designates rectangular coordinates onto the world map between latitudes 84° North and 80° South. Although not an angular system, these large quadrilateral grids are centered exactly on a line of longitude (central meridian) and use latitude and longitude coordinates to establish size.

The UTM system uses sixty zones (columns) that are 6 degrees apart and begin at the 180th meridian, advancing to the east. For example, Zone 1 is located between 174° and 180° West longitude, Zone 2 between 168° and 174° West longitude, and so on. In order for all the sixty zones to have its own origin (located at the equator and its central meridian), a slightly rotated Transverse Mercator projection was created for each zone. Using the central meridian of a zone as its origin assures that all spots within that zone are within 3 degrees of the centerline. The central meridian is exactly 6 degrees of longitude from the origin of the adjoining UTM grids. For example, the central meridian of Zone 1 is 177° West longitude, Zone 2 is 171° West longitude, and so on. The creation of sixty separate zones limits the distortion to less than .04 percent, making it an acceptable option, especially for large-scale maps.

Most USGS maps display the UTM grid zone in addition to an angular coordinate system, allowing you to identify a location by both its

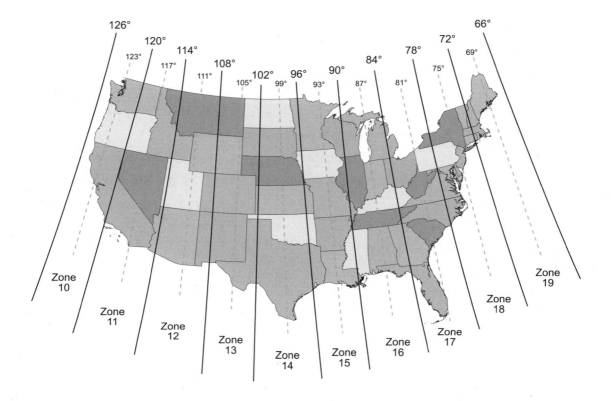

UTM zones.

latitude and longitude and its grid zone coordinates. The map's grid zone is often found within the marginal information at the bottom of the map. In the example shown on the facing page, the map is located in grid Zone 10, which spans from 126° to 120° West longitude.

UTM grid coordinates are expressed as a distance in meters to the east (called easting) and to the north (called northing). All easting coordinates relate to the zone's central meridian, which is assigned an easting value of 500,000 meters east. An easting of zero will never occur, since a 6-degree-wide zone is never more than 674,000 meters wide. All northing coordinates relate to the equator, which is given two different values. For locations north of the equator, the equator is assigned the northing value of 0 meters north. To avoid negative numbers, the equator is assigned the northing value of 10,000,000 meters north for locations south of the equator. Since a zone can have two of the same northing values (one north of the equator and one south), it is important to know which hemisphere of the zone you are in (northern or southern). The easting and

Mapped, edited, and published by the Geological Survey

Control by USGS and USC&GS

Topography by photogrammetric methods from aerial
photographs taken 1963.   Field checked 1965

Polyconic projection.   1927 North American datum
10,000-foot grid based on Washington coordinate system,
south zone

1000-meter Universal Transverse Mercator grid ticks,
zone 10, shown in blue

Land lines have not been established in this area

UTM zone
displayed on a
USGS map.

northing values are arbitrary figures and are therefore often referred to as
"false easting" and "false northing."

Coordinates of the UTM system depict an area of precision directly
related to the easting and northing value (coordinates based on the zone's
origin—central meridian and equator), which represents the bottom left
corner of a square. The size of the square depends on the number of digits
used and ranges from a 100,000-meter square to a 1-meter square. Within
a UTM zone, a combined (easting and northing) three- or four-digit coordinate represents a location to within 100,000 meters of precision, five or
six digits are within 10,000 meters, seven or eight digits are within 1,000
meters, nine or ten digits are within 100 meters, eleven or twelve digits to
within 10 meters, and so on. Since the easting distance of a zone is based
on a central meridian of 500,000 (false easting) and the zone's total distance (from its western to eastern edge) never reaches 1,000,000 (seven
digits), easting values will either drop the first number or start with a 0. In
order to avoid confusion, UTM coordinates are always read in order from
left to right and bottom to top (right and up = easting value first, northing
value second). For example, if your UTM designation was 0605000 mE,
5248000 mN (northern hemisphere), your location would be 0605000
easting (605,000-500,000 = 105,000 meters east of the central meridian)
and 5248000 northing (5,248,000 meters north of the equator). It is
common to see the coordinates written together as 11 06050005248000
(northern hemisphere), where the grid zone is 11 and the combined

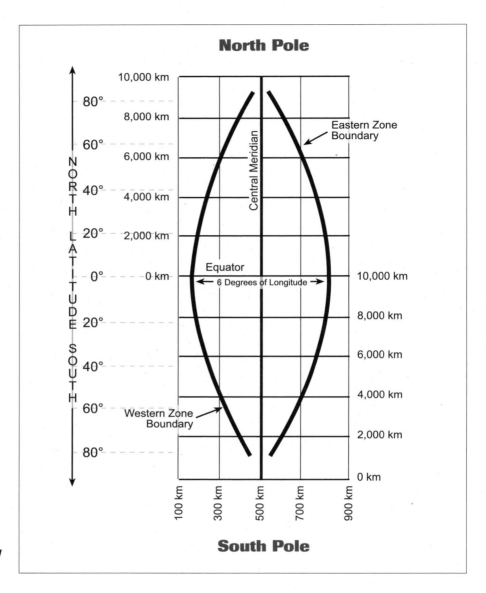

North Pole

10,000 km

80°

8,000 km

60°

6,000 km

Eastern Zone
Boundary

N
O
R
T
H

40°

4,000 km

Central Meridian

L
A
T
I
T
U
D
E

20°

2,000 km

0°

0 km

Equator
← 6 Degrees of Longitude →

10,000 km

S
O
U
T
H

20°

8,000 km

40°

6,000 km

4,000 km

60°

Western Zone
Boundary

2,000 km

80°

0 km

100 km   300 km   500 km   700 km   900 km

South Pole

UTM northing and easting concept.

coordinates represent 0605000 easting and 5248000 northing. In reality, these coordinates would probably be displayed as 11 6055248 (dropping the easting first zero and the last three zeros of both values). Table 3–2 represents the bottom left corner of a 1,000-meter square.

Most USGS topographic maps have a grid overlay or fine blue tick marks every 1,000 meters (1 km) that are located along the map's outer horizontal and vertical edges. Each marking is labeled relevant to its nor-

Table 3-2: Reading UTM Coordinates

Grid Zone	Usually given in the marginal information.
Coordinates	Right = easting value Up = northing value
Hemisphere	Is the northing value related to the Northern or Southern Hemisphere?

The total number of combined UTM coordinates determines precision (11 = zone).

Digits	UTM Coordinate	Easting Meters	Northing Meters	Grid Size
3 to 4	11 652	600,000	5,200,000	100,000 m.sq.
5 to 6	11 61524	610,000	5,240,000	10,000 m.sq.
7 to 8	11 6155248	615,000	5,248,000	1,000 m.sq.
9 to 10	11 615552484	615,500	5,248,400	100 m.sq.
11 to 12	11 61554524845	615,540	5,248,450	10 m.sq.
13 to 14	11 6155455248454	615,545	5,248,454	1 m.sq.

thing or easting value. To create less clutter, most maps omit the last three zeros and use a smaller type for designations greater then 100,000. For example, if you were located at 607,000 easting and 5,137,000 northing, it would appear as ^{6}07 and ^{51}37 on the map's edge (see illustration below). When using a USGS 7.5-minute quadrangle series (1:24,000 scale) or smaller map, it is doubtful you can calculate a position closer than 10 meters. The closest easting or northing value you will find will usually be a six-digit number (eleven or twelve digits when easting and northing are combined). In other words, the easting and northing values will drop the last zero. To find the value of the last two digits (after dropping the last 0), use the grid lines or tick marks that are closest to the point you are trying to locate. The easting is the value of the nearest grid line west of your location plus the distance east of that line; the northing is the value of the nearest grid line south of your location plus the distance north of that line. In the following illustration the inlaid symbol is located in the Northern Hemisphere, Zone 10, and 060750 easting, 513750 northing. This can also be written as 10 60750513750 Northern Hemisphere. The map illustrated for this example has blue tick marks for its UTM coordinates. For demonstration purposes, I have extended the tick marks onto the map.

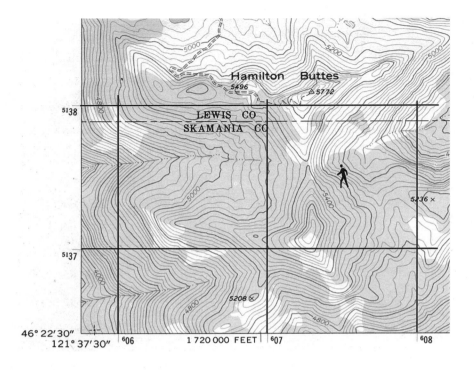

UTM coordinates.

In addition to zones, the UTM system provides rows that begin at 80° South latitude and end at 84° North latitude. All rows are 8 degrees apart, except for the top row, which spans between 72° and 84° North, making it 12 degrees wide. There are a total of twenty rows that advance in letter, from south to north, beginning at *C* and ending at *X*. *O* and *I* are omitted from the twenty-row alphabet in order to prevent confusion from similar appearing numbers. The letter designation is called the UTM latitude band letter. The Universal Polar Stereographic (UPS) system covers latitudes below 80° South and above 84° North (covered later). The UTM latitude band letter helps identify your position within a zone. The equator is the beginning of the *N* band; therefore, all bands higher than *N* are in the Northern Hemisphere. If you were located in western Washington State, using this system you would be located in Grid 10T (10 is the zone number and *T* is the latitude band letter). When known, the latitude band helps define your position within the zone. Most USGS maps, however, only provide the grid zone, without any mention of which latitude band the map relates to. In such instances, simply knowing which hemisphere the northing value relates to helps establish your northing position.

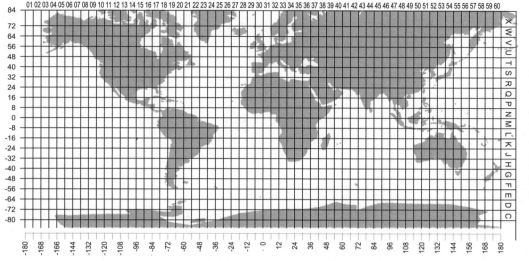

UTM Zone Number

UTM Latitude Band Letter

Universal Transverse Mercator (UTM) System

UTM zone number and latitude band letter.

Although you can find a distance or location by eyeballing a map's grid lines, using a UTM grid overlay will provide greater precision. To use the grid overlay, place it on the map with its edges aligned to the map's grid lines. Your UTM location can be determined using the tool's markings.

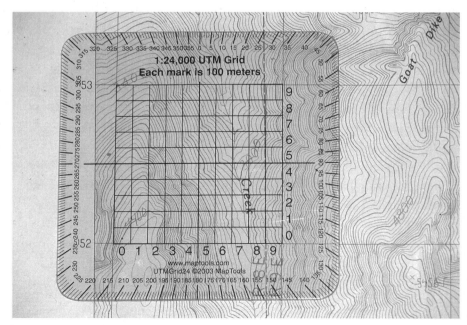

1:24,000 UTM Grid
Each mark is 100 meters

www.maptools.com
UTMGrid24 ©2003 MapTools

The UTM grid overlay.

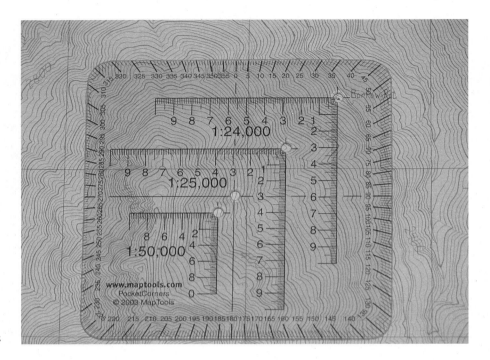

UTM corner ruler.

For even greater precision use a UTM corner ruler that provides an additional digit of precision beyond a UTM grid overlay. This tool allows you to determine a location to within a 10-meter square on 1:24,000 scale maps. Start by placing the top right corner of the corner ruler on top of the feature to be measured. Since the numbers of the UTM system always increase to the east and north, make sure the corner tool is placed so that its numbers are west and south of the feature you are measuring. Read the UTM coordinate values that cross the closest west grid line (gives easting) and south grid line (gives northing). To locate a UTM coordinate on the map, slide the ruler to the north and east until the desired distances are indicated at the UTM grid lines.

If you don't have a UTM grid tool, you can make one using the scale bars on the map. Place the corner of a piece of paper next to the kilometer measurement scale that is located at the bottom of the map. Using a pencil, mark the horizontal and vertical edges of the paper every 100 meters for 1 kilometer (ten markings on each edge). Number all marks starting with the corners, which should be labeled as zero.

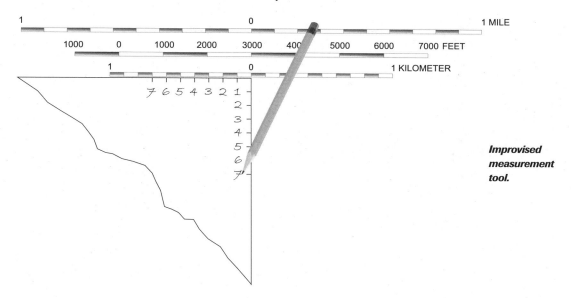

Scale 1:24,000

Improvised measurement tool.

Other Rectangular Coordinate Systems

Other rectangular coordinate systems include the Universal Polar Stereographic (UPS), Military Grid Reference (MGRS), and Township and Range (USPLSS).

Universal Polar Stereographic (UPS) Rectangular Coordinates. The UPS system covers the areas that the UTM system leaves out, which includes latitudes above 84° North and below 80° South. Similar to the UTM design, this grid system creates a false central origin that is located at both the North and South Poles and given coordinate values of 2,000,000 meters east and 2,000,000 meters north.

At the North Pole northing values are centered on the 0°/180° meridians and increase above 2,000,000 (the origin) as you move south on the 180° meridian (International Date Line) and decreases below 2,000,000 (the origin) as you move south on the 0° meridian (Prime Meridian). The easting values are centered on the 90° West/90° East meridians and increase above 2,000,000 (the origin) as you move south on the 90° East meridian and decrease below 2,000,000 as you move south along the 90° West meridian.

At the South Pole northing values are centered on the 0°/180° meridians and increase above 2,000,000 (the origin) as you move north

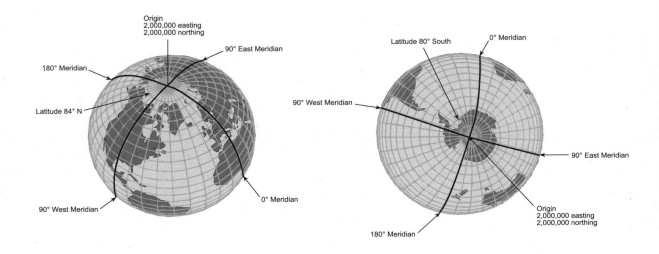

on the 0° meridian (Prime Meridian) and decreases below 2,000,000 (the origin) as you move north on the 180° meridian (International Date Line). The easting values are centered on the 90° West/90° East meridians and increase above 2,000,000 (the origin) as you move north on the 90° East meridian and decrease below 2,000,000 as you move north along the 90° West meridian.

Military Grid Reference System (MGRS). The U.S. Army created the Military Grid Reference System (MGRS) based on the Universal Transverse Mercator (UTM) concept. The MGRS uses the same grid zone identifiers (1 through 60) and latitude band letters (*C* through *X*) as seen with the UTM system. To further define your location, however, the MGRS system breaks each zone into smaller 100,000-meter squares that are identified with two letters. The column letters begin at the 180th meridian, run from west to east, and are lettered between *A* and *Z* (omitting *I* and *O*). Every 18 degrees this cycle repeats itself. The row letters begin at the equator and run between *A* and *V* (omitting *I* and *O*). Rows moving north of the equator advance from *A* to *V*. Rows moving south of the equator advance from *V* to *A*. Every 18 degrees this cycle repeats itself. Like the grid zones, these 100,000-meter squares are read from left to right and bottom to top. A grid zone designation plus two letters identifies a 100,000-meter area.

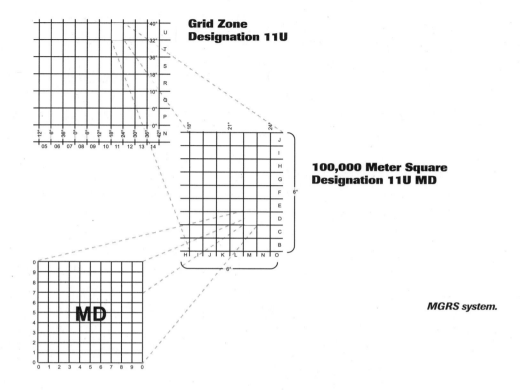

The MGRS designation 11U MD represents the 100,000-meter-square area much like the UTM coordinates 11 453 (Zone 11, 400,000 easting, and 5,300,000 northing) represent the lower left corner of the same 100,000-meter-square area. If two numbers follow the 100,000-meter-square designation (two letters), that represents the lower left corner of a 10,000-meter square. Four numbers represent a 1,000-meter square; six numbers, a 100-meter square; eight numbers, a 10-meter square; and so on. This rectangular coordinate system is found on Defense Mapping Agency maps.

Township and Range System (USPLSS). Surveyors use Township and Range grid systems. This system is printed on USGS topographic maps and can be useful for position determination when you're in the wilderness and its markers are seen. Township and Range grids use latitude and longitude lines (respectively) as an initial point (intersection of a baseline and principal meridian), building a grid system that moves outward in 6-mile increments. In other words, Township lines intersect the principal meridian (longitude line) every 6 miles north and south of the initial point; Range lines intersect the baseline (latitude line) every 6 miles east and west of the initial point. Each 6- by 6-mile square is called a Township. Both Township and Range lines are given numbers related to the initial point—Range numbers to the east and west, and township numbers to the north and south. For example, a Township of 3 north and Range of 2 east would lie between 12 and 18 miles north and 6 and 12 miles east of the initial point.

A Township is further broken down into 36 1- by 1-mile squares (640 acres) called sections. Each section is given a number between 1 and 36, beginning with 1 at the top right and increasing back and forth across the township until ending with the number 36 in the bottom right corner. Sections are further broken down into quarters of 160 acres each and are labeled by the position they hold (NE ¼, NW ¼, SW ¼, SE ¼). Finally, each quarter section is further divided into four blocks of forty acres each (commonly referred to as forties or 40-compass quadrant) that are also labeled by the position they hold. To compensate for the earth's curvature, every 24 miles (fourth Township and Range line) the initial point is corrected so that it realigns with actual latitude and longitude lines.

When describing a position using Township and Range the forty-acre block is given first, followed by the quarter section, section, and Township related to the initial point. For example, Township: T19N, R32W (6-mile square); Section: 24 (1-mile square); Quarter Section: NE ¼ (160 acres); Forties: NW ¼ (40 acres) would be displayed as NW ¼ of NE ¼, section 24, township T19N and R32W.

■ Declination Information

Understanding the relationship between true north, grid north, and magnetic north is extremely important when using a map and compass together. Failing to recognize the differences between them is a potentially fatal error.

True North

True north refers to any direction from our location to the North Pole. The easiest way to identify this direction on a chart or map is to find a longitude line, since all longitude lines point and converge at true north (and south). In fact, the angular coordinate system (latitude and longitude) is the only

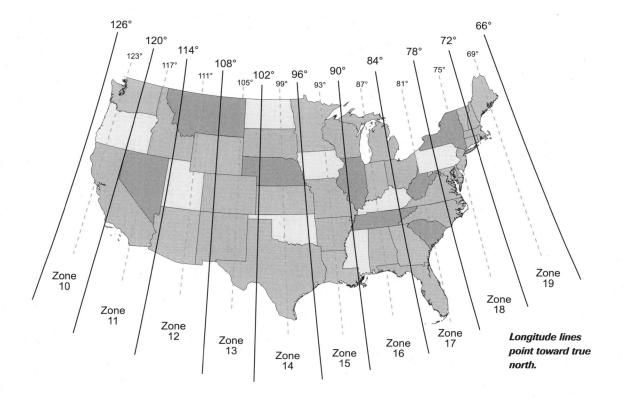

Longitude lines point toward true north.

one that accurately reflects the cardinal directions. Longitude follows a true north-south and latitude a true east-west direction. The declination angle difference between true north and that found in rectangular coordinate systems or a compass must be known and adjusted for as necessary.

Grid North

Grid north refers to the declination difference between true north and a vertical grid line of a rectangular coordinate system. The grid declination at the central meridian of the UTM system is always 0, since it falls on a line of longitude. Grid lines east of the central meridian have a declination to the east; grid lines to the west of the central meridian have a west declination. All values are relative to true north and increase the farther away from the central meridian and equator you are. For further information on the UTM setup, review the preceding Coordinate Systems section.

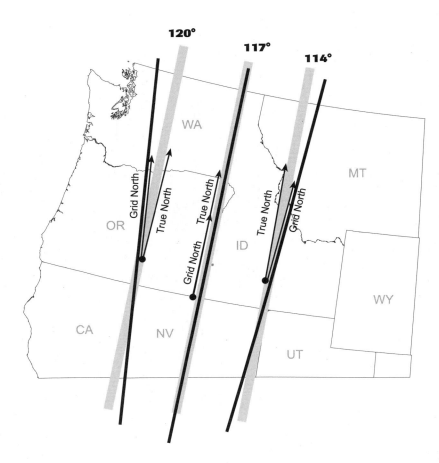

Grid north's relationship to longitude lines.

Magnetic North

Magnetic north refers to the direction the compass's magnetic north–seeking arrow points. Provided there is no magnetic interference, the compass arrow will point toward Prince of Wales Island, located in northern Canada (magnetic north). Isogonic lines—lines that represent a specific declinations path—provide the angle difference between true north and magnetic north. The only time these lines have a zero value is when your location puts magnetic north directly between you and true north. In such instances, the line is called an agonic line and the declination angle is 0.

The relationship between true north, grid north, and magnetic north is often referred to as "declination" on maps and "variation" on charts. Most maps display the declination as a three-lined diagram that identifies the true north line with a star, magnetic north with a full or half arrow

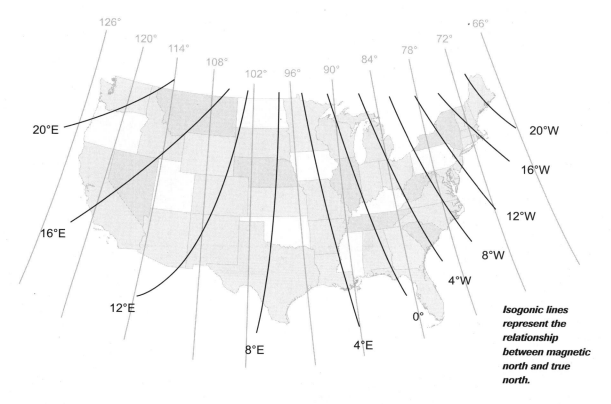

126° 120° 114° 108° 102° 96° 90° 84° 78° 72° ·66°

20°E

16°E

12°E

8°E

4°E

0°

4°W

8°W

12°W

16°W

20°W

Isogonic lines represent the relationship between magnetic north and true north.

and in some cases the letters *MN*, and grid north as a straight line and the letters *GN*. In addition to the lines, the declination angles between magnetic and true north and grid and true north are given. The importance of these declination angles is covered in Chapter 4.

Nautical charts use a compass rose to show the relationship of true and magnetic north. The compass rose has an outer ring that provides a true north heading without compensating for magnetic variation; 0 on the outer ring should be directly perpendicular to the chart. The middle ring provides the magnetic heading as it relates to your location on the map. It compensates for the variation between magnetic and true north and allows you to determine a heading without orienting the chart or using a protractor (provided you know where you are and where you are going). A reference to the amount of declination (variance) between true and magnetic north is listed in the center of the compass rose. Charts covering a large surface area will have several of these located within its borders. The purpose of this information will be discussed in more detail later in Chapter 5.

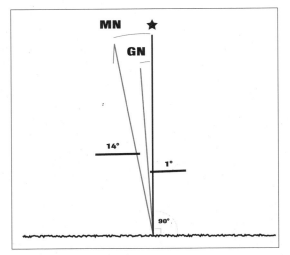

*Magnetic north and grid north
are west of true north.*

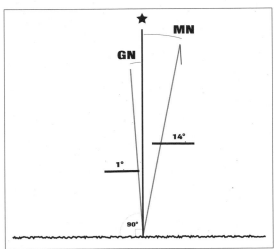

*Magnetic north is east and grid north
is west of true north.*

**Nautical charts
use a compass
rose to show the
declination angle
between true and
magnetic north.**

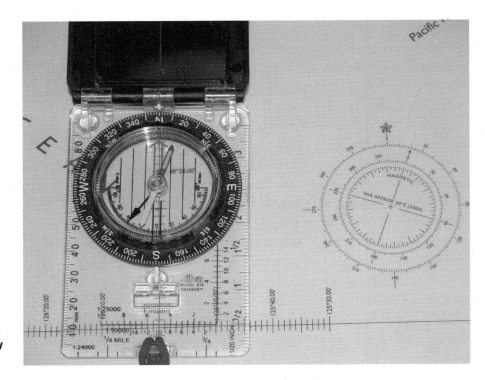

■ Horizontal and Vertical Datums

Contrary to popular belief, the Earth is not quite a sphere; its irregular shape makes measuring coordinates and altitude far more difficult. This irregular-shaped sphere is often called a "geoid," and it's the geoid's shell that is used in calculating the precise measurements of various points on the earth's surface. The earth's shape (geoid) and reference points used for map preparation are collectively called a "datum." There are two kinds of datum values: one for calculating relative horizontal positions and one for calculating relative vertical positions.

The most common horizontal datums in the United States are the older NAD27 (North American Datum of 1927) and the newer NAD83 (North American Datum of 1983). The WGS84 datum (World Geodetic System of 1984) is similar to the NAD83 and is the default datum for the GPS receiver. The most common vertical U.S. datums are the National Geodetic Vertical Datum of 1929 (NGVD 29), Local Mean Sea Level (LMSL), and the North American Vertical Datum of 1988 (NAVD88). Although most USGS maps were created using the older NAD27 and NGVD29 datums, updates will probably use horizontal datum NAD83 and vertical datum NAVD88. Using the wrong datum when combining two maps, transmitting coordinates, or using a GPS can cause errors of up to 200 meters or more. The type of datum used in the map design is usually listed in the marginal information. Additionally, some maps provide the

47° 22′ 30″
115° 37′ 30″   ⁶05   490 00(

PRODUCED BY THE UNITED STATES GEOLOGICAL SURVEY
CONTROL BY . . . . USGS, NOS/NOAA
COMPILED FROM AERIAL PHOTOGRAPHS TAKEN 1980
FIELD CHECKED 1982   MAP EDITED 1988
PROJECTION . . . . LAMBERT CONFORMAL CONIC
GRID: 1000-METER UNIVERSAL TRANSVERSE MERCATOR . . . . . . ZONE 11
    10,000-FOOT STATE GRID TICKS . . . . . . MONTANA, CENTRAL ZONE
                                    IDAHO, WEST ZONE
UTM GRID DECLINATION . . . . 1°04′ EAST
1988 MAGNETIC NORTH DECLINATION . . . . 18°30′ EAST
VERTICAL DATUM . . . . NATIONAL GEODETIC VERTICAL DATUM OF 1929
HORIZONTAL DATUM . . . . 1927 NORTH AMERICAN DATUM
To place on the predicted North American Datum of 1983,
move the projection lines as shown by dashed corner ticks
(13 meters north and 74 meters east)
There may be private inholdings within the boundaries of any
Federal and State Reservations shown on this map

*Datum as shown
on a USGS map.*

details needed to convert from one datum to another. One example is on the USGS map shown on the previous page.

■ Contour Lines

Contour lines are imaginary lines (superimposed on a map) that connect points of equal elevation. Charts, unlike maps, rarely use contour lines. Instead they list water depths as numbers and provide information regarding passageways and shallow areas that help the navigator avoid obstacles. Topographical maps use contour lines to reflect the land's elevation changes related to the map's vertical datum (often equivalent to mean sea level). The interval between two contour lines is usually found in the map's margins close to the bar scale. Each map uses a contour interval that best suits its size and the steepness of terrain; thus the contour interval between two maps is not always the same.

Contour lines are normally brown. In order to help the navigator calculate larger elevation changes, every fifth line is bolded. In addition, in relatively flat areas, dashed contour lines might appear between the regular lines. The dashed lines usually represent one-half of the contour line's regular intervals. Contour lines help provide information related to the terrain's elevation, slope, and shape.

Elevation

Your elevation or that of a destination can be obtained using contour lines. On most maps the fifth bolded line will provide a number value (in feet or meters) related to mean sea level. Using the fifth line's known elevation allows you to quickly identify an elevation by adding or subtracting the contour interval (distance between each contour line) for each line above or below the referenced line. Maps provide a numeric value for elevation of such items as peaks, road junctions, and benchmarks (surveyor's vertical junction points marked with an *X* and the letters *BM*).

Slope

Contour lines help identify the steepness of a slope that may fall within a route of travel. Lines that are close together represent steep terrain; lines far apart represent a more gradual, gentle slope.

Shape

Contour shapes help identify various land features, such as peaks, depressions, saddles, valleys, drainages, and ridgelines.

- **Peak.** A high point (mountain or hilltop). Contour line forms an enclosed circle.
- **Depression.** A low point. Contour line forms an enclosed circle with short in-pointing dashes from the inner surface.
- **Saddle.** A low area between two peaks. Contour lines usually form a U or V between the two peaks. Saddles provide easier passage through mountainous terrain.
- **Valley.** A large low-lying area. Contour lines are similar to a saddle, except the low area is much larger than the smaller passage found in a saddle.
- **Drainage.** An area with sharp, upsloping sides usually found close to a peak. Contour lines form a V pointing toward higher elevation. Year-round or intermittent creeks are often found in drainages.
- **Ridgeline.** An area with sharp downsloping sides usually found close to a peak. Contour lines form a V pointing toward lower elevation.

Three-Dimensional Terrain Features

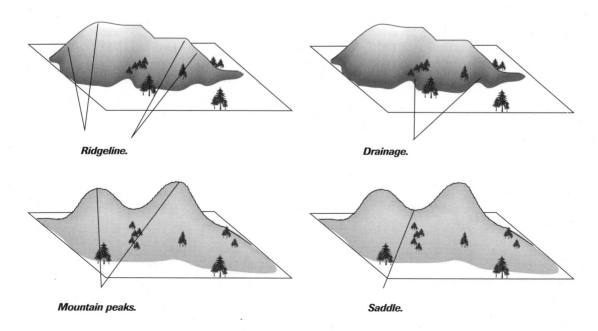

Ridgeline.

Drainage.

Mountain peaks.

Saddle.

Two-Dimensional Terrain Features

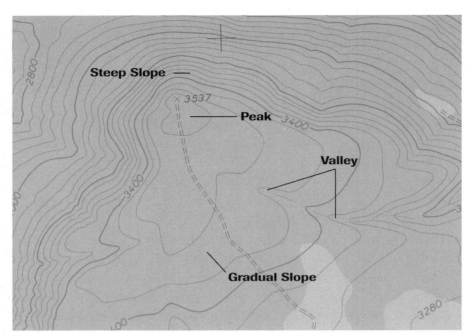

Steep slopes, gradual slopes, peaks, and valleys.

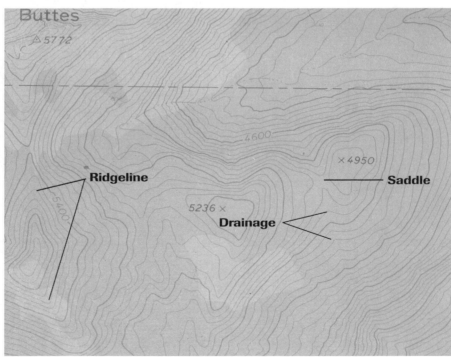

Saddles, ridgelines, and drainages.

■ Map Colors and Symbols

Maps provide a fair amount of information inside and outside the margins. Understanding the meaning of these various colors and symbols is a great navigation aid. When evaluating the accuracy of symbols, however, don't forget to check the map's date. Roads, buildings, and other features may have changed since the publication date and may be quite different than they appear to be on a map that is thirty years old.

Topographic Map Colors

- **Green.** Heavy vegetation, woods, scrubs, and orchards.
- **White.** Nonforested areas, such as rocks and meadows.
- **Blue.** Waterways, such as lakes, rivers, streams, swamps, marshes, and contour lines of glaciers.
- **Black.** Man-made structures, such as buildings, roads, and trails.
- **Red.** Prominent man-made items, such as major roads and surveying lines.
- **Brown.** Contour lines that show elevation.

Topographic Map Symbols

Map and chart symbols provide the viewer with a quick reference to physical, cultural, and political features. Physical features may include roads, rivers, cities, mountains, etc. Nonphysical features may include grid lines and forest boundaries. Unfortunately, many maps do not provide a comprehensive legend of what each symbol stands for; therefore, it is best to become familiar with your map's symbols before departure. The following guide to map colors and symbols is provided for review.

Topographic Map Symbols

Elevation

CONTOURS

Topographic

Intermediate	
Index	
Supplementary	
Depression	
Cut; fill	

Bathymetric

Intermediate	
Index	
Primary	
Index Primary	
Supplementary	

Boundaries

LAND SURVEY SYSTEMS

U.S. Public Land Survey System

Township or range line	
Location doubtful	----
Section line	
Location doubtful	----
Found section corner; found closing corner	
Witness corner; meander corner	WC / MC

Other land surveys

Township or range line	··············
Section line	··············
Land grant or mining claim; monument	--·--□
Fenced line	-------

BOUNDARIES

National	— —
State or territorial	— —
County or equivalent	— —
Civil township or equivalent	— —
Incorporated city or equivalent	— —
Park, reservation, or monument	—·—
Small park	-------

Land Surface Features

SURFACE FEATURES

Levee	Levee
Sand or mud area, dunes, or shifting sand	Sand
Intricate surface area	Strip Mine
Gravel beach or glacial moraine	Gravel
Tailings pond	Tailings Pond

MINES and CAVES

Quarry or open pit mine	
Gravel, sand, clay, or borrow pit	
Mine tunnel or cave entrance	
Prospect; mine shaft	x ■
Mine dump	Mine dump
Tailings	Tailings

VEGETATION

Woods	
Scrub	
Orchard	
Vineyard	
Mangrove	Mangrove

Buildings and Related Features

BUILDINGS and RELATED FEATURES

Building	■ □ ▭ ▭
School; church	
Built-up area	
Racetrack	
Airport	
Landing strip	-------
Well (other than water); windmill	○
Tanks	● ○
Covered reservoir	○ ▭
Gauging station	
Landmark object (feature as labeled)	⊗
Campground; picnic area	
Cemetery: small; large	† Cem

Topographic Map Symbols

Roads, Railroads, and Other Features

ROADS and RELATED FEATURES

Roads on Provisional edition maps are not classified as primary, secondary, or light duty. They are all symbolized as light duty.

Primary highway	
Secondary highway	
Light duty road	
Unimproved road	
Trail	
Dual highway	
Dual highway with median strip	
Road under construction	U.C.
Underpass; overpass	
Bridge	
Drawbridge	
Tunnel	

RAILROADS and RELATED FEATURES

Standard gauge single track; station	
Standard gauge multiple track	
Abandoned	
Under construction	
Narrow gauge single track	
Narrow gauge multiple track	
Railroad in street	
Juxtaposition	
Roundhouse and turntable	

TRANSMISSION LINES and PIPELINES

Power transmission line: pole; tower	
Telephone line	Telephone
Aboveground oil or gas pipeline	
Underground oil or gas pipeline	Pipeline

Water Features

MARINE SHORELINE

Topographic maps

Approximate mean high water	
Indefinite or unsurveyed	

Topographic-bathymetric maps

Moon-high water	
Apparent (edge of vegetation)	

COASTAL FEATURES

Foreshore flat	
Rock or coral reef	
Rock bare or awash	
Group of rocks bare or awash	
Exposed wreck	
Depth curve; sounding	3
Breakwater, pier, jetty, or wharf	
Seawall	

BATHYMETRIC FEATURES

Area exposed at mean low tide; sounding alarm	
Channel	
Offshore oil or gas: well; platform	
Sunken rock	

RIVERS, LAKES, CANALS, and Swamps

Intermittent stream	
Intermittent river	
Disappearing stream	
Perennial stream	
Perennial river	
Small falls; small rapids	
Large falls; large rapids	
Masonry dam	
Dam with lock	
Dam carrying road	
Perennial lake; Intermittent lake or pond	
Dry lake	
Narrow wash	
Wide wash	Wash
Canal, flume, or aqueduct with lock	
Elevated aqueduct, flume, or conduit	
Aqueduct tunnel	
Well or spring; spring or seep	
Marsh or swamp	

■ Chart Colors and Symbols

A large variation of colors and symbols can be used with charts. To best learn these, purchase a small booklet called *Chart No. 1*. This aid is published by the National Oceanic and Atmospheric Administration (NOAA) and National Image and Mapping Agency (NIMA) and provides the most comprehensive review of chart symbols. Take the time to review these symbols—in advance of your trip—and learn to recognize their meaning. Most nautical charts are published by the NOAA. The following colors and symbols are general guidelines on what you might see on a chart. For greater detail review *Chart No. 1*.

Nautical Chart Colors

■ **Yellow or gray tint.** Land areas on charts are often a yellowish or gray tint.

■ **Blue.** Shallow or shoal waters are often shown in blue.

■ **White.** Deepwater areas are shown in white.

■ **Shaded.** Shoal areas are often circled or shaded to give them greater visibility.

■ **Green.** Areas that may be submerged at high tide (sandbars, mudflats, and marshes) are often shown in green.

■ **Magenta.** Magenta is used for a fair amount of chart information because it is easier to read under red nightlights.

Nautical Chart Symbols

■ **Letters and numbers.**

  ■ **Feet, fathoms, and meters.** Bottom soundings (depth) are marked in feet, fathoms, or meters throughout the chart and relate to depths at mean low water.

  ■ **Slanting or Italic letters.** This lettering identifies submerged or floating features, with their height at mean high tide.

  ■ **Upright or Roman letters.** This type of lettering is used to identify features that are dry at high water.

■ **Lines.** Channel limits are often shown by lines.

■ **Solid lines with shading.** The shoreline is represented as a solid line, with the land portions shaded.

■ **Landmark symbols.** Land features on charts are often limited to major landmarks that help with navigation. These can include peaks, buildings, radio towers, and other prominent man-made and natural features.

■ **Man-made safety markers.** The location of man-made safety markers is labeled with a symbol and brief description.

    ■ **Lighthouses.** The elevated light helps the mariner avoid dangerous areas. In addition to light, lighthouses often have fog signaling and radio beacon equipment.

    ■ **Buoys.** Buoys are anchored floating markers that help vessels avoid dangers and navigate in and out of channels. Buoys come in several shapes and colors that help identify their purpose. Buoys located on the right side of a channel (leading in from seaward) are painted red and support even numbers (increasing from seaward). If a light is used, it will be red. Nun-shaped buoys (buoys with a cone-shaped top) are used when there is no light. Buoys located on the left side of a channel (leading in from seaward) are painted green and support odd numbers (increasing from seaward). If a light is used, it will be green. Can-shaped buoys (buoys with a cylinder shape) are used when there is no light. Buoys located at a junction or midchannel can be either nuns or cans and may or may not have numbers on them. Junction buoys are painted with horizontal red and green strips; midchannel buoys are painted with horizontal red and white strips. If a light is used, it will be white.

    ■ **Day markers.** Day markers are small signs held in place by poles. During daylight hours markers help vessels avoid dangers and navigate in and out of channels. Markers come in several shapes and colors that help identify their purpose. Markers located on the right side of a channel (leading in from seaward) are triangular shaped, painted red, and support even numbers (increasing from seaward). Markers located on the left side of a channel (leading in from seaward) are square shaped, painted green, and support odd numbers (increasing from seaward). Markers located midchannel are octagonal shaped.

    ■ **Lights.** Lights are described on charts by their behavior, height (at mean high water tide level), and projected visible range. For example, a chart that lists a light as "Fl 4sec 20ft 10M" is telling you that the light flashes every four seconds, is 20 feet above mean high water tide level, and has a predicted range of 10 nautical miles.

■ **Light behavior.** Table 3-3 notes light symbols and behaviors.

Table 3-3: Light Symbols and Meanings

Symbol	Meaning (light behavior)
F	Fixed light; a continuous steady light.
Fl	Flashing lights; a single flash at regular intervals where the duration of the flash is always less than the duration of darkness.
F Fl	Fixed light varied by bright flashes at regular intervals.
F Gp Fl	Fixed light varied by two or more bright flashes at regular intervals.
Gp Fl	Two or more bright flashes shown at regular intervals.
Gp Fl (1 + 2)	Bright flashes shown in an alternating sequence of numbers.
E Int	Flashing lights; a single flash at regular intervals, where the duration of the flash is equal to the duration of darkness.
Occ	Flashing lights; a single flash at regular intervals, where the duration of the flash is always longer than the duration of darkness.
Gp Occ	Two or more bright flashes shown at regular intervals (flash longer than darkness).
Gp Occ	Bright flashes shown in an alternating sequence of numbers (flash longer than darkness).

- **Light height.** When floating at sea level, the light's height is probably the most important factor of how well and far away it can be seen.
- **Visibility range.** Charts that list a light's projected visibility do so based on the brightness of the light. This **normal range** is calculated using a direct line of sight and doesn't account for the earth's curvature. If you're sitting on the floor of a life raft or deck of a sea kayak, the earth's curvature will reduce the light's visible distance. This distance is called the **geographic range** and can be calculated using the following formula:

Geographic range (miles) = square root of the light's height (in feet) + 1.5 miles

Chart and Map Care

A chart or map is a very valuable tool for identifying location and for traveling from one location to another. Take the time to protect it from damage. On trips where foul weather is expected, it is well worth the effort to laminate your map. On all trips, fold and store the map in either a clear plastic bag or a protective map cover. I often fold the map to expose the area I am in without removing it from the protective plastic cover.

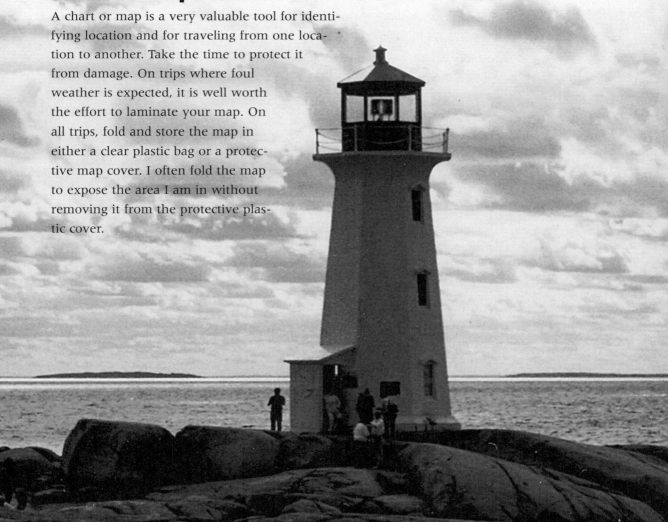

Chapter Exercises

Identify the chart/maps projection.

Is it Mercator, Transverse Mercator, Gnomeric, or another type of projection? Review the meaning of the projection found on your chart or map.

Identify the type of chart or map you are using.

How is the chart or map commonly used? Is it large or small scale? What is the ratio of one unit on the chart or map to actual distance covered?

Identify basic chart or map information found in the margins.

Things to identify include (not limited to) publishing date, title, ratio and distance, and adjoining maps. How does the publish date impact the accuracy of the map?

Identify angular coordinates (latitude and longitude) of a known location.

Using a chart or map, find the latitude and longitude of a known location. Remember that latitude lines are like the rungs of a ladder and increase to the north and south of the equator; longitude lines run perpendicular to latitude lines, increasing to the east and west of Greenwich, England (Prime Meridian).

Identify rectangular coordinates (UTM) of a known location.

Using a chart or map, find the UTMs easting and northing of a known location. Remember to identify your zone, read the easting value first, and to state which hemisphere you are in (north or south). Based on the number of combined UTM coordinates, how big is the grid you identified?

Identify the chart's or map's declination information.

Using the map's declination diagram or chart's compass rose, identify the difference between true and magnetic north. If using a map that provides UTM grids, identify grid north and how it relates to true north and magnetic north.

Identify basic contour line information and how it might impact your travel.

Using a chart or map, identify the elevation of a known location. From that location draw a line to another location that is at least 10 cm (approximately 4 inches) away, and identify the slope changes that occur between the two locations (lines close together represent steep terrain; lines far apart represent a gradual slope). Finally, take a look at the surrounding contour lines and try to identify peaks, depressions, saddles, ridgelines, drainages, valleys, etc.

Identify basic chart or map colors.

Identify basic chart or map symbols.

All About Compasses

Two years ago I watched a hiker try to orient his map while it was sitting on his truck's metal tailgate. He went through the process with great care, taking the time to box the magnetic north-seeking arrow. It was obvious that he knew how to orient a map. It was also obvious that he didn't understand how his compass worked. He didn't realize that nearby metal would disorient the compass magnet. Don't make the same mistake! Taking the time to understand the compass makes it easier to use.

Magnetic Forces Affecting a Compass

A compass provides direction using a rotating needle (or disc) that seeks out the earth's magnetic field and stops when it is aligned with the magnetic force. The northern end of the compass's needle points to an encircling ring of numbers that allow us to determine direction. A compass that uses a disc also has a northern end, but the numbers that help determine direction are located on the disc. The magnetic forces affecting a compass are magnetic north, local magnetic field influences, and magnetic interference.

■ Magnetic North

Compass arrows point to the magnetic north pole located where the earth's magnetic field is most concentrated. More specifically, the magnetic pole is located close to 74 degrees North latitude and 101 degrees West longitude (northern Canada), which is around 1,600 kilometers (1,000 miles) from true north. The difference between true and magnetic north (called declination for maps and variation for charts) is different from place to place and year to year because of the earth's never-ending magnetic shifts.

Magnetic North Pole **True North**

Magnetic north is approximately 1,000 miles from the true North Pole.

True South **Magnetic South Pole**

To further explain the difference between magnetic north and true north, take a look at the following illustration. Notice the line that passes through the Great Lakes and along the coast of Florida. This line is an agonic line, and a compass heading of 0 or 360 degrees would point toward both magnetic and true north. In other words, there is no magnetic variation. Lines with a variation between true and magnetic north are known as isogonic lines. The line that extends through Maine has a variation of 20 degrees west. Note that when this line is extended, the compass bearing of 360 is 20 degrees to the west of true north and the compass heading for true north is actually 20 degrees. The opposite would be true for the line extending through Washington. In this case, a compass bearing of 360 would be 20 degrees east of true north and the compass heading for true north is actually 340 degrees. Because of these variations, adjustments must be made in order to use a map and compass together (discussed in Chapter 5).

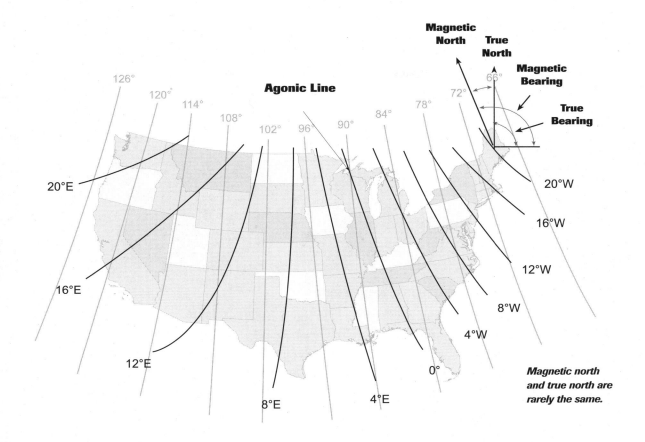

Magnetic North • True North • Magnetic Bearing • True Bearing

Agonic Line

126° 120° 114° 108° 102° 96° 90° 84° 78° 72° 66°

20°E
16°E
12°E
8°E
4°E
0°
4°W
8°W
12°W
16°W
20°W

Magnetic north and true north are rarely the same.

■ Local Magnetic Field Influences

Dips associated with the earth's magnetic field (at various locations) affect the compass's north-seeking arrow. These dips, called magnetic inclination, occur because the earth's magnetic field is almost perpendicular to the earth's surface at either pole. Only at the magnetic equator does the magnetic force run horizontal to the earth's surface. As a result, when close to the poles the compass's magnetic needle is pulled down (dips) away from horizontal. The needle's north end dips down in the Northern Hemisphere and its south end dips down in the Southern Hemisphere. To compensate for the dip, compass needles are made with a counterbalance specific to the area of intended use. A compass balanced for one zone would not work well in another zone. Suunto uses the magnetic inclination zones shown in the following illustration for compasses they market.

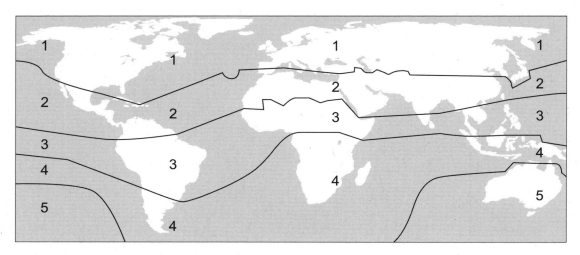

Magnetic fields.

■ Magnetic Interference

A compass's magnetic-seeking arrow is a nondiscriminatory device that seeks out any magnetic source. This includes automobiles (steel), buildings (electric currents), metal fencing, telephone lines, belt buckles, and knives. The magnetic north–seeking arrow is very susceptible to being pulled away when too close to such objects. It is best to stay a safe distance from power lines (60 plus meters), vehicles (20 meters), fencing and telephone lines (10 meters), and other handheld metal devices (3 meters).

Types of Compasses

A compass allows the traveler to identify direction, and although there are several types of compasses available, the most common styles are referred to as orienteering (baseplate), fixed dial, and magnetic card.

■ Orienteering (Baseplate) Compass

All orienteering compasses (also known as the baseplate compass) have a circular housing mounted on a rectangular base. Some also come with built-in clinometers, declination adjustability, and mirrors.

Orienteering Compass Nomenclature

Regardless of the type of orienteering compass you purchase, it should have a basic design that features a rectangular baseplate, circular rotating housing, and a magnetic north–seeking arrow.

Rectangular Baseplate. The sides of the orienteering compass's baseplate are often straight and have millimeter and inch markings that can be used to measure distances. These measurements may or may not be to the map's scale. When not to the map's scale, the markings can be used to measure distances via the map's distance guide (often located in the map's margins). The front of the compass has a direction-of-travel arrow that runs parallel to the long edge and perpendicular to the short edge. Compass headings are read from the point where the bottom of the direction-of-travel arrow touches the numbers on the edge of the circular compass housing. If the direction-of-travel arrow is not present or centered on the circular housing, your compass will probably have a stationary index line (sometimes called an index pointer). This nonmoving, short white line is either located on the baseplate next to the circular housing or inside the circular housing just beneath the moving numbers (it will be centered on the short wall of the baseplate and on the same side of the compass as the direction-of-travel arrow). Headings are read where the numbers touch or pass over this line (depending on which is used). The direction-of-travel arrow must always point toward the intended destination when a heading is being taken.

Circular Housing. A circular rotating housing rests and rotates on the baseplate. The housing's outer ring displays the four cardinal points (N, S, E, W) and degree lines that start at north and are numbered clockwise to 360 degrees. The bottom of the housing has an etched orienting arrow that points toward the north marking on the outer ring.

Magnetic Needle. The compass's north-seeking needle sits beneath the glass of the circular housing. It is free floating, with the magnetic north–seeking end of the needle often red. Magnetic north lies near Prince

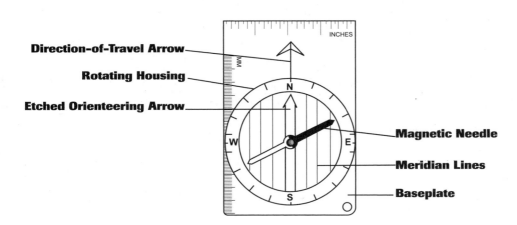

Basic orienteering compass.

of Wales Island in northern Canada, where the earth's electric currents are high. These currents are continually changing; thus the magnetic field they produce also changes. This means the exact location and declination for magnetic north also change over time.

Beyond the Basics. A no-frills orienteering compass will provide the basics. Depending on your budget, however, you may elect to purchase an orienteering compass with added features. Perhaps you travel in snow country and desire a clinometer or prefer the added precision found in a mirror compass so that you can sight the compass on a distant point while the magnetic needle is aligned with the north reference on the dial. Some compasses come with a dial that lets you set the magnetic declination so that a compass heading of 360 points toward true north (for the area you are in). If using a compass that can be set for a given magnetic declination, be sure it is set for the correct declination each time you begin a trip. The declination of your last venture may not be the same as your current one.

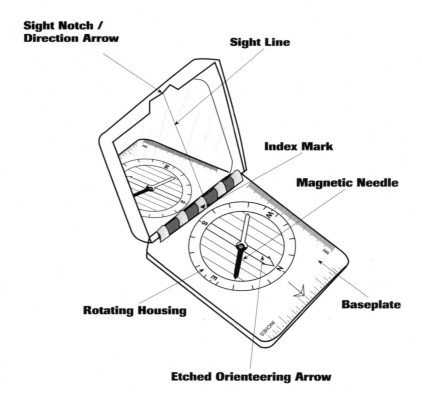

Sight Notch / Direction Arrow

Sight Line

Index Mark

Magnetic Needle

Rotating Housing

Baseplate

Etched Orienteering Arrow

Mirrored orienteering compass.

How to Hold an Orienteering Compass

To shoot a heading using an orienteering compass, point the direction-of-travel arrow at the identified landmark and turn its circular housing until the etched orienteering arrow boxes the magnetic needle (red end forward). Record the heading located at the point where the direction-of-travel arrow intersects the compass's circular housing. When shooting a bearing, hold the compass flat in your cupped hands so that the needle floats freely and the backside of the baseplate is parallel to your body's plane. If you need to adjust which way the compass is pointing, move the compass and your body as one. Doing this keeps the compass directly between the target and your line of sight. If the orienteering compass has a sighting device, bend the front section so that it is about 90 degrees to the baseplate, and use the mirror and sighting line to line up the intended target. At this point, turn the circular housing until the etched orienteering arrow boxes the magnetic needle, and find a heading using the same technique as done for a standard baseplate compass.

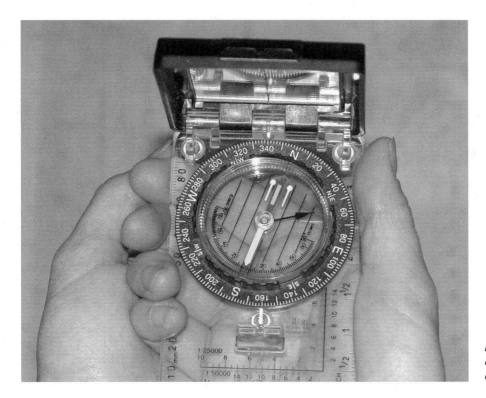

Holding an orienteering compass.

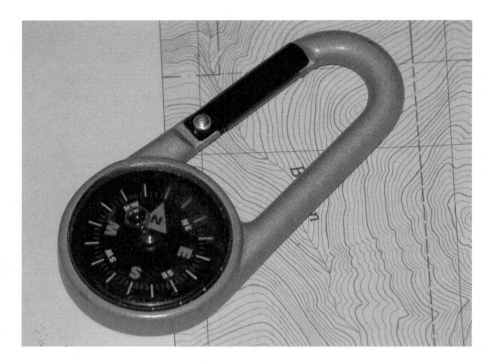

A small emergency fixed-dial compass.

■ Fixed Dial Compass

Fixed-dial compasses are an ideal small augment to your survival gear, but they don't provide enough accuracy for use as a primary tool. These tools have a free-floating needle that pivots and rotates on a bearing located inside a circular housing. The housing's outer ring displays the four cardinal points (N, S, E, W) and may or may not display degree lines starting at north and increasing clockwise to 360 degrees. A fixed-dial compass is held like an orienteering compass. Cardinal directions are determined based on the magnetic north heading for your location. In other words, cardinal directions are determined when the compass is held in such a way that the magnetic north–seeking arrow points to the magnetic north heading.

■ Magnetic Card Compass

Both the orienteering and fixed-dial compass use a free-floating needle that rotates on a pivot around a fixed dial. The magnetic card compass, however, joins the needle and dial on a card that sits on a pivot. The needle is finely balanced, allowing it to float freely with the arrow constantly aligned to magnetic north. The dial has cardinal directions (N, S, E, W) and is numbered between 0 and 360 degrees. With an orienteering compass, a heading is established only when the circular housing is turned and the north-seeking arrow is boxed. Providing the front of the compass points in the same direction you're facing, the heading from magnetic card compasses is found directly under the index (lubber) line.

Magnetic Card Compass Nomenclature

The most widely known magnetic card compass is the military lensatic compass. Other well-known types include the marine and the automobile compass.

Military Lensatic Compass. The military lensatic compass has three major components: the cover, the base, and the rear-sighting lens.

- **Cover.** The compass cover protects the floating dial. It contains the sighting wire (front sight) and two luminous sighting slots or dots used for night navigation.
- **Base.** The body of the compass comprises a floating dial, a bezel ring, and a thumb loop.
  - **The floating dial.** The floating dial is mounted on a pivot so that it can rotate freely when the compass is held level. Printed on the dial in luminous figures are an arrow and the letters *E* and *W.* The arrow always points to magnetic north. The floating dial has an outer scale that denotes miles and an inner scale that denotes degrees. For our purposes, the only scale that matters is the one that represents degrees. The floating dial is encased by a flat piece of glass that also supports a fixed black index line.
  - **The bezel ring.** This is a notched device that clicks when turned. It has 120 notches, and each click is equal to 3 degrees. Knowing the number of degrees for each click is an aid when trying to set your compass to a heading for night travel—something I strongly discourage. The short, luminous line that rotates with the bezel ring can be used to help you stay on course. Providing the desired heading falls under the fixed black index line, you can rotate the bezel ring until the luminous line is aligned with the north-seeking arrow. Once set, you can quickly check your direction of travel by realigning the luminous line and the north-seeking arrow.
  - **The thumb loop.** This loop is attached to the base of the compass and is used to help support the compass when shooting a heading.

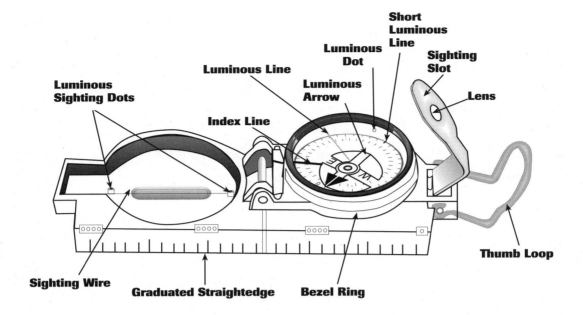

Luminous Sighting Dots

Luminous Line

Index Line

Luminous Arrow

Luminous Dot

Short Luminous Line

Sighting Slot

Lens

Thumb Loop

Sighting Wire

Graduated Straightedge

Bezel Ring

The military lensatic compass uses a magnetic card.

■ **Rear-sighting lens.** The lens helps increase precision when reading an azimuth. In addition, just above the lens there is a slot that can be used in conjunction with the front-sighting wire when shooting a heading. Beware: When the rear-sighting lens is closed more than 45 degrees, it locks the floating dial in place. Don't make this mistake when trying to take a reading.

Marine and Automobile Compasses. In most instances, marine and automobile compasses are mounted on the vessel or car and have been adjusted to account for magnetic deviation caused by forces specific to the boat or vehicle (engine, anchor, etc.). This adjustment makes it unpractical to dismount the compass for use with land navigation unless you know the deviation and can adjust for its absence (when establishing direction). If you happen to have a marine or automobile compass that has not had a magnetic deviation adjustment, it can be used for land navigation in the same way as any similar compass might be. If attached to the vessel or car, the lubber line is aligned with the front of the vessel or auto so that all headings represent the direction of travel. On land, as long as the front of your compass is pointing in the direction of your intended travel, headings are read directly below the lubber line.

How to Hold a Magnetic Card Compass

Military Lensatic Compass. Point the front of the compass at the identi-fied landmark so that the landmark is centered on the compass's sighting

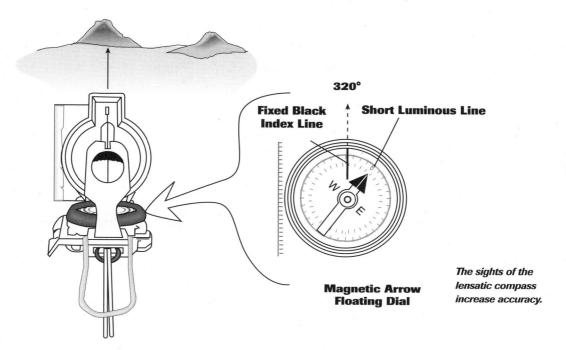

320°

Fixed Black Index Line

Short Luminous Line

Magnetic Arrow Floating Dial

The sights of the lensatic compass increase accuracy.

wire. While holding the compass level and steady, read the heading below the stationary index line. When shooting a bearing, hold the compass by sliding your thumb through the thumb loop and resting its main compartment on top of your thumb and closed fist. Bend the forward half of the compass so that it forms a 60- to 90-degree angle between it and the back section (actual compass). Next, lift up the compass's sighting slot and lens until a 45-degree angle is formed. Finally, raise the compass to your cheek so that the landmark can be seen and centered on the sighting wire (which is centered on the sighting slot) while you use the magnifying lens to read the heading under the stationary index line. Be sure to move the compass and your body in the same manner as discussed for an orienteering compass.

Maritime Compass. When using a handheld marine compass, point the front of the compass at the landmark and read the heading under the fixed lubber line. When using a deck-mounted marine compass, point the front of the vessel at the landmark. If handheld, position the compass to your body in the same manner as discussed for an orienteering compass.

Creating Your Own Compass

A compass that provides general cardinal directions can be improvised using a piece of steel (needle, paper clip, etc.), something that floats, and a

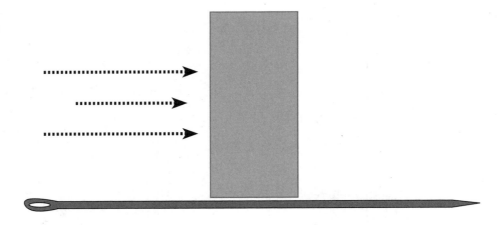

Stroke the magnet across the steel ten to twenty times.

magnet. In order to work, the piece of steel will need to be magnetized.

The first step is to turn the needle (or paper clip) into a magnet. The easiest way to do this is with another magnet, stroking the magnet along the needle ten or twenty times as shown above.

Next you'll need a container (improvised from your gear or Mother Nature) that can hold water and something that floats (cork, leaf, etc.). Place the float in the water and the needle on the float. This frictionless (free-floating) method allows the needle to seek out magnetic north (provided there isn't any interference). Once the needle has stopped moving, it should be lined up with north and south. Determining which direction is north or south, however, requires the use of the sun, stars, and terrain features.

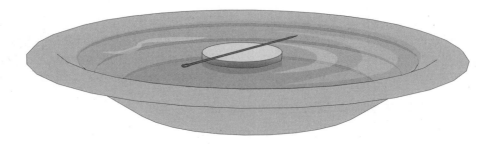

The needle needs to float without obstruction.

Chapter Exercises

Identify magnetic declination.

Take a look at your map or chart and identify its magnetic deviation. Is it to the east or west of true north?

Identify the type of compass you have.

What type of compass are you using? Look at every aspect of it. Identify its basic parts (baseplate, housing, magnetic needle). How does each of the parts interact to provide a magnetic north reference? Does it have a clinometer or other elaborate feature? If it does, practice using it.

Adjust for magnetic declination.

If your compass has the ability to adjust for the magnetic declination (meaning a compass heading of 360 degrees points to true north) and you are not on an agonic line, practice making this adjustment.

Identify the effects of magnetic interference.

While standing at least 20 meters away from your car, hold your compass so that the magnetic-seeking arrow is free floating. While observing the compass needle, begin walking toward the car. How close can you get before the needle is drawn off magnetic north and toward the car? Try this on different types and sizes of vehicles to see the impact of each.

Create a magnetized needle.

Using a speaker magnet or any other source you can find, make a magnetized needle compass as outlined in this chapter. Be sure to do it away from any metal interference. Once the steel has settled into a specific direction, pull out your compass and see if its magnetic north is the same as found using the magnetized needle.

These rescuers take a moment to find cardinal direction and location.

SECTION III

Finding Cardinal Direction & Location

In order to travel from one point to another, first you must be able to identify where you are. Hopefully, you can. If you don't know exactly where you are, however, knowing your general location will be the key to helping pinpoint your exact position. Without this knowledge you might not even be looking at the right map (especially if you're traveling by car, boat, or plane).

This section provides details on how to find cardinal directions and your location using a map and compass and celestial aids.

C H A P T E R 5

Using a Map & Compass

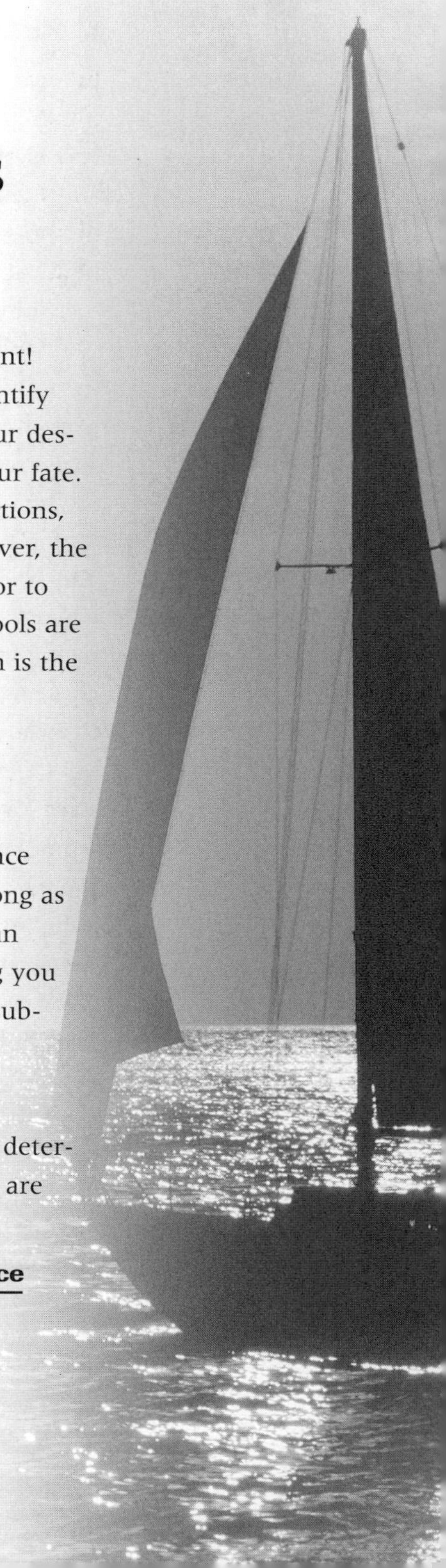

Understanding the nomenclature of a map and compass is important! Using them correctly in the wilderness is crucial. The ability to identify your location and plan a route of travel keeps you in charge of your destiny. Otherwise you are relying on luck and memory to control your fate.

The map and compass are excellent tools for identifying directions, location, resources, and how to get from point A to point B. However, the skill of using a map and compass is one that should be learned prior to departing into the great outdoors. Without this knowledge these tools are nothing more than added weight. Identifying your general location is the first step in map and compass use.

Dead Reckoning: Finding Your General Location

Dead reckoning is a mathematical process that calculates the distance traveled using your speed and time of travel as shown below. As long as you know your starting point and the time your trip began, you can determine your location based on your rate of travel and how long you have been moving. Any stops that alter the time frame should be subtracted from the total time.

Dead Reckoning: Rate × Time = Distance

The resultant distance can be applied to your line of travel to determine a general location. Also, as long as two of the three elements are known, the third unknown can be determined.

$$\text{Time} = \frac{\text{Distance}}{\text{Rate}} \qquad \text{Rate} = \frac{\text{Distance}}{\text{Time}}$$

■ Rate: How Fast

In a car the rate of speed relates to miles or kilometers per hour. Most maps use kilometers as the preferred unit of measurement. If you need to convert kilometers to miles or vice versa, 1 kilometer is equal to 0.6214 mile and 1 mile is equal to 1.609 kilometers. Mariners measure a vessel's speed in knots per hour and distance traveled in nautical miles. Most charts use a nautical mile as the preferred unit of measurement. A nautical mile is equal to 1 minute of latitude, 1.852 kilometers, and 1.1508 miles.

A backpacker's rate of speed is impacted by his or her physical fitness, the terrain, and the amount of weight carried. As a rule, a backpacker covers 1 to 3 miles per hour. Determining your average rate of speed requires some effort on your part. Take several trips where distances are known, and calculate the amount of time it takes to get from point A to point B. Record the information along with how much gear was carried and what type of terrain was covered. Over time you'll establish your average rate of speed, and this information can be applied to the dead reckoning formula. Another way to accomplish the same goal is to purchase an electronic pedometer (tracks distance covered) that can be used to establish your average rate of speed (Rate = Distance/Time).

Getting dead reckoning to work in a plane, car, or boat requires a constant awareness of the vehicle's speed. In a drifting boat, however, you won't have this luxury. Determining your speed in such an instance requires the use of a chip log. To create a chip log, attach a heavy floating object to a long heaving line and tie two knots in the line. Place the first knot so that it touches the water after the container has settled and the second knot at a premeasured distance from the first. Make sure the floating object used is heavy enough to maintain contact with the water. In other words, counteract the wind effect. To determine your rate of speed, set the container into the water, and as the line passes between your hands, record the amount of time that passes between hand contact with the first and second knot. To calculate your speed, plug this number into the following formula.

$$\text{Speed in knots} = \frac{0.6 \times \text{feet between marks}}{\text{Seconds of time between knots}} = \text{feet/second}$$

A speed of 1 knot per hour is equal to 1.15 statute miles per hour, or 1.69 feet per second. There are 5,280 feet in 1 statute mile. Since winds and currents change, your rate of speed should be evaluated on a regular basis. Constant awareness plays a major role in determining your general location.

■ Time: How Long

Provided you noticed the time of departure and what time you stopped, you can determine the distance traveled. It is important to recognize direction changes and establish a new starting time and location when each occurs. If any stops are made, subtract that time from the total time used in the formula.

■ Distance: How Far

Knowing how fast and how long you've traveled is not enough. You'll also need to know the starting point and the heading taken. To establish a heading when adrift, shoot a compass heading (azimuth) on a chip line and add or subtract 180 degrees from that figure. If on foot and you have a pedometer, distance may be known and can be used to establish your rate of speed (rate = distance/time) or estimated time of travel (time = distance/rate). If you don't have a pedometer and you are on *flat, open* terrain, you can establish gross distances using a map and the top of an easily identifiable landmark (seen on the horizon). First calculate the distance to the horizon (even if landmark bottom is not seen) by taking the square root of your eye height above the ground (in feet) and dividing by 0.5736.

$$\sqrt{\text{Eye height above ground in feet} / 0.5736} = \text{distance to the horizon in statute miles}$$

Next apply the same formula to the identified landmark's height (as noted on the map) and add that to the already calculated horizon distance. The result is a rough estimation of the object's distance from your location.

$$\sqrt{(\text{Identified landmark height in feet} / 0.5736)} + \text{distance to the horizon in miles} = \text{distance to the object in statute miles}$$

Knowing how far you have traveled or the distance to an object is extremely helpful when trying to determine your general location. Once you have a general idea of where you are, use the map and compass to hone in on your exact location. The first step in this process is to orient the map.

Orienting a Map

Orienting a map to the lay of the land is extremely helpful when you don't know where you are. The process allows you to orient a two-dimensional map to the surrounding terrain—both seen and unseen. Once done, the map, compass, and identified landmarks can be used to identify your exact location. For best results on land, get to high ground where you can see as many landmarks as possible. At sea, your relationship to land and the earth's curvature might impede your view. For best results, identify landmarks when your vessel is cresting a wave.

Open the map and place it on a flat, level, and protective surface, such as a tarp or plastic bag. Next identify the magnetic variation (declination) found within the map or in its legend, and set your compass appropriately. This is an important step! The map is drawn to true north (North Pole), but the compass points toward magnetic north (near Prince of Wales Island in northern Canada). Forgetting to identify the variation is a serious error, since a 360-degree map heading is not necessarily a 360-degree compass heading. To establish the *compass's* true north heading, use the following rules.

- **East is least.** If the declination is to the east, *subtract* it from 360 degrees to establish the compass heading to true north.
- **West is best.** If the declination is to the west, *add* it to 360 or 0 degrees to establish the compass heading to true north.

Magnetic Declination

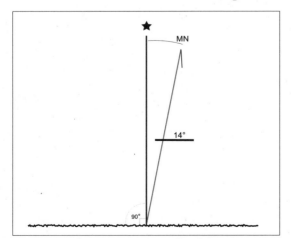

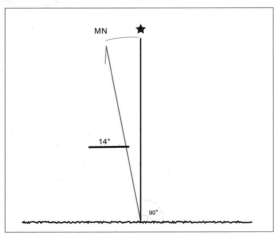

East is least—subtract magnetic declination from 360 degrees.

West is best—add magnetic declination to 360 degrees.

Once the compass's true north heading has been established, the next couple of steps will depend on the type of compass and map or chart you are using.

Oriented map using an orienteering compass.

■ Orienteering Compass

Rotate the compass's circular housing until the bottom of the direction-of-travel arrow touches the compass's true north heading. Place the long side of the compass on the map, parallel to a longitude line and with its direction-of-travel arrow pointing toward the map's north end. Next rotate the map and compass until the floating needle is centered inside the orienting arrow (red end forward) of the compass's baseplate. This is called "boxing the arrow" and is key to using an orienteering compass. Double-check the compass heading to make sure you didnt move the circular housing. Providing the heading is correct, the map is oriented.

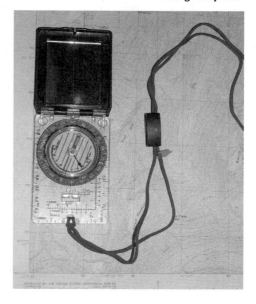

■ Magnetic Card Compasses

Lensatic and maritime compasses have floating dials that display a numerical heading. The dial sits on a pivot with the 360-degree heading directly above the magnetic needle mechanism. When 360 degrees is directly below the stationary index line (lubber line), the front of the compass is pointing toward magnetic north. Place the long side of the compass's on the map—parallel to a longitude line—and rotate the map and compass until the compass's true north heading (adjusted for the given declination) can be read below the stationary index line. Make sure the top of the compass is pointed toward the north end of the map. At this point the map is oriented. If you're using a maritime compass attached to a vessel, the lubber line will be oriented to the front of the vessel. Orienting the map may require maneuvering the vessel (unless you have a chart with a compass rose).

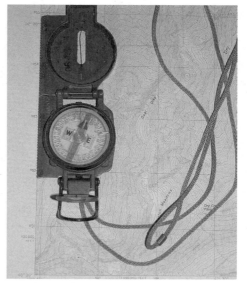

Oriented map using a magnetic card compass.

■ Orienting with a Compass Rose

Most charts use a compass rose to show the amount of declination for a given area. Larger charts will have several of these within the margins. The compass rose closest to your location is the one you should use. A compass rose has an outer ring that shows true north as it relates to the chart and a middle ring that shows true north as it relates to a compass. To orient the chart, lay the compass on the chart (parallel to a longitude line and pointing toward the north end) and rotate both until the compass's heading of 360 (below the lubber line) is in line with the inner ring's 0 degree heading. In the example provided, you would see a heading of 340° in line with the outer ring's 0°. If you prefer, you can ignore the inner ring and simply add the west variation to 0, using this heading and the outer ring to orient the map.

Once the map or chart is oriented, keep it in place by weighing down the edges using rocks, sticks, or other heavy objects. At this point you can use the map, compass, and surrounding terrain to identify your location.

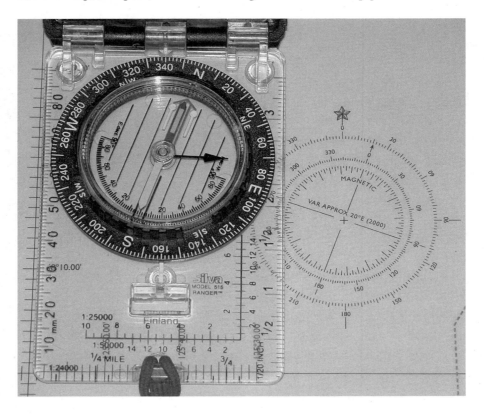

Oriented chart using a compass rose.

Terrain Evaluation Related to a Map Feature or Line of Travel

If you are on a referenced line such as a trail, road, or creek, finding your location may be as simple as evaluating the surrounding terrain. The same might be true if you have been moving in a straight line (on foot, in a car, or in vessel) and it can be referenced to a map. Identifying the land features in proximity to your position will help you recognize your location on your route of travel. Your ability to relate the seen terrain to its map portrayal is the key to success. For details on identifying map terrain, read below. If you have no referenced line, you'll need to identify a prominent land feature and use your compass to create a line of position.

Angulation: Line of Position

Angulation is the process of finding your location by shooting a heading off a prominent landmark, drawing it on an oriented map, and using terrain evaluation to establish where you're at related to the line. A prominent landmark might include such man-made items as a road, building, bridge, or lighthouse and such natural items as a stream, mountain, or large clearing.

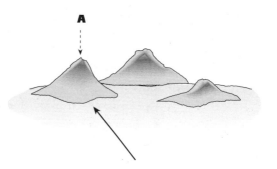

To angulate, use the following steps:

■ Step 1: Get to High Ground

On land get to high ground and in a large clearing where you can see as many landmarks as possible. At sea your best bet is to identify land features when cresting the top of a wave.

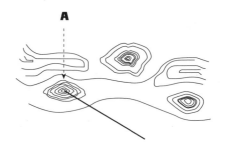

Angulation.

■ Step 2: Orient the Map

Orient the map or chart (see preceding) and weigh down its edges.

■ Step 3: Identify Prominent Sea/Landmarks

Identify a prominent land or sea feature (buoys and lights) that is sure to be displayed on the map.

Land Features

Relating a seen land feature to its two-dimensional map representation is an art that takes lots of practice. The best way to learn this skill is to put the map aside and pull out a pencil and paper. Try to think of the landmark by its contour (review Chapter 3 for information on contour lines), distance, and elevation in relationship to where you are.

Contour Lines. Draw the feature using contour lines. Does it have any ridgelines? If it does, are they steep or gradual descents? Is there a peak, saddle, or depression? Is it a clearing, swamp, or lake? Draw it in its entirety before referring to the map. On charts, land features are often shown as a symbol, making this step unnecessary.

Distance–Related to Your Position. Although a gross calculation, the following can be used to estimate how far the land feature is from your location. Write down your distance estimation. It will help you later.

■ **In treed terrain.** From 1 to 3 kilometers you should be able to see the individual branches of each tree. From 3 to 5 kilometers you should be able to see each individual tree. From 5 to 8 kilometers trees will look like a green plush carpet. At greater than 8 kilometers, not only will the trees appear like a green plush carpet but there also will be a bluish tint to the horizon.

■ **In flat open terrain.** In open terrain a gross distance can be calculated once the top of a prominent landmark becomes visible on the horizon. To apply this formula you must first calculate how far you are from the viewed horizon. To do this, take the square root of your eye height above the horizon in feet divided by 0.5736. The answer is in statute miles.

$$\sqrt{\text{(Height to center of eye} + \text{ground elevation)} / 0.5736}$$
$$= \text{statute miles to the horizon}$$

Next apply the same formula to the object's height above the ground and add that to the already calculated horizon distance. The result is a rough estimation of the object's distance from your current location.

$$\sqrt{\text{(Height of the object above ground} / 0.5736)} + \text{distance to the horizon}$$
$$\text{in miles} = \text{distance to the object in statute miles}$$

Elevation—Related to Your Position. Does the landmark appear to be at a higher or lower elevation than you? Write down your perception. It will help you later.

Sea Features

Charts provide symbols for land features, buoys, and lights. It shouldn't be too hard identifying man-made features like a lighthouse or large building that can be used when trying to establish a line of position.

■ Step 4: Shoot an Azimuth (compass heading) of the Sea/Landmark

Once you have positively identified a map's landmark, use your compass to establish a heading from your position to it. The process of this step depends on the type of compass you are using. For details on how to hold a compass and shoot an azimuth, refer to Chapter 4.

■ Step 5: Recheck the Map's Orientation

While you're shooting an azimuth off your landmark, it's not uncommon for the map to lose its orientation due to wind or perhaps an accidental bump from your boot. Make sure it's still oriented before proceeding further.

■ Step 6: Plot the Line

Once you've identified a landmark and a compass heading to it, it's time to plot the line on your map. If you're using an orienteering compass, turn the circular housing until the heading—to your landmark—touches the bottom of the direction-of-travel arrow. Regardless of the type of compass you're using, place its long side on the map so that the left front tip is centered on the known landmark. Without moving the map, rotate the compass until either the magnetic-seeking arrow is boxed (orienteering compass) or the heading is under the stationary index (lensatic or maritime compass). For a chart, place the left tip of a straightedge on the identified landmark and, while keeping the tip in place, rotate its edge around until it crosses the compass rose (or parallels it) at the desired heading. Make sure you are using the middle ring and read the heading from the side closest to the landmark. Finally, use a straightedge to lightly pencil a line—from the landmark down—until it passes well through your presumed general location.

■ Step 7: Find Your Location

Visually evaluate your surroundings, interpreting what you see to its map representation. Use the contour, presumed elevation, and distance from the identified landmarks to help pinpoint your location. Your position should be somewhere on or close to the line you've drawn.

Table 5-1: Steps to Angulation

Steps	Key Points
1. Get to high ground.	Better view of surrounding land features.
2. Orient the map.	Relates two-dimensional map to the lay of the land.
3. Identify prominent sea/land features.	This step is the crux of success.
4. Shoot an azimuth.	From your position to the identified point.
5. Recheck map's orientation.	If the map moved even a little, the line of position will be off.
6. Plot the line.	From the landmark through and beyond your presumed general location.
7. Find your location.	Evaluate the surrounding terrain as it relates to the drawn line.

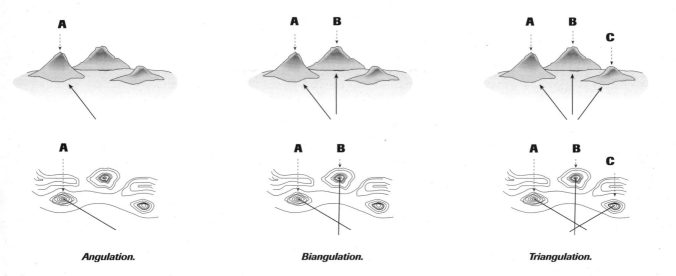

Angulation.   **Biangulation.**   **Triangulation.**

Biangulation: Using Two Lines of Position

Biangulating helps better pinpoint your location by using two lines of position. The process is the same as outlined for a single line of position; however, the intersecting lines provide a better idea of where you are. For best results try to find two landmarks that are around 120 degrees apart. In general, use the lines' intersection as a starting point when evaluating the surrounding terrain to determine your position.

Triangulation: Using Three Lines of Position

Triangulating is perhaps the best way to determine your location. By plotting a third line of position to the biangulation process, a "triangle of error" is formed between the three. The created triangle provides a starting point for identifying your position. You should be located within or around the triangle. For best results use three landmarks that are 120 degrees apart.

Hopefully you'll never get disoriented and need to figure out exactly where you are. However, learning these skills in advance can mean the difference between relying on someone else to rescue you and a short trip to that well-traveled road. Practice, practice, practice!

Chapter Exercises

Orient the map.

Orient the map to a given magnetic variation. At first use the one found within the map's margins. Next practice using made-up declinations. After all, if you travel outside your general location, sooner or later you'll find yourself in an area with a different magnetic variation from what you're used to. Remember: If magnetic north is *east* of true north, *subtract* the amount from 360; if magnetic north is *west* of true north, *add* the amount to 360.

Take a road trip.

On your next road trip, use the dead reckoning formula and see if you can determine your location on a map (perhaps when someone else is driving and you have taken a quick nap). Remember: Rate x time = distance. If you're on a reference line, like a road, finding your position should be relatively easy.

Evaluate your trekking pace.

Next time you take a hike, calculate your traveling speed. As noted previously, the average backpacker travels between 1 and 3 miles per hour. Doing this exercise several times will give you a general idea of your average traveling speed under a multitude of scenarios (gear carried and terrain covered). Applying this information to the dead reckoning formula is a great way to establish a quick idea of your location.

How well can you draw a map?

With an awareness of your general location and an unobstructed view of the surrounding terrain, draw a map (contour representation) of the prominent land features. Pay attention to peaks, ridgelines, depressions, etc. Once you have drawn as much detail as you think you can, pull out a topographical map of the area and see how well you've done. This skill is something you need to become proficient in. The ability to translate a seen land feature to the map's two-dimensional representation is key to finding a line of position (angulation, biangulation, or triangulation).

Angulate, biangulate, and triangulate.

Practice identifying multiple land features using contour, elevation, and distance as they relate to your position. At first do this from a known location and later from an unknown one. Identifying from an unknown place might require a blindfold and a friend who can drive. Do this exercise on a day when you can reciprocate and both of you can practice from both a known and an unknown location. Once you have established your general location and identified the major landmarks, see if you can recognize your position by plotting one or multiple lines of position.

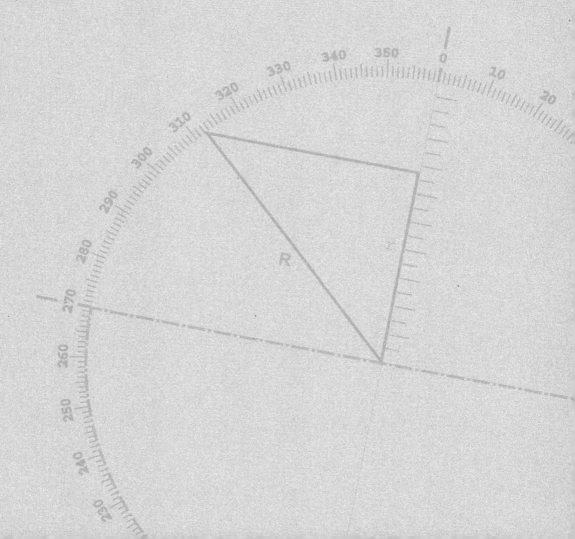

Using Celestial & Other Aids

In an ideal world, you'll never need a map and compass and not have one. But this isn't an ideal world. What would you do if your compass broke or your map was misplaced? How would you get back home? In 1990 an acquaintance of mine set his pack down to scurry up a hill and capture the spectacular view. The sun was out and the wildflowers provided myriad stunning colors. After enjoying the moment, he headed back to his gear—only to discover it was no longer there. His search was fruitless, and he began to panic when he realized he was disoriented and unaware of which direction to take to safety. With nothing but a shirt on his back and a water bottle, he spent a cold night huddled under a tree. Fortunately for him, a rescue team found him the next morning. What went wrong? Of course the obvious failure was leaving his gear behind and not having a map and compass on his person. What could he have done to avoid this unfortunate outcome?

One solution—he could have oriented himself to the sun while going uphill and used this information to guide him back to the gear he left behind. By failing to orient his uphill travel, he didn't realize his return route was taking him down the wrong side of the peak. My friend ended up in a different canyon far from his perceived location and gear. He was lucky that rescue was swift. Celestial aids such as the sun and constellations can augment your ability to establish your current location and navigate from point A to point B.

The Sun

The sun is the closest star to the earth and provides the heat and light necessary to sustain life. As the earth rotates on its axis, the sun rises to the east in the morning and sets to the west in the evening. This movement across the sky marks the passage of time during the day. The relationship between the sun and the earth is a helpful tool for finding cardinal directions and your current location. Since the sun can be harmful to your eyes, avoid looking directly at it whenever possible.

■ The Sun and Earth Relationship

Common sense would suggest that the sun is north of your position when you are in the Southern Hemisphere and south when you're in the Northern Hemisphere. Don't be tricked, however, into thinking this way. The earth's axis (an imaginary line that runs between the North and South Poles) is tilted 23 degrees 27 minutes (relative to the sun with its north end pointing toward Polaris), and it orbits around the sun in an elliptical (oval) pattern.

As the earth moves around the sun, it rotates on its axis. It takes one day (23 hours, 56 minutes, and 4.1 seconds) for the earth to complete one rotation on its axis. For navigation purposes (as you'll see later) it is helpful to break this rotation down into hours and minutes—the earth rotates 15 degrees each hour (360 degrees/24 hours = 15 degrees) and 0.25 degree every minute (15 degrees/60 minutes = 0.25 degree). It takes one year (365 days, 5 hours, 48 minutes, and 46 seconds) for the earth to complete one revolution around the sun. Since the earth's axis is tilted, two spheres are used to describe its relationship to astronomical bodies—celestial sphere (based on the earth's axis) and ecliptic sphere (based on

Tilt of the earth's axis as it relates to the sun.

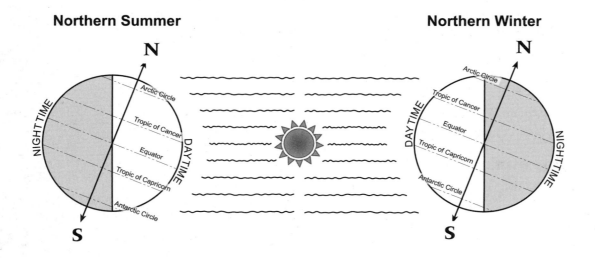

Northern Summer

N

NIGHTTIME

DAYTIME

Arctic Circle

Tropic of Cancer

Equator

Tropic of Capricorn

Antarctic Circle

S

Northern Winter

N

DAYTIME

NIGHTTIME

Arctic Circle

Tropic of Cancer

Equator

Tropic of Capricorn

Antarctic Circle

S

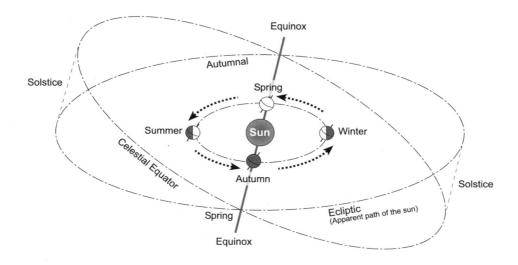

the sun's axis). As a result of the earth's tilt, the north and south celestial poles are tilted 23 degrees 27 minutes away from the north and south ecliptic poles, respectively.

Celestial poles and ecliptic spheres.

- ■ **Celestial sphere.** The equator and the north and south celestial poles are simply projections of the earth's geographic equivalents into space. The celestial sphere is oriented to the earth's north-south poles and equator.

- ■ **Ecliptic sphere.** The ecliptic equator (east-west line) and the north and south ecliptic poles (north-south line) are projections that arise from the sun's center. The ecliptic sphere is oriented to the sun's north-south poles and equator.

The earth's tilt (celestial equator) related to the sun's path (ecliptic equator) causes the sun to deviate from a true east-west passage (related to the earth). This deviation, also called declination, directly relates to the celestial and ecliptic spheres and ranges between 23° 27' North and 23° 27' South latitude, depending on the time of year. The sun reaches its maximum declination values on the longest and shortest days of the year, the solstices (23° 27' North declination on June 21 and 23° 27' South declination on December 21), and at this time the distance between the celestial and ecliptic equators is at its highest point (23° 27'). The sun declination is at its minimal value (0°) when it crosses the equator during the equinoxes (March 21 and September 23), and at this time the ecliptic and celestial equator intersect

Declination of the sun as it relates to solstices and equinoxes.

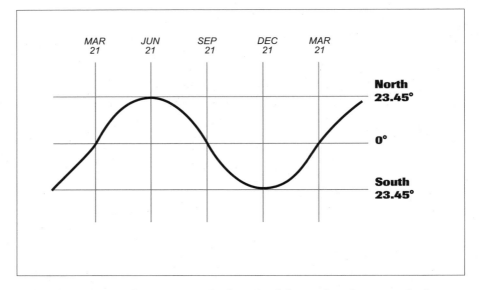

each other. During the equinox, the length of day and night is equal. The sun's declination change is greatest near the equinoxes (perhaps as much as 24 minutes a day) and slowest near the solstices. Understanding the earth-sun relationship is very helpful for finding direction and position.

■ Finding Cardinal Direction from the Sun

The sun provides several avenues for finding the four cardinal directions. In a crunch, knowing these skills will help when trying to find your way out of a situation or maintain a course of travel.

The Stick and Shadow

Near midday, all shadow tips move due east and are accurate within 10 degrees (or thereabouts) for two to three hours on either side of local apparent noon (shortest shadow of the day). This is true no matter what your location or time of year. During morning and evening hours, however, the stick-and-shadow method can be off by a significant amount. The exception is during the equinoxes, when it is accurate all day long. Using the sun to find direction at sunrise and sunset is discussed later.

As close to, yet before, local apparent noon as practical, on a flat surface scrape away debris and vegetation until a 3-foot-square bare-ground surface is all that remains. Find a 4-foot-long stick and sharpen it at both ends. Next, with the stick perpendicular to the ground, force the downward end into the dirt so that the shadow of the upward end is centered

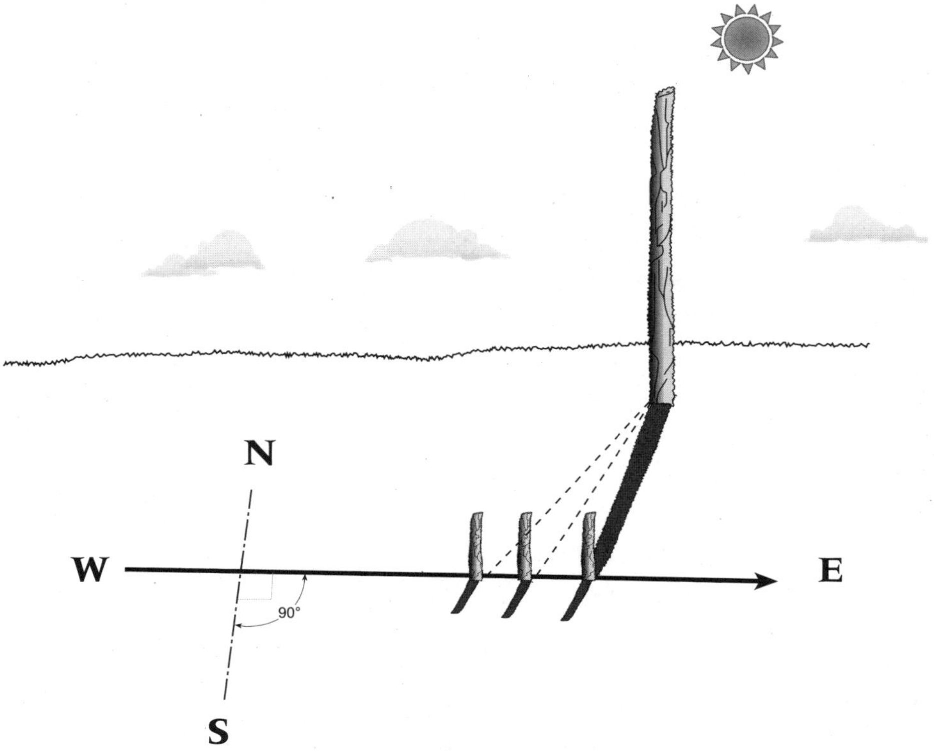

N

W

90°

E

S

on the area you prepared. Try to get the stick as perpendicular to the ground as you can. Mark the shadow tip with a twig (or other appropriate material). Every five minutes, place another twig at the shadow tip's new location. Watch as the shadow gets shorter and then longer. The shortest shadow occurs when the sun is either due north or south of your location (depends on which hemisphere you are in). Connect two equal-distance shadow tips (from the stick and midpoint) using a straight line. This line represents east and west. Since the sun rises in the east and sets in the west, the first marking on the shadow line is west and the second one is east. Creating a line perpendicular to the east-west line provides a north-south reference. This line should occur close to the location where the shortest shadow was seen.

The earth's changing relationship to the sun creates obstacles when using a stick and shadow in the tropic and polar regions.

The Tropic Regions. During the summer solstice, the sun's rays shine directly over the tropic of Cancer (23° 27' North); during the winter solstice the suns ray's shine directly over the tropic of Capricorn (23° 27'

South). Between these dates, the sun could be north or south of the equator (depending on the season) anywhere between 23° 27' North and South. This poses no problem—simply realize that the first shadow is west and that the subsequent shadows move toward the east. A perpendicular line to the east-west line allows you to find which way is north or south.

The Temperate Regions. The stick-and-shadow method works best in the temperate latitudes (between 23° 27' and 66° 33' North and South latitude). The shadow always moves from west to east (opposite the sun's movement which is from east to west), and the sun is always due south in the Northern Hemisphere and due north in the Southern Hemisphere at local apparent noon (shortest shadow of the day).

The Polar Regions. Beginning with the summer solstice, latitudes above 66° 33' North (Arctic Circle) may never see the sunset, and latitudes below 66° 33' South (Antarctic Circle) may never see the sunrise. During the winter solstice things change—latitudes within the Arctic Circle may never see the sunrise, and latitudes within the Antarctic Circle may never see the sunset. The sun's position on the horizon and its constant presence—or lack thereof—make the stick-and-shadow method impractical in regions greater then 66° 33' North and South latitude. The sun can still help in determining your cardinal directions, provided you know when local apparent noon is. At local apparent noon, the sun is due south of your position in the Arctic and due north of you in the Antarctic.

Local Apparent Noon

At local apparent noon in the temperate latitudes (between 23° 27' and 66° 33' north and south latitude), the sun has reached its highest point and is due south of your position in the northern latitudes and due north of you in the southern latitudes. Local apparent noon is not necessarily 12:00 P.M. Local apparent noon can be determined using a twenty-four-hour watch and a simple mathematical formula.

Finding Local Apparent Noon (LAN)

(Time of sunrise + time of sunset)/2 = local apparent noon

For example, if sunrise was at 0700 and sunset at 1930:

(0700 + 1930)/2 = 1315 (or 1:15 P.M.)

Sunrise is the time when the top of the sun first appears on the horizon; sunset is when it disappears below the horizon. The horizon used needs to be nonobscured and equal in height at both sunrise and sunset. In our example, 1315 hours is local apparent noon, and the sun should be directly north or south of you at that time. Drawing a straight line from your position toward the sun and a second one perpendicular to the first is all you'll need to establish the cardinal directions (N, S, E, W).

If the horizons (sunrise and sunset) are not equal, use a kamal to establish similar heights. A kamal helps you create a false yet equal horizon—taking clouds, haze, rock formations, and other obstructions out of the picture. The kamal is a simple device consisting of a string and a small flat object like a credit card. Attach the flat object to the line, and tie a knot on its other end at the position that allows you to create a taut line when the knot is held between your teeth and you're holding the flat object with an extended arm. For best results, attach line to both ends of the flat object

A kamal helps when clouds or terrain obscure the horizon.

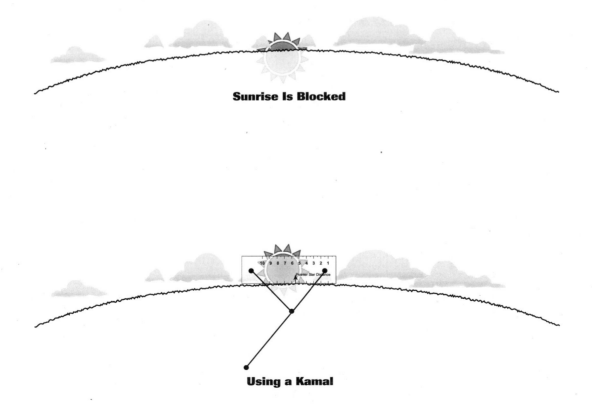

Sunrise Is Blocked

Using a Kamal

and bring them together (about 10 inches beyond the card) with an over-hand knot so that they are centered on the card (see the illustration on the previous page). Attaching line at both ends gives you better control, keeping the card steady when relating it to the horizon. To use a kamal, while holding the knot between your teeth, hold the flat object (keep the line tight) so that its bottom touches the horizon. Sunrise is the time when the top of the sun first appears above the top of the card; sunset is when it disappears below the top of the card.

Another method of finding local apparent noon is to establish the shortest shadow (of the day) cast by the stick-and-shadow method. The short shadow is a result of the sun's reaching its highest point in the sky. Since the actual time can fall anywhere between 1100 and 1300 hours, it is best to begin marking your shadow tips at around 1100. For optimal accuracy, mark the shadow tips every minute (the earth rotates ¼ degree a minute, 15 degrees an hour, and 360 degrees in twenty-four hours) until you have identified the shortest shadow (local apparent noon).

Using Sunrise and Sunset

If you have an unobstructed horizon, cardinal directions can be calculated at sunrise or sunset. The exact direction of sunrise and sunset, however, will hinge on your latitude and the time of year. During fall and winter the sun has a southern declination (see preceding) and rises south of east. During spring and summer it has a northern declination and rises north of east. The sun's declination is greatest (rising north or south of due east) for around one month on each side of the solstices and smallest (rising to within 5 degrees of due east) for about one week on each side of the equinoxes.

The angle difference between the rising sun and due east (or the setting sun and due west) is called the amplitude of the sun. When the sun has a north declination, its amplitude is north; when the declination is south, the amplitude is south. However, don't confuse the sun's amplitude with its declination! The only place where they are equal is in the tropic latitudes. The sun's amplitude in other latitudes depends on the date and your latitude and can vary greatly. Provided you know the sun's maximum amplitude for your location (found in the amplitude almanac), you can calculate its amplitude at other times of the year. The only thing you need is a compass rose (if you don't have one, make one—it's not that hard to do).

1. Label the four quadrants of a compass rose (N, W, S, E) with the dates of the equinoxes and solstices, being careful to put the solstices on the vertical line (June 21 at 000°, September 22 at 090°, December 21 at 180°, and March 20 at 270°).

2. Draw a horizontal line (from your present date) so that it intersects the north-south vertical line (the line connecting 0 and 180). Since there is more than ninety days in each of the four quadrants, you'll need to do a little math to establish where to locate the date. In other words, convert the date to an angle on the compass rose. To do this, divide the number of days from the preceding equinox or solstice by the number of days that occur during that quarter, and multiply that figure by 90 degrees. This subsequent figure is the number of degrees beyond the preceding equinox or solstice that correlates with the date used. For example, if the date is May 1, the angular value for that date would derive from the following equation: (43/93) X 90 = 41.61. Adding 41.61 to 270 (last equinox) gives a 311.61° angular value for May 1.

Table 6-1: **Finding the Date-to-Angle Relationship**

(# Days from *last* equinox / # days in that quarter) X 90 = **Number of degrees beyond the last equinox or solstice that correlates with the date used**

Quadrant	Dates	# of Days in 2004
One	June 21 to September 21	93
Two	September 22 to December 20	90
Three	December 21 to March 19	89
Four	March 20 to June 20	93

---

3. Make a second line perpendicular to the first so that it spans between the first line and the compass rose east-west line. This line should be placed directly over the compass rose north-south line. Label this line *r*.

4. Draw a third diagonal line between the date and the intersection of the compass rose north-south and east-west lines. Label this line *R*. The combination of these three lines creates a triangle.

5. Divide the length of the vertical line *(r)* by the length of the diagonal line *(R)*, and multiply that ratio by the maximum amplitude for your location. The measurements can be done in any unit you want, as long as you use the same one for each line. It is the ratio of the two measurements that is used.

(r/R) X maximum amplitude for your location = estimate of the sun's amplitude

6. The sun's amplitude is max at the solstice when r/R = 1 and is zero at the equinoxes when r/R = 0.

Math Tidbit

Converting degrees to minutes is a simple process. Since there are 60 minutes (') in a degree, simply divide however many minutes you have by 60. In this example 23° 27' was converted as follows:

27/60 = 0.45;   **thus 23° 27' is equal to 23.45°**

For example, if $R = 2"$ and $r = 1.3125"$ where the maximum amplitude is 34 (this value is based on a 45° north latitude),

(1.3125/2) X 34 = 22.31° North

(Calculation based on a date of May 1).

As you can see, precision in math and measurements is key to accuracy in determining the sun's declination using this method. To establish the sunrise bearing, subtract north amplitudes or add south amplitudes to 90 degrees. For example, if the sun's amplitude is 22.31° North, the sunrise bearing would be 67.69°. To establish sunset bearings, add north amplitudes or subtract south amplitudes to 270 degrees. Once these bearings are known, cardinal directions can be established.

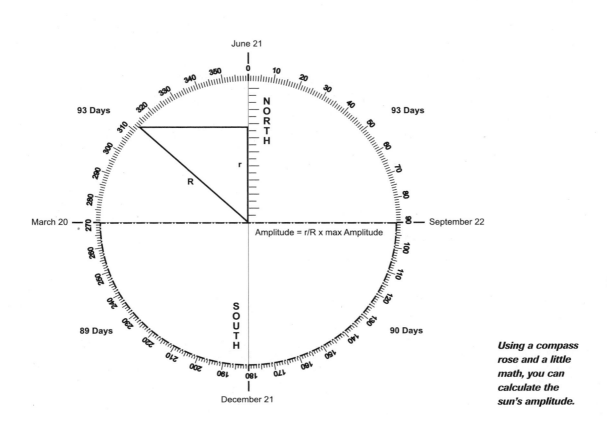

Using a compass rose and a little math, you can calculate the sun's amplitude.

Amplitude = r/R x max Amplitude

June 21

March 20

September 22

December 21

NORTH

SOUTH

93 Days

93 Days

89 Days

90 Days

Table 6-2: **Amplitudes**

Northern Amplitude	Southern Amplitude
90 degrees – Amplitude = Sunrise Bearing	90 degrees + Amplitude = Sunrise Bearing
270 degrees + Amplitude = Sunset Bearing	270 degrees – Amplitude = Sunset Bearing

If math isn't your favorite thing, you can get a similar result by plotting the maximum amplitude (north and south) and creating a scale between the two extremes. In other words, for latitudes with maximum amplitudes of 34°, mark the compass rose south and north ends with that value. The center of the compass rose is zero. Halfway between 0° and 34°, make a mark and label it 17°; continue halving the line until multiple values are created. At this point draw a horizontal line (from your present date) so that it intersects the north-south vertical line (the line connecting

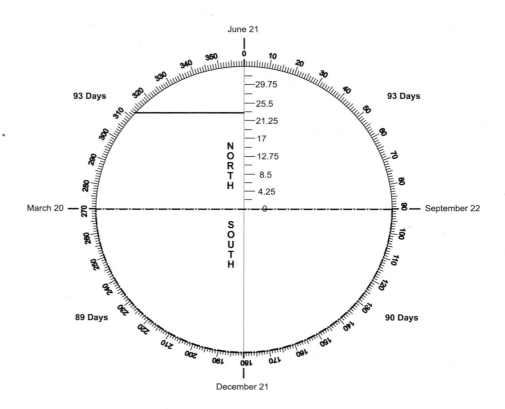

A rough scale can be used to find the sun's amplitude.

0 and 180). Don't forget to convert the date to its compass rose angle equivalent (see preceding). The point where the horizontal line intersects the north-south line is a rough estimate for the sun's amplitude for your location and date. The illustration shown uses May 1 and provides a rough value of around 23 degrees (pretty close to the 22.31° value found using the math-based model). Subtracting this northern amplitude value from 90 degrees provides a sunrise bearing of 67 degrees.

As a rule, the values in Table 6-3 can be used for maximum amplitudes. For greater precision, refer to other amplitude tables.

Table 6-3: Amplitude Values

Latitude	5	10	15	20	25	30	35	40	45	50	55	60
Maximum Amplitude	24	24	24	25	26	27	29	31	34	38	44	53

Using a Watch

Similar to the stick-and-shadow method discussed earlier, a watch can be used to find cardinal directions. Recall that near midday, all shadow tips move due east and are accurate within 10 degrees (or thereabouts) for two to three hours on either side of local apparent noon. This is true no matter what your location or the time of year. The watch method is a gross method of determining direction and is prone to major error. In a pinch, however, it may provide a heading that intersects a well-traveled road.

Using a Watch in the Northern Hemisphere. Keeping the watch level, point its hour hand toward the sun and draw an imaginary line between its hour hand and twelve o'clock (one o'clock if daylight saving time). The line represents a gross southern heading. With a known southern heading, a second line drawn perpendicular to the first is all that needed to establish N, S, E, W.

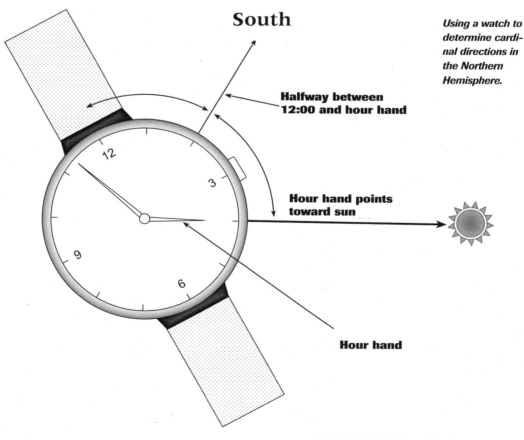

South

Halfway between
12:00 and hour hand

Hour hand points
toward sun

Hour hand

Using a watch to determine cardinal directions in the Northern Hemisphere.

Using a Watch in the Southern Hemisphere. Keeping the watch level, point its twelve o'clock symbol (one o'clock if daylight saving time) toward the sun and draw an imaginary line midway between the twelve o'clock symbol and the hour hand. The line represents a gross northern heading. With a known northern heading, a second line drawn perpendicular to the first is all that needed to establish N, S, E, W.

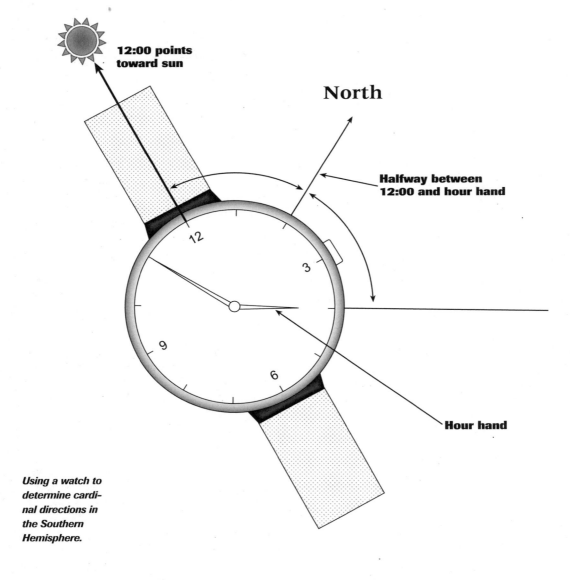

12:00 points toward sun

North

Halfway between 12:00 and hour hand

Hour hand

Using a watch to determine cardinal directions in the Southern Hemisphere.

Table 6-4: Cardinal Directions Using the Sun

Method	Key Points
Stick and Shadow	Not useful in polar regions. The first shadow tip is west and the second east. For best outcome, perform within two to three hours of local apparent noon.
Local Apparent Noon (LAN)	At LAN the sun is at its highest point in the sky and due south (or north) of your location. At that moment the sun has reached its midpoint between sunrise and sunset—producing the shortest shadow of the day.
Sunrise and Sunset	The sun's position, related to the earth, falls between 23° 27' North and South latitude (sun's declination). Unless it passes directly overhead, you will need to add or subtract its amplitude to establish cardinal directions of sunrise or sunset. Don't forget: Amplitude and declination are not the same.
Watch	For best outcome, perform within two to three hours of local apparent noon. Don't forget to adjust for daylight saving time.

■ Using the Sun to Find Latitude and Longitude

Latitude can be approximated using the sun's position at sunrise and sunset and local apparent noon. Local apparent noon is also useful for establishing longitude. The steps outlined here are presented for use in unforeseen situations and not as a substitute for good planning, terrain evaluation, constant awareness, and dead reckoning.

Finding Latitude Using the Sun's Angle at Sunrise and Sunset

Perhaps the quickest and easiest way to find latitude is to track the sun for one to two hours after sunrise or before sunset (as it moves eastward). Unless you have a sextant, you'll need to improvise a way of finding this angle. One method for doing this uses a stick. The stick allows you to create a straight line between the sun's current position and its rising point. The angle created by connecting the sun, its rising point, and the horizon can be used in the following formula.

Latitude = 90 degrees – rising angle of the sun (or setting angle)

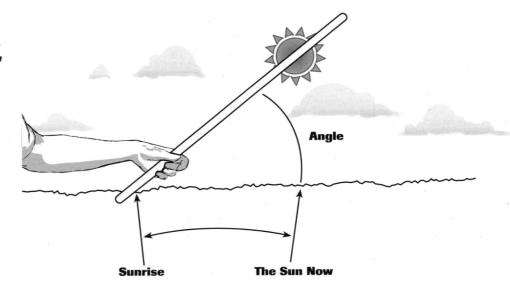

The angle of sunrise or sunset can be used to find your latitude.

Angle

Sunrise　　　　**The Sun Now**

For this method to work, the rising and setting angles need to be taken when the sun has reached its maximum east or west location related to the horizon. In addition, the horizon must be clearly visible—without obstructing terrain. This technique is at its worst when used in high north latitudes around the winter solstice. At that location and time, the sun comes up south of east and moves farther from east as it rises. Under ideal circumstances you'll have a protractor. Better yet, you'll have a sextant. If you don't have either, improvise the necessary tool from whatever materials you have available. If you have a compass rose, it provides a perfect template.

If by chance you missed sunrise (or want to calculate the angle at sunset), you can estimate the location. However, this requires that you know the time of sunrise or sunset and have a watch. Use an improvised ruler made from a straight 2-foot-long stick that has 1-inch interval marks along its side. The ruler is used to relate degrees to hours using the rule, "1 inch per 10 minutes at 2 feet," which is equivalent to the sun's movement of 15 degrees per hour. This formula is based on a hand-to-eye value of 2 feet (using an outstretched arm) and predicts the sun's movement at 1 inch every 10 minutes. To apply, hold the stick by placing your thumb at the mark equal to how much time has passed since sunrise (or until sunset). For example, if 40 minutes have passed, you'd place your thumb at the 4-inch mark. Position your arm in such a way that your arm, your

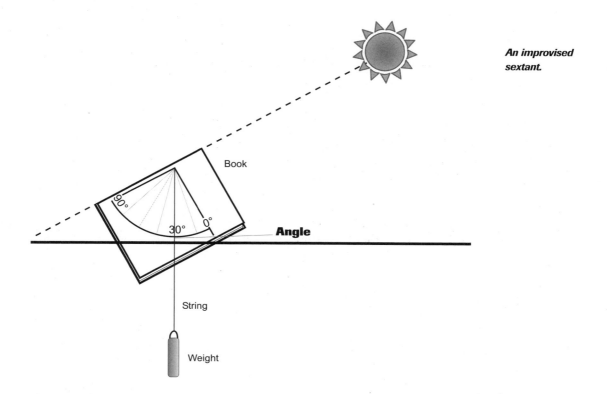

An improvised sextant.

thumb, and the sun create a straight line, and rotate the stick until the free end touches the unobstructed horizon. The angle between the stick and the horizon can be applied to the preceding formula to find latitude. Once again, a protractor (brought along or improvised) is a useful tool for establishing these angles.

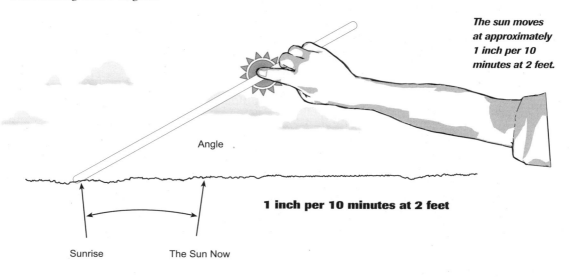

The sun moves at approximately 1 inch per 10 minutes at 2 feet.

1 inch per 10 minutes at 2 feet

Finding Latitude Using the Sun at Local Apparent Noon

The stick-and-shadow method for finding cardinal directions (described earlier) can also be used to establish your current latitude provided you can calculate the sun's declination. The sun's declination can be found in almanacs, or it can be calculated using the previously mentioned methods for finding amplitude (see Finding Cardinal Direction Using Sunrise and Sunset). If you decide to calculate the sun's declination, be sure to use 23.45° as the maximum amplitude value (equal to the sun's maximum declination).

If you know the sun's angular distance (to the horizon at local apparent noon) and its declination, these values can be used to determine your latitude. The formula used is a constant. Addition and subtraction values, however, change depending on north or south orientation of its various elements.

Table 6-5: **Determining Latitude**

Distances	North	South
Latitude	+	−
Sun declination	+	−
Looking north/south toward the sun, zenith distance	+	−

Using the appropriate signs, the formula for finding latitude is:

Latitude = Sun Declination − (Zenith Distance)

Zenith Distance = 90 degrees − sun's angular distance at local apparent noon

The angular distance of the sun is the angle between it, the horizon, and your position at local apparent noon (when the sun is due north or south of you and it produces the shortest shadow of the day). Again, unless you have a sextant you will need to improvise one. To do this, run a line from the top of the stick to the end of the shortest shadow. Hopefully you'll have a protractor, but if you don't, improvise one from whatever material you can scrounge up. Tie one end of a string to the center of the protractor and the other end to a heavy object (so that it keeps the string tight and allows the object to move freely). Line up the bottom of the protractor with the string, and read the value under the string. This value is the sun's angular distance as it relates to your position. An example of an improvised sextant can be found under Finding Latitude Using the Sun's Angle at Sunrise and Sunset (discusssed earlier in this chapter).

If the sun was south of your location and you obtained a 60-degree angle (from your stick and shadow at LAN) on May 1, you could find your latitude.

Table 6-6: Finding Latitude at Local Apparent Noon (LAN)

Steps	Key Points	Example
Sun's angular distance at LAN	Angle created between the stick and its shadow at LAN.	60°
Sun's declination and value	(r/R) x 23.45° = sun's declination. (1.3125/2) x 23.45 = 15.39° North (for May 1). A northern declination value is positive; a southern declination is negative.	15.39° North Negative value
Zenith distance value	You are looking south, so the zenith distance value is negative; if looking north, it would be positive.	Negative value
Find latitude	Latitude = Declination – (Zenith Distance). Latitude = 15.39 – (– (90 - 60)) = 45.39.	45.39° North latitude

If you are in the tropic latitudes and the sun passes directly overhead, your latitude is equal to the sun's declination. For a review on how to find the sun's declination, refer to Using Sunrise and Sunset earlier in this chapter. To review procedures for creating a stick and shadow and finding local apparent noon, refer to The Stick and Shadow earlier in this chapter.

Finding Longitude Using Local Apparent Noon and Greenwich Mean Time

Longitude can be calculated from the sun's movement, which is from east to west covering the globe (360 degrees) every twenty-four hours. Remember that longitude lines are north-south-running lines numbered between 0 and 180 degrees east and west of Greenwich, England (longitude 0°). There are twenty-four separate time zones, each covering 15 degrees of longitude. The center of the Greenwich time zone is the Greenwich meridian (longitude), which is 0°. The centers of all other zones are at 15 degrees of longitude intervals. The borders between zones are located 7 degrees, 30 minutes on either side of the centers. The central meridian of every time zone is the "standard" meridian of that zone.

Since Greenwich, England, is at longitude 0° and the sun moves 15 degrees an hour (from east to west), you could determine your longitude if you know the date and time in Greenwich (known as Greenwich Mean Time, or GMT). If you were in a time zone that is five hours behind Greenwich, your longitude would be 75° W (15 degrees x 5 hours = 75 degrees). You are in a west longitude when the sun passes after Greenwich and an east longitude when it passes before (as related to sunrise, LAN, or sunset).

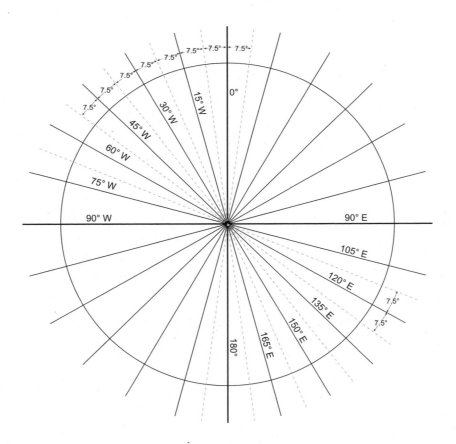

Table 6-7: Determining Longitude by Greenwich Mean Time (GMT)

U.S. Time Zones	Central Longitude	Hours Added to GMT
Eastern	75°	5
Central	90°	6
Mountain	105°	7
Pacific	120°	8

During daylight saving time (between the first Sunday of April and the last Sunday of October), one hour should be subtracted from the calculations.

Precision in this method requires the use of tables that display local apparent noon (LAN) for Greenwich Mean Time (GMT). LAN for your location can be established using the shortest shadow of a stick and shadow or the midpoint between sunrise and sunset. Be as precise in your time measurements as you can. Once LAN values are known (GMT and your location), you can calculate the longitude for your present position. For example, on December 11, 2004, while in the PST zone (west of GMT) you determine LAN occurred at 12:01. On this date the almanac shows GMT's LAN as 11:53. Since the PST zone is eight hours ahead of GMT, you'd add eight hours to the PST figure, making it 20:01. To calculate your longitude, subtract GMT from PST (20:01 - 11:53 = 8:08). LAN occurs at your longitude eight hours and eight minutes beyond GMT. Since the sun moves 15 degrees an hour and 15 minutes every minute, your location would be 122° W longitude.

15 degrees X 8 hours = 120 degrees

15 minutes X 8 minutes = 120 minutes or 2 degrees

Your longitude = 120 degrees + 2 degrees = 122° West

Table 6-8: **Time and Sun Angular Relationship**

Time Lapsed	Sun's Movement
24 hours	360 degrees
1 hour	15 degrees
4 minutes	1 degree
1 minute	15 minutes
4 seconds	1 minute
1 second	15 seconds

For best results, set your watch to GMT or your local equivalent before heading out. In addition, know how well your watch keeps time and make any necessary adjustments. For example, if your watch was set to a precise time when you departed but loses four seconds a day, you'll need to factor this into your time for sunrise, sunset, or LAN.

Table 6-9: **Determining Latitude/Longitude Using the Sun**

Method	Key Points
Latitude by sun's angle at sunrise/sunset	Latitude = 90 degrees − rising (or setting) angle of the sun. Must be done within one to two hours of sunrise or sunset.
Latitude by local apparent noon	Latitude = sun declination − (zenith distance). Zenith Distance = 90 degrees − sun's angular distance at local apparent noon. Although the formula is a constant, addition and subtraction values change depending on north or south orientation of its various elements.
Longitude by LAN and GMT	If you know GMT and LAN you can establish your longitude based on the time difference and the sun's movement of 15 degrees an hour.

The Stars

Like the sun, stars are a great option for defining cardinal directions and your present location. The concepts are simple: Circumpolar stars rotate around the north or south sky pole, respectively (tightly around a high northern or southern latitude), never dip below the horizon, and can be seen all night long. A central star, Polaris, can be seen from the Northern Hemisphere. The Southern Hemisphere, however, has no central star. Noncircumpolar stars rotate around a specific earth latitude (never changes), rise and set on the horizon (following an east-west path), bear due north or south when they reach maximum height in the sky, and can only be seen at certain latitudes and times of year.

Table 6-10: **Navigation Value of Stars**			
Type of Star	**Rotation**	**Visibility**	**Navigation Usefulness**
Circumpolar	Around the earth and sky poles.	As a general rule, never dip below the horizon.	Finding latitude and cardinal directions from the north or south sky pole.
Noncircum-polar	Around earth latitudes away from its poles.	Depends on time of year and latitude.	Finding latitude and cardinal directions at star rise, maximum height, set, and angle.

Stars that circle the earth over southern latitudes have a southern declination; those that circle over northern latitudes have a northern declination. Thus, southern stars rise south of due east and set south of due west, and northern stars rise north of due east and set north of due west. Like the sun, stars also move from east to west at a rate of 15 degrees an hour.

■ Finding Cardinal Direction from the Stars

A bright night sky does much more than help you see where you are going. Those sparkling lights have been used for centuries, helping maritime and land travelers determine direction and position. Don't overlook the stars—learn their meaning and how they can be used in navigation. You never know when they might come in handy.

Circumpolar Stars in the Northern Hemisphere

In the Northern Hemisphere, Polaris (North Star) provides an excellent method of determining direction at latitudes above 5° North. Like other stars, it rotates around the sky's northern pole, but the movement is so small it is hardly noticed. Its actual location (related to the northern sky) is 89° 12' North, and it rotates around the sky's pole at a radius of 48 minutes. Contrary to popular belief, Polaris is not the brightest star in the sky. The easiest way to find the North Star is to first identify Cassiopeia or the Big Dipper. The Big Dipper looks like a cup with a long handle. Cassiopeia is made up of five stars that form a large *M* when above Polaris and a *W* when below (its opening faces Polaris). These two constellations rotate counterclockwise around the sky's northern pole (on opposite sides), and Polaris can be found halfway between them—at the very end of the Little Dipper's handle. Polaris is one of several stars that make up the Little Dipper, a smaller version of the Big Dipper.

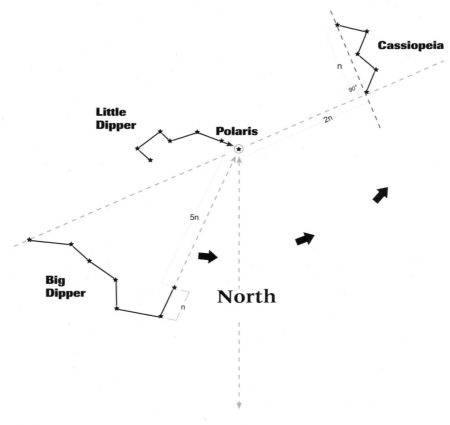

The Big Dipper and Cassiopeia make finding Polaris easy.

When both constellations cannot be seen, you can still find Polaris or determine your cardinal direction by doing one of the following:

- **Big Dipper.** At the forward tip of the Big Dipper, Polaris can be found by extending a line, straight off the Dipper's two forward stars, approximately five times the distance between the two stars.

- **Cassiopeia.** At a right angle from the base of Cassiopeia's trailing side (side where the *W* is slightly flattened), Polaris can be found by extending a line approximately two times that of the *W's* (or *M's*) base.

As a rule, Polaris is within 48 minutes of true north. The location of the Big Dipper and Cassiopeia provide the key to this variance.

- Polaris is due north when Cassiopeia is directly above or below its location.

- Polaris is 48 minutes east of true north when Cassiopeia is to its right.

- Polaris is 48 minutes west of true north when Cassiopeia is to its left.

North can also be found when only one constellation is visible and clouds or other obstacles obscure Polaris. Simply mark a stick with appropriate distances (five times the distance of the Big Dipper's two forward stars or two times the distance of Cassiopeia's base), and use it to calculate the North Star's location by holding the stick so that it represents the line you'd normally use (from the constellation).

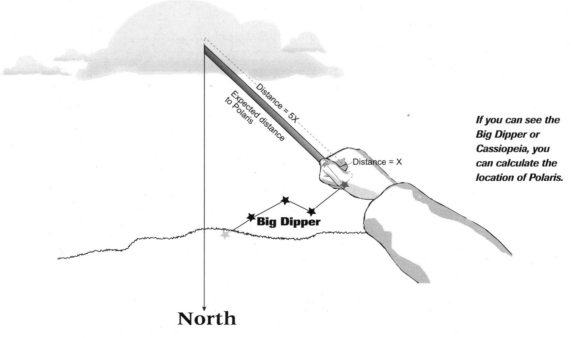

Distance = 5X

Expected distance to Polaris

Distance = X

If you can see the Big Dipper or Cassiopeia, you can calculate the location of Polaris.

Big Dipper

North

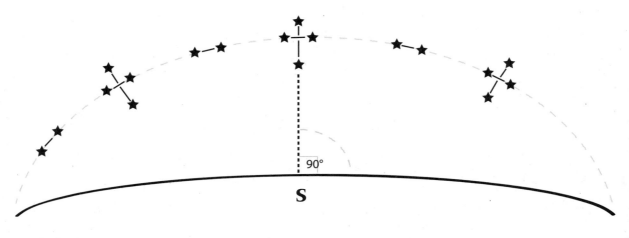

90°

S

The Southern Cross moves from east to west.

Circumpolar Stars in the Southern Hemisphere

In the Southern Hemisphere, the Southern Cross provides an excellent method of determining direction. The Southern Cross moves from east to west. It rises on its side (south-southeast), climbs into the sky until it is upright (directly over due south), and sets on its opposite side (south-southwest). Two bright pointer stars (Pointer Stars) follow the Southern Cross and point toward its forward movement.

To establish a southern heading, extend an imaginary line downward from the long axis of the Southern Cross (the upright portion of the cross). Draw another imaginary line perpendicular to the center of the Pointer Stars. A third line, which extends down from the intersection of the preceding two, represents a southern direction. If the Pointer Stars cannot be seen, south is located at the far end of a line extended five times the distance between the two stars creating the long axis of the Southern Cross (from the base of the cross).

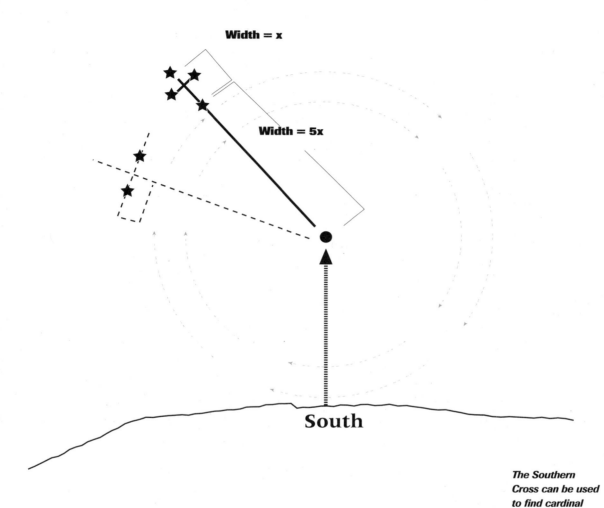

Width = x

Width = 5x

South

The Southern Cross can be used to find cardinal directions.

The Noncircumpolar Stars of Orion

Orion the Hunter is perhaps the best noncircumpolar constellation used for finding cardinal direction. Orion circles the earth (east to west) almost directly above the equator and can be seen from both the Northern and Southern Hemispheres from November through April. Orion has a rectangular shape with two shoulder stars, two leg stars, and three stars that create a belt across its middle. The leading star of Orion's Belt (called Mintaka) rises exactly due east and sets exactly due west.

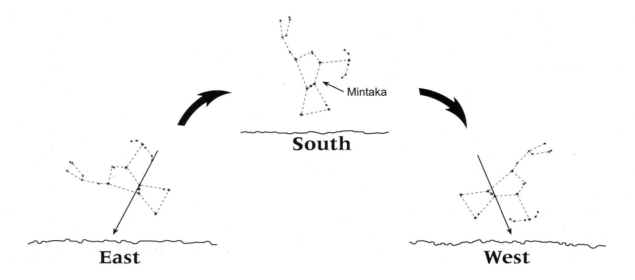

South

East

West

Mintaka

Orion the Hunter (shown in the Northern Hemisphere) moves from east to west directly over the equator.

Unless you are located at the equator, Orion will not rise directly due east or set due west of you. If you know your latitude and have an unobstructed view of the horizon, however, you can calculate Orion's rising and setting direction. The rising angle equals 90 degrees minus latitude. This heading can be used to establish cardinal directions.

In the Northern Hemisphere, Orion rises on its side, stands up to the south-southwest, and sets on its opposite side. In the Southern Hemisphere, Orion can be seen standing on its head as it moves across the sky.

When Orion is standing up or on its head (Southern Hemisphere), Mintaka can be used to create a night version of the stick and shadow

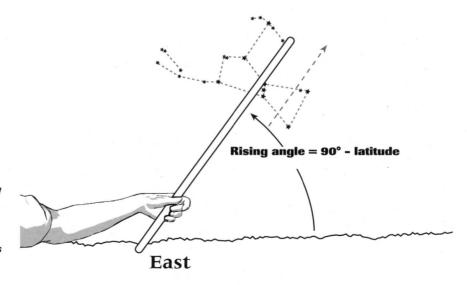

Rising angle = 90° - latitude

East can be found from Mintaka's rising angle, which is equal to 90 degrees minus your latitude.

East

(covered in, the noncircumpolar star passing directly overhead).

If you missed the rising of Mintaka and know your latitude, you can quickly find cardinal directions using its rising angle. The rising angle is equal to 90 degrees minus your present latitude.

To find Mintaka's rising point, use a stick to create the correct angle between the stick, Mintaka, and the horizon. Knowing Mintaka's rising point is helpful for finding cardinal directions. For optimal results, this method should be used within two to three hours of Mintaka's rising. Beyond that time, inaccuracies of 10 degrees or more will occur. Once you have done your calculations, use a stick to create the correct angle between the stick and the horizon when its upward end crosses Mintaka.

The Noncircumpolar Stars of Scorpius

In Greek mythology, Scorpius was a scorpion that killed Orion. The legend further states that the two constellations were placed at opposite ends of the sky, with the sun between them, to avoid future conflicts. True or not, the location of each constellation and the earth's yearly rotation around the sun make Orion visible from November to April and Scorpius from May to November. During the transitional time, Orion can be seen disappearing below the western horizon at about the same time Scorpius becomes visible to the southeast (examples relate to the Northern Hemisphere). Scorpius travels directly overhead at latitude 40° South (headfirst from east to west) and is visible between 40° North and 90° South

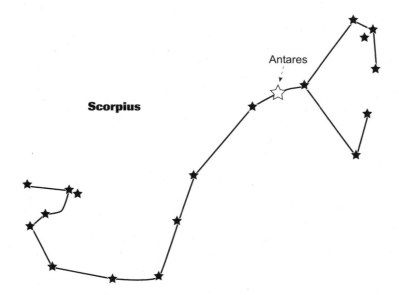

Antares

Scorpius

During summer months, Scorpius can be used to find cardinal directions.

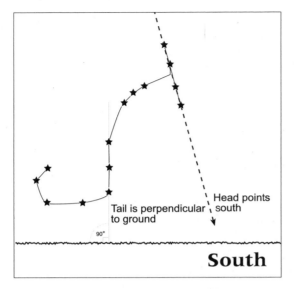

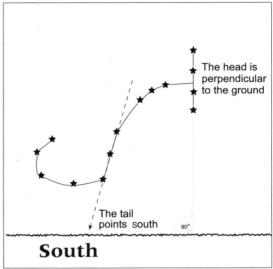

Perpendicular tail = head points south.   *Perpendicular head = tail points south.*

latitudes. The constellation forms a *J* and actually looks like a scorpion with a head, body, and tail. Its brightest star, Antares, has a reddish tint and is located in the scorpion's neck. Finding Antares is often the key to finding Scorpius.

In the Northern Hemisphere, Scopius crawls across the southern sky close to the horizon. In the Southern Hemisphere it passes high in the sky. At higher northern latitudes, Scorpius can only be seen when it passing to the south (at its highest point in the sky). The ability to find due south, however, depends on the orientation of Scorpius's head and tail. As a rule, when the tail is perpendicular to the horizon, the *head* stars point south; when the head is perpendicular to the horizon, the *tail* stars point south.

The Noncircumpolar Stars Passing Directly Overhead

All noncircumpolar stars passing directly overhead can be used to find cardinal directions. This is true no matter where you are, since all stars rise in the east and set in the west. To find east, west, north, and south, simply watch the direction of the traveling star. Since the star is moving west, a line showing its path represents an east-west line, and a line perpendicular to that gives north and south.

Since these stars move from east to west, a night version of the stick and shadow can be used to establish a general guide for the cardinal directions. For this technique, use the same setup as used in the stick-and-shadow method, and tie a piece of line to the top of the stick. Make sure the line is long enough to reach the ground and then some. Lie on your back so that the stick is between the star and your head and so that the free end of the line rests next to your temple. Position yourself so that the noncircumpolar star, the taut line, and top of the stick are all in line with one another. The line represents the star's shadow. Place a rock at the point where the line touches the ground, and repeat the process every five to ten minutes. Similar to the stick and shadow, the first mark is west and the second one is east. A perpendicular line will aid you in determining north and south.

If you plan to travel at night, you should find and use a sturdy 7-foot-long walking stick. When walking, keep the stick in front of you to protect your face from branches and to ensure that the ground is there before you put your foot down.

Table 6-11: Cardinal Directions Using the Stars

Star Type	Key Points
Circumpolar Stars	The sky's north pole can be found using Polaris. The sky's south pole can be found using the Southern Cross.
Noncircumpolar Stars	Mintaka (Orion) travels directly over the equator and gives east-west direction when appearing and disappearing on an unobstructed horizon. When not visible, Scorpius provides another option.
Noncircumpolar Overhead Stars	All stars move from east to west; thus any star that passes directly overhead offers an east-west line.

■ Using the Stars to Find Latitude

In order to find latitude from the stars, you will need to determine a star's altitude above the horizon or how close it is to traveling directly overhead. Without a sextant (or improvised sextant, discussed under Finding Latitude Using the Sun at Local Apparent Noon), finding a known star's altitude is extremely crude yielding a 60-nautical-mile error for every 1

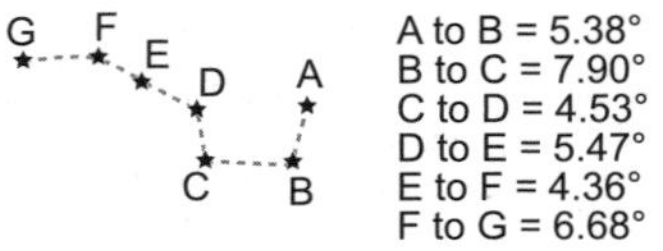

Big Dipper

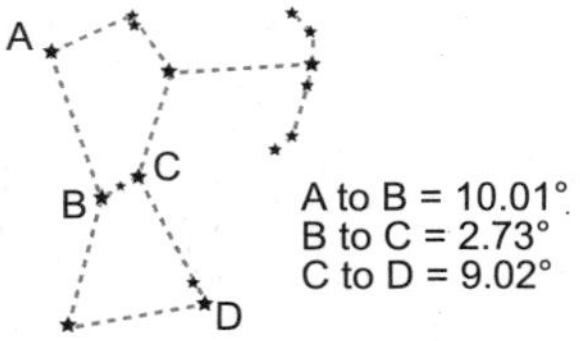

A to B = 5.38°
B to C = 7.90°
C to D = 4.53°
D to E = 5.47°
E to F = 4.36°
F to G = 6.68°

Orion

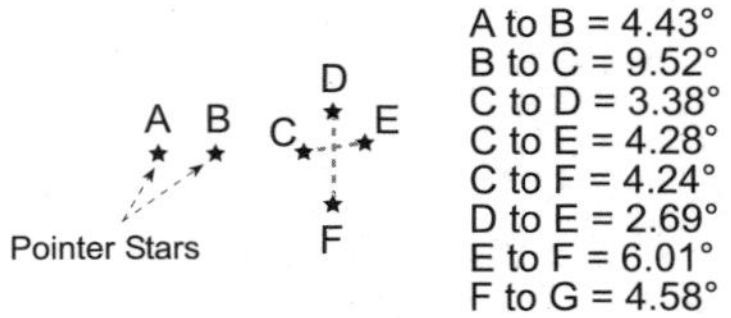

A to B = 10.01°
B to C = 2.73°
C to D = 9.02°

Southern Cross

Pointer Stars

A to B = 4.43°
B to C = 9.52°
C to D = 3.38°
C to E = 4.28°
C to F = 4.24°
D to E = 2.69°
E to F = 6.01°
F to G = 4.58°

Knowing the distance between known stars is helpful when trying to calibrate a kamal.

degree of star-height error. One method of decreasing this potential error is to make and calibrate a kamal. During the day the kamal is a great tool for establishing sunrise and sunset when the horizon has an obstructed view. At night it is very useful when trying to find latitude based on a star's altitude. To use the kamal for this purpose, however, it needs to be calibrated. In order to calibrate the device, you will need to know the distances between some of the potentially visible stars, as shown in the following illustration.

The first step for making the kamal useful for measuring angular distance is to make a scale on one of the card's long sides (inches, centimeters, etc.). Next, holding the kamal as discussed earlier (knot in mouth and arm held straight out), place the end of the card on one of the known stars and mark the distance between it and a second known star. Transforming the star's degree measurement into the unit scale created on the card requires a little math. The formula for making this happen is:

$$\text{Star distance} / \text{unit measurement} = \frac{\text{degrees per one unit of}}{\text{measurement on your scale}}$$

For greater precision, perform calibration checks on several known stars and find the average between all solutions. To find an average of several solutions use the following formula:

$$\frac{\textbf{(Solution 1 + Solution 2 + Solution 3)}}{\textbf{The number of solutions added together}}$$

Knowing the angle distance of each unit on the kamal makes it a useful tool for determining your latitude using a star's angular height on the horizon. To use the kamal, place the knot in your teeth, fully extend your arm (knot should be placed so that this step creates a taut line), and hold

Created Card Scale
Unit measurement of choice (inches, centimeters, etc.)

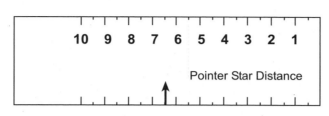

Distance between Big Dipper's pointer stars = 5.38°
Unit distance equivalent on this created scale = 6.5

Calibration Formula
5.38°/6.5 units = 0.83° per unit

the kamal with the top edge aligned with the star and your thumb aligned with the horizon. To measure the distance along the kamal's edge to the star's angular height, read the unit measurement that is found directly above your thumb. Although gross angles can be done using a stick and the horizon, for increased accuracy use the kamal whenever possible.

Once you have the kamal made, take the time to evaluate distances that allow quick reference—for example, the distance between two fingers when your arm is held out straight (often close to 2 degrees) or the spread distance between thumb tip and little finger when your arm is held out straight (often close to 20 degrees).

Finding Latitude Using Polaris

Since Polaris lies almost directly over due north (90° North latitude), its angular height on the unobstructed horizon is equal to your latitude. At the North Pole, Polaris is directly overhead, creating a 90-degree angle between it and the horizon. This angle decreases by 1 degree for each degree of latitude you make to the south. In other words, your latitude is equal to the angular height of Polaris. Polaris is rarely seen below latitude 5° North; thus this technique only works in the Northern Hemisphere. If unable to create the kamal card, improvise a sextant using a protractor or compass rose (discussed earlier).

Latitude = angular height of Polaris

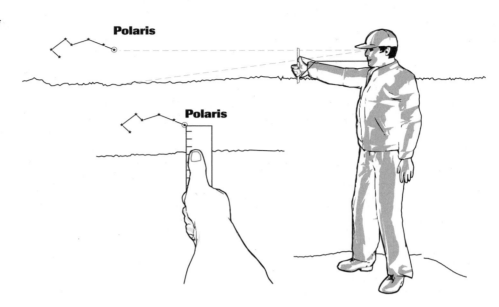

Identifying the angular height of Polaris using a kamal.

Polaris

Polaris

Finding Latitude Using the Southern Cross

In the Southern Hemisphere, the Southern Cross is a great tool for establishing your latitude. Unlike Polaris in the Northern Hemisphere, however, it isn't as close to the sky pole. The upper star of its long axis, Gacrux, is located roughly at latitude 57° South. The lower star on the long axis, Acrux, is located roughly at latitude 63° South. When these two stars form an imaginary line perpendicular to the horizon, the Southern Cross is at its highest point in the sky and directly due south of your location (at latitudes greater than 57° South). The first step to finding your actual latitude is to find your latitude relative to a known star, like Acrux. To do this, use a kamal to measure the angle distance between the horizon and Acrux and apply it to the following formula:

**Your latitude relative to Acrux
= 90 degrees − Acrux angular distance**

This is not your latitude, it is the latitude relative to Acrux. To calculate your latitude relative to the poles and equator,

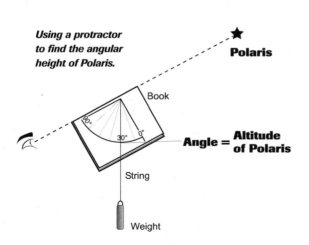

Using a protractor to find the angular height of Polaris.

Polaris

Book

90°

30°   0°

Angle = Altitude of Polaris

String

Weight

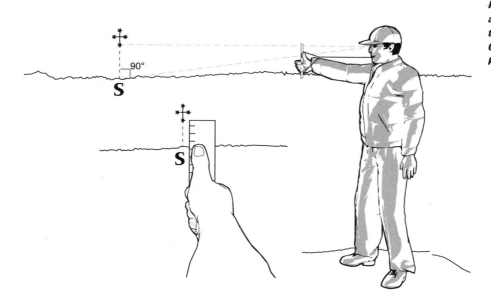

use the following (negative answer implies Southern Hemisphere; positive answer implies Northern Hemisphere):

Actual latitude = your latitude relative to Acrux − 63 degrees
(latitude path of Acrux)

Finding Latitude Using Orion

Mintaka, the leading star in Orion belt, travels directly over the equator (0° latitude). Its location makes it very useful for establishing latitude from its rising or setting angle or the angle created when it has reached its highest point in the sky (seen standing upright from the north and on its head from the south). The formulas are simple:

Latitude = 90 degrees − Orion's rising or setting angle (using Mintaka)

Latitude = 90 degrees − Mintaka's angle when it has reached its highest point in the sky

If Orion is north of you, you are in the Southern Hemisphere; if Orion is south of you, you are in the Northern Hemisphere. For best results, use a kamal to determine Mintaka's rising, setting, and highest point angles.

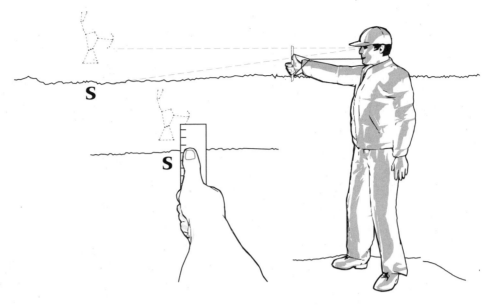

Finding the angular height of Mintaka using a kamal.

Finding Latitude Using Overhead Stars

Since all stars rotate around specific latitudes, those stars that pass directly overhead can be used to determine your latitude. The difficulty in this formula is identifying the star and then deciding if it is directly overhead.

Table 6-12: Finding Latitude Using the Stars

Stars	Key Points
Polaris	Latitude = angular height of Polaris.
Southern Cross	Latitude can be found as long as you can relate your latitude relative to Acrux to your actual latitude.
Orion	Latitude = 90 degrees – angular height of Mintaka. For best results, take the angular height of Mintaka within two hours of rising or setting or when Orion has reached its maximum height in the sky.
Overhead Stars	Since stars rotate around specific latitudes, stars that pass directly overhead can be used to determine your latitude.

Chapter Exercises

Find cardinal direction using the sun.

1. *From a stick and shadow.* Within two hours of LAN, use a stick and shadow to establish an east-west and a north-south line.

2. *Find local apparent noon (LAN) using a stick and shadow.* Within two hours of when you believe LAN will occur, make marks using the stick and shadow until you find the shortest one. At that time, the sun is at its highest point in the sky and should be due south or north of your location.

3. *From the sun's rising angle.* Since an unobstructed view of the horizon is necessary, this method may require a trip to the desert or beach. Take a lunch and make it a day. Within two hours after sunrise or before sunset, shoot a heading off the sun, adjust for its amplitude, and calculate where due east is (or due west in the case of a setting sun).

4. *With your watch.* Within two hours of LAN, establish the cardinal directions using your watch. Be sure to adjust for daylight saving time when appropriate.

For each exercise above, check for accuracy using an equivalent compass heading (be sure to adjust for the magnetic variation). Remember, a compass heading to true north is not necessarily 360 degrees. When the north-seeking arrow is boxed, the heading under the stationary index line must point the compass to true north not magnetic north.

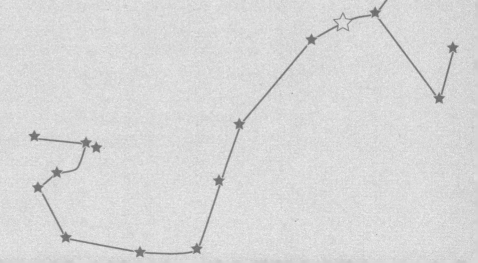

Find latitude and longitude using the sun.

1. *Latitude from the sun angle at sunrise or sunset.* This exercise can be done at the same time you practice finding cardinal directions (remember that trip to the beach?). Within two hours after sunrise or before sunset, use a stick or kamal and calculate the sun's rising or setting angle. Latitude = 90 degrees − rising (or setting) angle of the sun.

2. *Latitude from the sun angle at local apparent noon (LAN).* Find local apparent noon using the stick-and-shadow technique listed above. you'll need your calculator for this exercise. Find the sun declination and the zenith distance, and plug these values into Latitude = sun declination - (zenith distance). Remember, although the formula is a constant, addition and subtraction values change depending on north or south orientation of its various elements.

3. *Longitude from GMT and LAN.* Before you start, set your watch so that it represents your local time relative to Greenwich Mean Time (GMT). In addition, look up GMT's local apparent noon (LAN) for that date. Find LAN for your location using a stick and shadow. Add or subtract the time zone figure relative to GMT. Add if you're in a western longitude, subtract if you're in an eastern longitude. In the example I used, I was in PST, so I added eight hours to my LAN time. Subtract GMT's LAN from your adjusted LAN time, and calculate longitude by multiplying the answer by 15 degrees per hour and 15 minutes per minute (if your LAN time is before GMT's LAN, subtract it from GMT). Remember, if you're in west longitudes the sun passes you after Greenwich; in east longitudes it passes before (as related to sunrise, LAN, or sunset).

For each exercise above, check for accuracy using a map of your location that provides latitude and longitude measurements.

Find cardinal directions using the stars.

1. *From circumpolar stars.* In the Northern Hemisphere use the Big Dipper and Cassiopeia to pinpoint Polaris. In the Southern Hemisphere use the Southern Cross to find due north.

2. *From noncircumpolar stars.* This exercise requires an unobstructed view of the horizon. Another trip to the beach may be necessary. During winter months, find due east and west using Mintaka (leading star on Orion belt). During summer months, find due east and west using Scorpius.

3. *From overhead stars.* On a clear starry night set up camp, kick your feet back, and try to identify the stars that pass directly overhead. Once you identify them, check the almanac to see what declination (latitude) they have, and compare that to the latitude to your location. Stars that pass directly overhead travel on a precise east-to-west line.

For each exercise above, check for accuracy using an equivalent compass heading (be sure to adjust for the magnetic variation). Remember, a compass heading to true north is not necessarily 360 degrees. When the north-seeking arrow is boxed, the heading under the stationary index line must point the compass to true north not magnetic north.

Find latitude using the stars.

1. *Latitude from the angular height of Polaris.* In the Northern Hemisphere use the angular height of Polaris to find your latitude: Latitude = angular height of Polaris.

2. *Latitude from the Southern Cross.* In the Southern Hemisphere find the angular height of Acrux relative to your position and use this information to find your actual latitude: Latitude = your latitude relative to Acrux - 63 degrees.

3. *Latitude from Orion.* During winter months find your latitude from the angular height of Mintaka (when Orion has reached it maximum height in the sky): Latitude = 90 degrees - angular height of Mintaka.

4. *Latitude from overhead stars.* Once you have mastered the identity of stars relative to your location, identify your latitude from those stars that pass directly overhead.

For each exercise above, check for accuracy using a map of your location that provides latitude and longitude measurements.

Learning to navigate is the catalyst that allows us to enjoy nature with confidence.

SECTION IV

From Navigation to Travel

Navigation is more than the art of planning a trip and establishing a route from one point to another. It includes the *act* of traveling—the moving part that actually gets you safely from your starting point to your destination. Navigation without good travel techniques is a lesson only half learned—a toolbox without the tools.

This section will show you how to apply those tools to your trip—starting with planning a basic trek and moving on to terrain-specific travel techniques for unique environments. The key to learning navigation is to get out there and do it. The more you use your skills, the more they'll become second nature—and the safer all your travels will be.

This section provides details on basic and advanced travel techniques.

CHAPTER 7

Basics of Land Travel

Applying navigation to land travel begins with the basics. Here you'll learn how to pack and carry your backpack, a six-point checklist for route-finding, basic hiking techniques, and how to navigate on nighttime treks, as well as a reminder to review your basic survival kit.

Before departing into any environment, leave an itinerary with someone you can trust, and establish check-in times to let them know you are OK. Be very specific! Let them know where your car will be parked, who is traveling with you (along with their contact person), what gear you are taking, camping sites, side trips, destination, return time, and whom to contact should you be late (names and phone numbers of police, rangers, etc.). If you don't check in, your contact can let rescuers know your intended route of travel and initiate a search long before you might otherwise be missed. Doing this is like purchasing insurance! You hope you never need it, but when you do need it, you are sure glad it is in place. Don't forget to call your contact immediately upon leaving the wilderness. Otherwise a big—and completely unnecessary—search could be initiated, putting rescuers at potential risk.

When planning a route of travel, consider the terrain and how well you can meet your needs. What type of vegetation, ground surface, and slope issues might arise for the given route? Can troublesome obstacles be avoided using a dogleg route or following contour lines? Does the route provide campsites, water sources, and potential emergency exits to well-traveled roads, towns, etc.? Finally, if you're using a map or guidebook, how old is it? Although the contour should be the same, water sources could now be dry and man-made features (roads, buildings, etc.) could have changed. If you think your reference is outdated, contact the local ranger to discuss available resources in the area of intended travel.

How to Pack and Carry a Backpack

The type of pack you carry depends on your personal preference. As a rule, internal-frame packs provide better balance and are used for cold days, off-trail hikes, and rough terrain. External-frame packs allow better airflow between the pack and your back and are used for hot days, trail hikes, and level terrain. Use the following guidelines when packing either type for a trip.

- **On-trail.** When on-trail hiking organize your gear so that the heavier items are on top and close to your back. This method focuses most of the pack's weight on your hips, making it easier to carry.

- **Off-trail.** Organize the pack so that heavy items are close to the back (from the pack's top to its bottom) so that the majority of the pack's weight is carried by your shoulders and your back, affording you better balance.

Regardless of which packing method you use, make sure to pack your larger survival items so that they can be easily accessed, and carry a smaller survival kit on your person. Pad items that might gouge your back or can easily break.

Route-Finding: The Six-Point Checklist

Planning a trip requires daily objectives that end when you reach your final destination. Each day's trek may or may not point toward the final objective, since each trek must consider the terrain (safety issues) and how well it meets your needs (water, campsites, emergency exits, etc.). Also, each day may require several dogleg treks in order to meet that day's objective. Regardless of the route taken (direct or otherwise), take the time to plan your trek—using my simple six-point checklist, outlined here. If you're traveling in a direct line, one six-point checklist is all that you'll need. If your trip is a dogleg, however, it is best to make a six-point checklist for each trek needed to complete the trip. The six-point checklist includes heading, distance, pace count, terrain evaluation, point description, and estimated time of arrival (ETA). These points are discussed in the following sections.

■ Point 1: Heading

The first step in planning your trek is to establish a heading that is safe and meets your needs. Several methods of finding and maintaining a heading are covered here.

Finding a Heading from Point A to Point B

A heading from point A to point B can be found using a compass and oriented map, compass meridian lines and map, protractor and map, map alone, or just a compass.

Using a Compass and Oriented Map. To establish a route with a compass, use the following steps:

- Orient the map.
- Lightly draw a pencil line from your current location to your intended destination.
- Place the top left edge of the compass on your intended destination.
- Rotate the compass until the left edge is directly on and parallel to the line you drew.
- Next rotate the compass housing, keeping the base of the compass stationary until the floating magnetic needle is boxed inside the orienting arrow (red portion of the needle forward).
- Read the compass heading at the point where the bottom of the direction-of-travel arrow touches the numbers of the circular compass housing. This heading is the field bearing to your intended destination.
- Before taking this heading as gospel, double-check to make sure the map is still oriented.

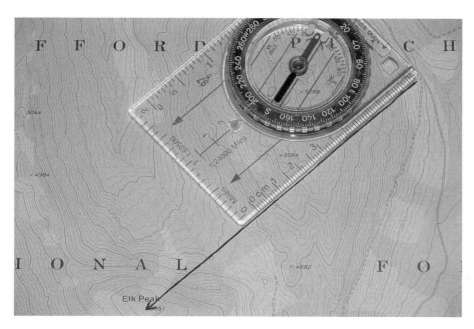

A compass heading acquired from an oriented map.

Using Compass Meridian Lines and Map. If you have an orienteering compass that has meridian lines, these lines can be used to establish a heading. To establish a route using the orienteering compass meridian lines, use the following steps:

- Lightly draw a pencil line from your current location to your intended destination.
- Place the top left edge of the compass on your intended destination.
- Rotate the compass until the left edge is directly on and parallel to the line you drew.
- Next rotate the compass housing, keeping the base of the compass stationary, until the meridian lines are parallel with a longitude line (make sure the north end of the meridian lines point toward the north end of the map).
- Read the compass heading at the point where the bottom of the direction-of-travel arrow touches the numbers of the circular compass housing. This heading is based on true north and must be converted to a compass heading.
- To establish a magnetic compass heading, the magnetic declination must be added (if west) or subtracted (if east) from the heading found. This adjusted heading is the field bearing (compass heading) to your intended destination.

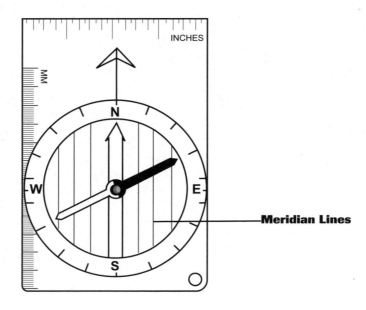

Meridian lines can be used to establish a compass heading.

Using a Protractor and Map. Many types of protractors can be used with a map in order to find a heading. Regardless of the type (full-circle, half-circle, square, or rectangle), all have an outer edge marked in degrees and a central index mark. To establish a route using a protractor, use the following steps:

- Lightly draw a line that connects your current location with your intended destination.
- Place the central index mark of the compass at a point where the drawn line crosses a vertical (north-south) grid line or longitude line (the line you use makes a difference in which magnetic declination you use—grid north or true north).
- Keeping the index mark at this point, align the 0° to 180° line of the protractor with the vertical grid or longitude line.
- Read the protractor angle at the point directly over the drawn line. This heading is based on true north (if using a longitude line) or grid north (if using a vertical grid line) and must be converted to a compass heading.
- To establish a magnetic compass heading, the magnetic declination must be added (if west) or subtracted (if east) from the heading found. Be

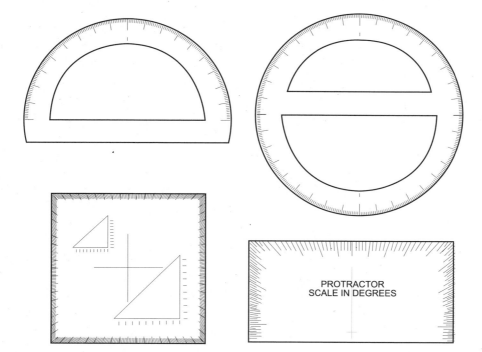

PROTRACTOR
SCALE IN DEGREES

Protractors can be used to establish a heading.

sure to use the appropriate declination (magnetic to grid or magnetic to true) when establishing the compass heading. This adjusted heading is the field bearing to your intended destination.

Route-Finding with Only a Map. Why anyone would venture into the wilderness without a compass is beyond my comprehension. But it happens. If it should happen to you, don't forget all the aids Mother Nature provides. Cardinal directions (N, S, E, W) can be found using the constellations, stick and shadow, and your watch. These gross headings can be used to orient a map, determine a heading to the nearest well-traveled road, and maintain a route of travel until you get there. For further details on how to use this information, refer to Chapter 5.

Route-Finding with a Compass Alone. A map is an extremely important piece of gear—one that all backcountry travelers should carry. If you don't have a map, I can only hope that you know an emergency heading to a well-traveled road (or town or building) in the vicinity. To determine this heading, use the following steps:

■ Hold the compass level, and turn the circular housing until the intended heading meets the stationary index line (the point where the bottom of the direction-of-travel arrow touches the numbers of the circular housing).

■ Next, while keeping the bottom of the compass level with the ground and its back end parallel to your body plane, turn your body and the compass until the magnetic north–seeking needle is boxed directly over and inside the orienting arrow (red portion of the needle forward).

■ Double-check the heading to make sure it hasn't changed. Provided it hasn't, the destination can be found boxing the magnetic needle, taking a course that coincides with the direction-of-travel arrow.

Maintaining a Heading from Point A to Point B

A heading that isn't heeded can lead to extreme course deviations. In other words, trust your compass! Staying true to your heading is easy, provided you use one of the following methods.

Point-to-Point Navigation. With the compass's heading established and your body perpendicular to the direction-of-travel arrow (eyes forward), pick a prominent landmark that is in line with your field bearing. Walk to that point and repeat the process on another landmark that falls in line with your heading. This method allows the traveler to steer clear of obstacles.

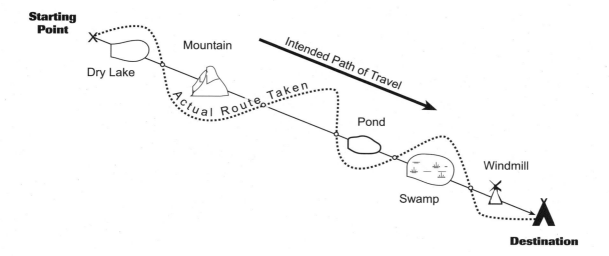

Following the Compass. This technique will vary slightly, depending on the type of compass used. Regardless of the type, the compass is held level while keeping the magnetic needle boxed (orienteering compass) or the appropriate heading under the lubber line (magnetic card compass). A course of travel is maintained by constantly adjusting your forward motion so as to maintain the proper compass heading (body perpendicular to the direction-of-travel arrow).

Contour Navigation. Getting from point A to point B using contour navigation is an advanced skill that is well worth learning. The ultimate goal is to reach your destination while using the easiest terrain available. This is rarely a direct path and often requires you to travel a greater distance. However, it is a path that conserves energy, since it avoids steep grades, drainage slash, and other nasty obstacles that consume our time and get-up-and-go. A prime example of how this method might be used can be seen in treks that cross a drainage. This path leads the navigator down a steep grade, through dense vegetation (often found in drainages), and back up a steep grade. A better option is to follow the ridgelines around the drainage, avoiding the grade changes and slash. This technique, however, requires a constant awareness of the surrounding landscape and understanding of how the terrain relates to the map.

Point-to-point navigation allows you to circumnavigate obstacles.

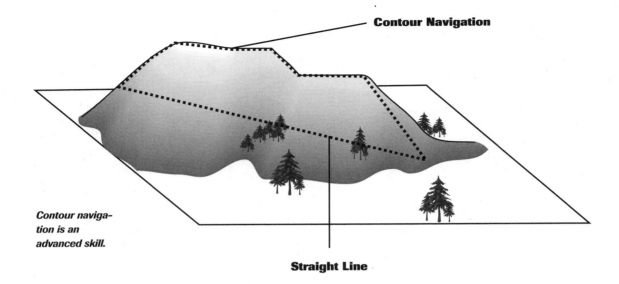

Contour Navigation

Contour navigation is an advanced skill.

Straight Line

■ Point 2: Distance

Distance from one point to another can be measured using nautical miles, statute miles, and kilometers. Most charts and maps provide a usable scale within the marginal information. The map's bar scale is created specific to that map and provides an ideal tool for establishing a distance from one point to another. The scale can be used in one of two ways:

- **Mark the distance on paper.** Place a piece of paper so that its edge creates a line between your location and your destination. While holding the paper in place, make a mark at both places. Move the paper to the bar scale, and measure the distance between the two points.

- **Create a paper scale.** Place a piece of paper next to the bar scale and mark its edge, forming a line that replicates the various measurements of the scale. The paper can then be used to measure the distance from one point to another when its edge is placed to align with the direction of travel, with zero at the starting point. The distance from point A to point B is where the paper scale meets the destination on the map.

For larger charts, latitude lines are helpful when trying to determine a distance. Remember that 1 degree of latitude is equal to 60 nautical miles (about 69 statute miles). Therefore, 1 minute of latitude is equal to 1 nautical mile (about 1.15 statute miles). The same, however, is not true for longitude lines. These lines get closer together the farther north and south you go from the equator. Longitude lines should not be used for measuring distances. Grid lines on a UTM scale can be used for measuring distances, regardless of which line (vertical or horizontal) is used (referenced to the bar scale or with a protractor).

■ Point 3: Pace Count

The pace count relates distance to a more tangible process. A pace is every time the same foot hits the ground. For example, each time your left foot strikes the ground, you count one pace. When converting distance to pace count, the terrain must also be considered, since it is doubtful your pace on level terrain is the same as on a steep grade. Over time you will develop a feel for your pace count and how it should be adjusted for various terrains. For now, however, start with a few generic values that have worked for me. On fairly level terrain I estimate 650 paces per kilometer and double that ratio when my trek involves a steep or treacherous path.

■ Point 4: Terrain Evaluation

Take the time to list all natural and man-made features that are visible during the trek. These features may include roads, buildings, towers, rivers, marshes, clearings, ridgelines, and drainages. In addition to listing terrain features, take the time to calculate how many paces it takes to reach each one. This is extremely helpful—once one feature has been passed, your attention can focus on the next. A properly done terrain evaluation helps provide a heightened awareness related to your location within your route of travel.

■ Point 5: Point Description

In addition to evaluating the terrain, establish the appearance of your final location and its surroundings. Consider this the last feature of your terrain evaluation. This step is very helpful when the pace count has been met but you have not reached the final point. More often than not, this problem stems from underestimating the number of paces needed to reach the destination. However, this is not always the case. In such instances, understanding the terrain that surrounds your final destination is helpful. Is there a peak to the left of the destination? Does the destination rest on a ridgeline? Is there a marsh or stream crossing at the final point? The more

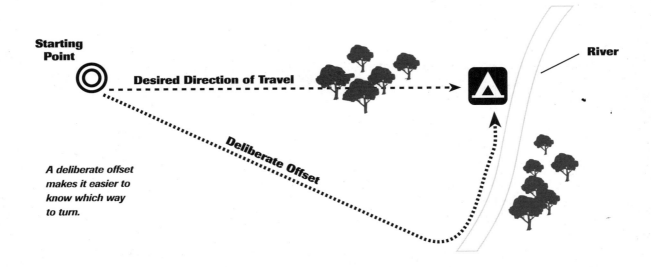

Starting Point

Desired Direction of Travel

River

Deliberate Offset

A deliberate offset makes it easier to know which way to turn.

detail that goes into describing the final point, the easier it will be to establish your location relative to it.

When traveling to a destination located on a road, river, or trail, a deliberate offset (to one side) is very helpful when trying to decide where the final point is (vehicle, camp, etc.). Use a heading several degrees to one side of your final location (the longer the trek, the smaller the offset should be). Once the road or stream has been reached, your destination should be to the right when offsetting left and to the left when offsetting right.

■ Point 6: Estimated Time of Arrival

Alone, estimating your time of arrival has limited value. But when used with the other five components, it helps you make decisions. It will take time and practice to establish time frames for the various terrains. At first, a route estimated to take eight hours may actually take twelve hours. In such instances you may need to reevaluate and actually stop at an alternate campsite for the night. Over time you will gain a better idea of how much time to allot for specific terrains and be able to set more realistic goals on the distance to travel each day. An ETA, like a pace count, is unique to you.

Table 7-1: The Six-Point Route-Finding Checklist

Point	Description
1. Heading	Compass heading from point A to point B.
2. Distance	Distance measured from point A to point B.
3. Pace Count	Number of paces between each terrain feature and total paces from point A to point B.
4. Terrain Evaluation	Be aware of and document each prominent land feature between point A and point B.
5. Point Description	Understanding how the final point should look is key to knowing your destination has been reached.
6. ETA	Estimated time of arrival may be altered by terrain and other features.

Basic Hiking Techniques

When hiking, it is important to see the big picture—to recognize the route's obstacles and plan a trek that meets your needs, while keeping you headed toward your final destination. Make every effort to pick an appropriate route, conserve energy, and avoid environmental risks. Some methods of accomplishing this are listed below.

■ Pick Your Route Wisely

During a navigation class, students are taught to use a straight line to get from point A to point B. This is an important skill to master. The next step is to learn the terrain and how to conserve energy by moving from point A to point B with the least amount of elevation loss and gain. The ability to use the terrain not only saves energy but also helps keep you oriented and aware of your current location. If you have developed this skill, take the time to look at both options—point-to-point versus terrain navigation. Choose a route that meets your basic needs while reducing safety risks. If you're in a group, sit down and review the map, the terrain, and the experience of the team. If the trek and conditions warrant, make sure everyone has an ice ax and knows how to use it (for details on ice axes, see Chapter 12). Proper preparation will greatly decrease the risk of ending your trek with a bad outcome.

■ Breaking Trail and Setting the Pace

If you are traveling in a group, it is doubtful that everyone has the same stride and physical ability. This is not the time to prove how macho you are. A pace should be set that is comfortable for everyone. In addition, the lead person should change on a regular basis, allowing everyone the opportunity to break trail, especially since the lead will expend much more energy than those who follow.

■ Going Uphill: The Kick Step

When going up a snow or scree slope, using a kick step will help stabilize your footing and make the trek much easier for those behind you. If going straight up, plant the toe of your boot with enough force to create a step that supports the ball of your foot. This doesn't take much energy—the weight of your boot and swing of your lower leg is all it should take. If you are leading a group, make sure your stride accounts for the shortest member of the team. For more control during an uphill ascent, lean forward (sideways if traversing) until your body is perpendicular to the earth's natural surface (not that of the hill).

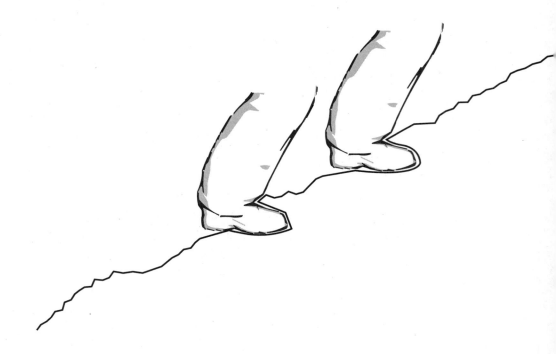

Kick step.

Plunge step.

■ Going Downhill: The Plunge Step

When going down a snow or scree slope, the plunge step provides down-hill stability in the same way the kick step does when going uphill. The only difference is that your heels rather than your toes are kicked into the slope. When going downhill, lean backward until your body is perpendicular to the earth's natural surface (not that of the hill).

■ Traversing a Slope

Crossing the slope in a zigzagging diagonal pattern is a quick and easy method for getting up or down a hill, especially when the slope's steepness is too exhausting. On snow or scree slopes, a kick step can be used to stabilize the foot, but instead of kicking the toe of your boot into the snow or scree, kick the uphill side of your boot so that at least half its width is making solid contact with the snow or scree.

Traversing a slope.

■ Conserving Energy: The Rest Step

When walking uphill, use a rest step, locking the knee with each step. This process takes the weight off the muscle, allowing it to rest, and places it on the skeletal system. For best results, you'll need to take a short pause with each step.

■ Use Available Trails

It only makes sense—when a trail follows your direction of travel, use it. Animals make trails by constantly taking a route that has the least amount of obstacles. Following such trails helps you conserve energy. To avoid getting lost, make sure you check the trail's heading at regular intervals. Blindly following a trail is not wise, since an animal's trail often heads toward its water, shelter, or food source; odds are it will eventually deviate from your course.

■ Avoid Overheating

Heat loss is energy loss. Avoid it whenever possible by taking frequent breaks and adjusting clothing as needed.

■ Crossing a Creek

Before crossing a creek, loosen your pack's shoulder straps and undo your waistband so that you can quickly remove the pack if you fall in. Cross the creek at the shallowest location you can find, using a diagonal downstream route. If you have one, use a long walking staff to support your body and decrease the current's impact on your legs. To decrease the current impact, place the stick on the upstream side of your position so that a V forms with you in its center.

Night Navigation

Last year I taught a group of students the art of advanced navigation. One of the first lessons: Avoid night navigation at all costs! Night navigation is extremely dangerous! There are many unseen obstacles, it is hard to evaluate the terrain, and the pace count increases significantly. With that said, we went on to perform several night navigation maneuvers, including one in an open area that allowed us to use the stars as our guide and one in dense forest that required close adherence to our compass heading. In an attempt to increase safety, in both instances I had students use a 7-foot-long walking stick (procured from Mother Nature). The stick helped students evaluate their next step (ensure that ground is there) and protect their face and eyes from unseen small twigs or other head-high obstacles. I have seen people get corneal abrasions from small branches and heard stories of night travelers walking off cliffs or falling through a false floor, jungle vegetation that extends beyond the earth's surface.

■ Open Terrain

When the skies are clear, traveling at night is not too bad—provided the terrain is without obstacle. In such cases, a heading can be established using a compass and maintained using either a compass or the stars. The walking stick is key to understanding the earth's surface beneath your feet and making each step safe.

■ Dense Forest

In a dense forest it can be very dark at night—to the point that you can't see more than a foot in front of your nose. My recommendation is to avoid this type of travel at all cost. If you do choose to travel at night, you will need a compass with an illumination feature in order to stay on your heading. Using a flashlight will destroy your night vision; use one only when you have enough battery power for the whole trek. In addition, a walking stick is extremely valuable for protection. If the conditions are extreme (very dark) and you are in a group, each member should have physical contact with the person in front of him/her (hand on shoulder), feet ought to be moved in a shuffling manner, and there should be constant communication about upcoming obstacles throughout the line.

Survival and Safety Gear

Each environment presents a different obstacle. Make sure you carry the gear necessary to meet your basic and survival needs. Take the time to do your research and pack appropriately. Make sure to consider your five survival essentials when packing and preparing a survival kit. Take the time to review the basic survival kit contents covered in Chapter 2.

Chapter Exercises

Find a heading.

Practice finding a heading using the various methods discussed in this chapter (oriented map, compass meridian lines, protractor). Do the headings match? Which method did you prefer?

Calculate a distance and estimate a pace count.

Take a road trip and, using an established heading, calculate a distance from point A to point B and estimate a pace count. Walk the route, keeping a precise pace count and paying attention to the exact type of terrain covered. Perform this process on several routes, and compare the pace counts and type of terrain covered with each. A trend should be obvious. Use the trends to create a reference of your estimated pace count over specific distances and terrains.

Evaluate the terrain, including the final point.

When doing each of the preceding exercises, write down a detailed terrain evaluation of what to expect during the trek and at the final point. During the trek, try to identify each feature listed—relating its appearance and pace count to what you expected. How well did you do? The more details you establish up front, the better your constant awareness and odds of knowing where you are at all times.

Estimate your time of arrival.

Estimate a time for the trek and evaluate how close you came. Keep a log, and use trends to form a reference of expected ETAs for the various terrains.

Travel in Unique Environments

The wilderness is not one-size-fits-all. It comprises several unique environments—each with potential obstacles that must be considered during a wilderness outing. A brief summation of travel in snow and ice environments is provided here, along with more in-depth coverage of travel in desert, jungle, and water environments, both river and coastline. Terrain is one of the many factors that make up an environment—it's the physical characteristics of the land you'll be dealing with on your wilderness treks. For further details on travel over rough land, snow, and ice terrain, including rock and glaciers, refer to Chapter 5.

Travel on Snow and Ice

Snow and ice regions are located in northern and southern latitudes roughly above and below 35 degrees. On average they receive 10 to 40 inches of precipitation a year. Snow affected by warm weather turns to a wet, slushy substance that makes for difficult travel. Snow affected by cold is frequently dry and powdery, often forming large drifts that must be negotiated.

■ Snow and Ice Climates

Winter begins December 21 in the Northern Hemisphere and June 21 in the Southern Hemisphere. In the Northern Hemisphere winter officially ends on March 21, but in reality it can last up to six months, depending on your location. In addition to snow, the beginning and end of winter often bring freezing rain and sleet.

Snow Climates

Snow climates are found in the interior continental areas of the two great landmasses of North America and Eurasia. The north side usually borders the tundra climate and the southern side borders a temperate forest. There are two kinds of snow climates: the continental subarctic and the humid continental.

Continental Subarctic. The continental subarctic climate is known for its wide temperature extremes, which can range from -100 degrees to 110 degrees Fahrenheit. They have long, cold, snowy winters and short summers, along with seasonal extremes of daylight and darkness. These climates are found in Alaska to Labrador and Scandinavia to Siberia.

Humid Continental. The humid continental climate has four seasons. Its summer, however, tends to be cooler and shorter than in other temperate zones, and a high percentage of its precipitation is snow. These climates are found in New England and westward beyond the Great Lakes region into the Great Plains and into the prairie provinces of Canada.

Ice Climates

Ice climate terrain varies greatly. These climates are found in the tundra and on continental glaciers located in Greenland and the Antarctic. The tundra has steep terrain, snow and ice fields, glaciers, and very high wind conditions. The continental glaciers are windswept ice that is moving slowly toward the sea. Both areas are desolate and provide a harsh environment. There are three kinds of ice climate: marine subarctic, tundra, and the ice cap.

Marine Subarctic. The marine subarctic climate is known for its cloudy skies, strong winds, and high rainfall. This climate is found on windward coasts, on islands, and over wide expanses of ocean in the Bering Sea and North Atlantic, touching points of Greenland, Iceland, and Norway. In the Southern Hemisphere the climate is found on small landmasses.

Tundra. The tundra climate is known for its permanently frozen subsoil. The tundra's level ground, proximity to ocean, and persistent cloud cover keep it cold even during summer. These climates are located between the polar ice cap and the timberline of North America and Eurasia.

Ice Cap. Ice cap climates are just that—ice. Areas where this can be found include Greenland, Antarctic continental ice caps, and the larger area of floating sea ice in the Arctic Ocean.

■ Snow and Ice Terrain: Things to Consider

In addition to avalanches (covered in Chapter 12), snow and ice terrain has many other obstacles that should be considered before the backcountry traveler hits the trail. The terrain, running and standing water, and trees and rocks are just a few problem areas that should be considered.

Terrain Issues

Cornices, glaciers, and crevasses are perhaps the biggest terrain risks (besides avalanche) faced by the snow and ice hiker.

Cornices. Cornices are wavelike formations that extend from the downwind side of a ridge or peak. This can pose a problem for the hiker in two ways. First, if you're hiking below a cornice, there is the risk of it fracturing and your being caught in an avalanche. Second, if you're above a cornice (approaching from the windward side), there is a risk of the cornice

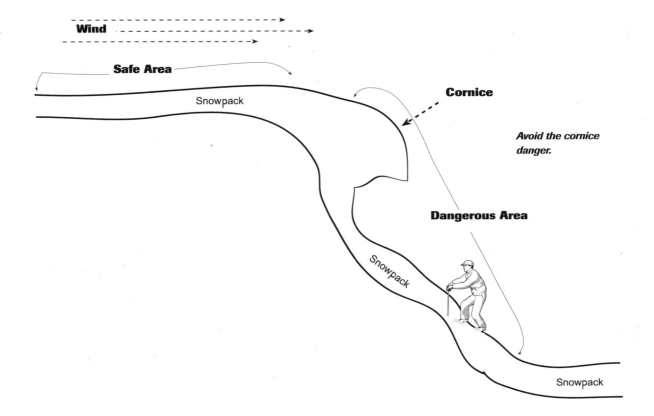

Avoid the cornice danger.

fracturing and taking you for a ride. Don't be caught in either scenario! Try to recognize a cornice in advance by identifying wind patterns and looking at similar ridges in the area. Do they have cornices? If you must cross below a cornice, cross no higher than two-thirds of the way up the ridge. Doing this should give you time to escape should the cornice break free. Do not cross on top of a cornice. Be alert; recognize this threat early, and select routes that avoid this hazard.

Glaciers. Glaciers are basically rivers of snow and ice that form when the existing snow doesn't completely melt before the next year's snowfall. The glacier's lower layers melt, only to be replaced by a new top layer. Falling on a glacier can provide a long ride if you're not prepared. Be sure to wear crampons for added traction, carry an ice ax to self-belay and arrest, and when necessary rope up with fellow team members (all covered in Chapter 12).

Crevasses. Crevasses are cracks in a glacier, formed when the glacier stretches or bends too fast, and are often 100 feet deep. When crossing a glacier, it is best to avoid crevasses unless you are well versed and trained in crevasse crossings and rescue. If a crevasse is in your path, try to cross close to the top, where the glacier is more stable. Crevasse crossing and rescue techniques are covered in Chapter 12.

Running and Standing Water

Water is necessary for life! However, crossing water (creeks, rivers, pond, lakes) in snow and ice regions is not without risk. These risks include loss of gear, hypothermia—and drowning.

Creeks and Small Rivers. After filling your water containers, it is time to cross the creek or river. Take the time to survey the area. Look for a shaded area with a large amount of snow and where no water can be seen. The snow is often more stable at these sites, but there is no guarantee. Loosen your shoulder straps, undo your waistband, and take off your skis or snowshoes. This will make it easier to remove the pack if you fall in and will prevent your skis or snowshoes from trapping you in the water. Before crossing, find a long pole and use it to evaluate the snow's depth and stability before taking each step. Finally, cross one person at a time. If you fall into a small waterway like these, getting out should be relatively easy. The biggest problem here is hypothermia.

Lakes, Ponds, and Large Rivers. Lakes, ponds, and large rivers often freeze in extremely cold environments. Their stability, however, is not a given, and crossing large bodies of ice should be avoided whenever possible. If you can, go around. The potential risk associated with breaking through is too high. If there is no other option, cross close to shore, at the outer corners of bends, or in passages that are more prone to be shallow. Stay clear of areas that have logs, stumps, or rocks piercing through the ice. The radiant heat from these items weakens the surrounding ice.

The greatest risks from falling in a large body of ice-covered water are hypothermia and drowning. Getting out is not as easy as you might think. If a member of your group falls through the ice, do not run onto the ice to rescue the person. From a safe place, try to reach the person using a long, sturdy object. If others are present, form a chain of bodies (lying flat with each person holding the ankles of the next) from a secure location to the victim. If you are the one who fell in, do everything you can to keep your head above the water's surface. To get out, put your hands in front of you, keep your body flat on the water's surface, and use a flutter kick to propel yourself onto the ice. If you're unable to get out of the water, keep your arms on the ice surface—even if they freeze in place. This will prevent you from going beneath the surface and give the rescue team more time.

Trees and Rocks

Trees, saplings, and rocks that breach the snow's surface do so because of the radiant heat they produce and the prevailing winds. These areas can become huge unseen sump holes that pull you down when you breach the surface. Don't walk close to exposed saplings and rocks.

■ Snow and Ice Hazards: Things to Consider

Avalanche and crevasse risks are perhaps the greatest threat to a snow and ice hiker. However, more people suffer injury and death from exposure. Avalanche safety is covered in Chapter 12. Other snow and ice hazards are listed below.

Dehydration

My experience has shown that people tend to drink less water in cold climates. This can prove to be a fatal error. The body is burning off a tremendous amount of calories to warm itself—a process that consumes the body's water. That water must be replaced. Take the time to drink and replace your water supplies.

Exposure Injuries

Exposure-related injuries include hypothermia, frostbite, immersion foot, and snow blindness. Make sure you are prepared to enter this environment. Wear and carry the correct attire to prevent these injuries, including sunglasses that provide 100 percent UV protection and a hat and gloves to prevent rapid heat loss. Wear boots and socks that keep your feet dry, and change socks at the first sign of moisture. Take the time to warm up your water whenever you can. Don't forget the sunscreen! The sun reflecting off snow can cause a pretty good burn.

Whiteouts

The best thing to do in a whiteout is go to ground. Make sure you carry enough survival gear to meet your five survival essentials should you get caught in a whiteout. Better to wait until you can see than to walk off a cliff!

Altitude Sickness

Plan your trip to allow several days of acclimatizing at the higher altitudes. Your body needs to adjust. Set this time aside—or risk having to cancel your trip after developing an altitude-related illness.

■ Snow and Ice Travel: Key Points

Snow and ice travel can be a wonderful, even spiritual experience, or it can be the worst trip of your life. It all depends on how you prepare for the trip you take. Most issues related to travel in a snow and ice climate are covered in Chapter 12; however, some basic concepts are listed below:

■ Consider a trek that keeps you on a safe, avalanche-free ridgeline. Travel at the two-thirds point keeps you out of the deep snow and slush found in drainages and below the drifts often found at the highest elevations.

■ It not uncommon to have GPS and cell phone failure in these environments. Believe this! If you use a GPS, stay aware of your location, and make sure your map and compass skills are honed in case the GPS can't lock in or its batteries fail. Decrease the battery failure risk by replacing batteries before each trip and keeping them warm while on the trail.

- Depending on the trek, you may or may not be able to use constellations. Use constellations when you can, but keep that compass close by.

- The person breaking trail and setting pace often does the most work. Change this position on a regular basis.

Desert Travel

Deserts are considered any area that receives less than 10 inches (25 cm) of precipitation a year. Based on this criterion, deserts cover approximately 15 percent of the earth's surface.

■ Desert Climates

Deserts are not all hot, barren, and sand covered. In fact, only 20 percent of the world's deserts are covered in sand. The rest are gravel plains (50 percent), barren mountain ranges, rocky plateaus, and salt marshes. Deserts are located in hot or cold regions and often have large temperature swings between day and night. Deserts are classified by their location and weather pattern as high-pressure deserts, rain shadow deserts, continental deserts, or cool coastal deserts.

High-Pressure Deserts

High-pressure deserts are located between 20 and 30 degrees latitude (on both sides of the equator) and in both polar regions. The high atmospheric pressure of these areas force dry air to descend and absorb much of the area's moisture.

High-Pressure Deserts in the Polar Regions. The words *cold* and *desert* aren't often used together. Cold polar regions, however, do meet the definition of a desert. Although temperatures rarely exceed 50 degrees Fahrenheit, these areas have less than 10 inches of precipitation a year.

High-Pressure Deserts between 20 and 30 Degrees Latitude. At latitudes between 20 and 30 degrees (north and south of the equator), the descending air is so dry it absorbs the area's moisture. Temperatures at these locations can reach as high as 130 degrees Fahrenheit. Most of the world's deserts are located in this area.

Rain Shadow Desert

Rain shadow deserts are located on the downwind side of a mountain range just beyond the point where the wind cools and dumps its moisture. The dry wind absorbs the area's moisture, creating the desert.

Continental Desert

Continental deserts are located in the center of large continents just beyond the point where winds have lost most of their moisture. The dry wind absorbs the area's moisture, creating the desert.

Cool Coastal Desert

Coastal deserts are perhaps some of the driest in the world. These deserts are the result of the cold ocean currents that parallel the western coastline near the tropics of Cancer and Capricorn. Here the cold ocean current touches a warm landmass and results in almost no moisture transfer, causing the dry descending air mass to become even drier.

■ Desert Terrain: Things to Consider

Desert terrain can come in many forms, and each form presents a different problem for the traveler. Traveling in a desert at the poles is much different from traveling in a southern California desert. Do your research, and prepare for the type of terrain your desert offers. Some of the terrains you might encounter are outlined here.

Dunes

Walking on sand is a hard task that rapidly depletes the hiker's energy. Like snow, sand tends to give way, making each step that much harder. To decrease this impact, stay on the wind-packed side of a dune whenever you can.

Canyons and Similar Structures

It is easy to get lost in a canyon's maze. Carefully research your trip, and carry a good map of the area. In addition, flash floods can occur in a canyon path. Avoid canyons during peak flash flood season. At other times be wary, and keep a constant eye out for potential escape routes.

Rocky Peaks

The climb up a rocky peak is often not the problem. The climb down, however, can present the climber with a significant problem and perhaps lead to a fall and injury. Before heading up a rocky peak, think about the trip downhill.

Dry Lakes

Dry lakebeds are often hard crusty surfaces that are devoid of visible land-marks, making it difficult to identify your location. This type of travel mandates carrying a GPS and keeping an accurate pace count.

Lava Beds

Lava beds present the traveler with uneven and hard-to-negotiate terrain that often cannot be circumnavigated. For areas requiring a direct path from one rock to the next, establish a balanced posture before moving from your current location to the next.

Loose Rock Surface

A desert with multiple loose rocks sets the traveler up for stone-bruised feet, twisted ankles, and stress fractures. Wear shoes or boots that provide the needed protection and support, and maintain a constant awareness to avoid the potential threats that lie in your path.

■ Desert Hazards: Things to Consider

The desert presents many potential hazards, and each should be considered before your trek begins. Evaluate potential water sources and terrain issues, and talk to the local rangers before you depart. Don't rely on information that may be old and outdated.

Water

Without water you will die! If you are thirsty, you are already dehydrated. You can live a long time without food but only days without water. On average, drink at least a pint of water an hour for temperatures below 100 degrees Fahrenheit and a quart an hour in higher temperatures. Pack enough water to meet your needs, and make sure there is a water source on your trek. Discuss your trip with the local authorities, including the availability of accessible water. Be leery of hearsay information from the locals, as it may be outdated or just wrong. Never ration your water! Instead decrease your water loss by rationing sweat and staying out of the midday sun. If necessary, adjust or delay your trip when there's no water on your trek.

Extreme Temperatures

Nonpolar deserts are known for their hot days and cold nights, and high temperatures may make day travel inadvisable. If the risk of exposure injury is too high, travel during early morning and late afternoon. In addition, decrease the threat of an exposure injury by covering as much of your body as you can. Wear full-length pants, long-sleeved shirts, sunglasses, and a hat that shades your head and neck. These clothes should be made from synthetic sun-protective fabrics that have an ultraviolet protection factor (UPF) rating of 30 or more. Clothes should be baggy and multiple layered so that layers can be removed or added as needed. An outer nylon shell should also be brought for protection from the wind. Wear sunscreen on exposed areas to avoid painful sunburn.

Sandstorms

In sand-covered deserts, sandstorms not only hamper travel but also present the traveler with equipment- and health-related issues. Eye injury, skin irritation, and electronic failure can all result from sand's abuse. Take the time to find shelter, and be sure to protect yourself and your gear from these exposure risks.

Flash Floods

Avoidance is the key to flash flood survival. Stay away from dry riverbeds, canyons, and other depressions during flash flood season. Flash floods often originate far from your location, making it hard to judge the risk when traveling on a hot, sunny day. A flash flood can easily sweep you up and carry you away.

Mirages

Unlike the television and movie portrayal of mirages, they are not illusions of a hamburger stand or naked ladies. A mirage will actually present as a "sheet of water" where none exists. This appearance is created when alternate layers of hot and cool air distort light. Awareness of your route's water sources is key. Don't travel for hours trying to reach a mirage water source—you never will.

■ Desert Travel: Key Points

Desert travel covers many types of environments, from a snow-covered field to a steep canyon wall to never-ending waves of sand. Each condition presents unique challenges that must be met. Other than water and exposure considerations, there isn't a lot more to desert travel than what this book has already covered. Some of the basics are listed here:

- Consider traveling during early morning or late evening in hot deserts. If there is adequate moonlight, consider traveling at night. If the terrain is treacherous, you may need to travel during the day, when visibility is at its best.

- Sand dune travel isn't much different from arctic travel. Whenever you can, hike on the wind-packed side of a slope, kick step when going uphill, and plunge step when going down.

- Constellations provide a good augment to your navigation.

- Many deserts are basically flat, making them ideal for using a GPS.

- The lack of landmarks hampers navigation.

- The person breaking trail and setting pace often does the most work.

- Distances often seem closer than they really are, making for a journey that seems never to end.

- In sandy deserts keep your mouth shut—unless you like eating sand.

Jungle Travel

Jungles (also known as tropical rain forests) are located near the equator, where temperatures average 80 degrees Fahrenheit (27 degrees Celsius) and precipitation exceeds evaporation. Although jungles cover less than 7 percent of the earth's surface, they contain more than 50 percent of the earth's plant and animal species.

▪ Jungle Terrain

Making your way through the thick vegetation is one of the challenges of jungle travel. A typical rain forest has three layers of vegetation.

Ground Layer

A jungle ground layer consists of small plants, palms, and saplings. These plants receive a limited amount of sunlight but have managed to adapt and thrive. The density of these plants is dependent on the amount of light that gets through the upper canopy—the more light, the denser the ground layer.

Middle Layer

Large shrubs and midsized trees form a middle layer between the ground and the upper canopy.

Top Layer

The jungle top layer consists of a blanketing canopy of treetops that capture most of the available rainwater and sunlight. The canopy height averages between 65 and 165 feet (20 to 50 meters).

■ Jungle Terrain: Things to Consider

In some locations, jungle travel is relatively easy. In others, the ground vegetation can seem like an unending and impenetrable wall. Some of the obstacles you might encounter are listed here.

Canopy Density

The difficulty associated with jungle travel is dependent on how much sun breaks through the upper canopy. The more sun, the denser the lower layers. When possible, you should travel on rivers or established trails. When this isn't an option, a walking stick or sharp machete can be used. Use the walking stick to push vegetation out of the way and the machete when the walking stick isn't enough. If using a machete, your swing should be controlled, with a down-and-out path. This technique helps avoid cuts and expends the least amount of energy.

Ridgelines

Although following ridgelines might seem like a good idea, they often have abrupt edges or, worse yet, a false floor. False floors are like snow bridges, occuring when vegetation connects two surfaces separated by a long drop. Breaking through one of these may lead to a long, potentially fatal, fall.

Foliage

Avoid grabbing brush and plants when walking in dense vegetation. Ground-level foliage often supports sharp edges and thorns that can easily cut or puncture your skin. Either use a stick to push the vegetation aside or wear thick leather gloves.

Quicksand

Quicksand does exist—just not as Hollywood portrays it. Quicksand can be found close to the mouth of large rivers or flat shores. It will often look like the ground around it, except it will be devoid of vegetation. The sand-and-water mixture is often held in place by firm soil walls and a clay bottom. Contrary to popular belief, quicksand can and will hold your weight, as long as you lie flat and put your arms and legs into a spread-eagle position. This posture helps you stay afloat by dispersing your body weight over the surface. A swimming motion can then be used to reach the edge of the quicksand and get out.

■ Jungle Travel: Key Points

Traveling in a jungle requires advanced skill, and unless you have received navigation training related to this environment, use a guide. Be sure to check references, and try to talk to previous students before signing up. Some basic problems with jungle travel are listed here.

- Trust your compass. The jungle is one environment where terrain navigation is not the best method. It is too easy to get lost when vegetation obscures the terrain. It is better to use a straight-line heading and reach your destination than to suddenly realize you can't see the terrain well enough to evaluate where you are.

- Whenever you can, follow rivers, streams, or game trails that are on your heading.

- Before going on a jungle trip, consider taking a canoe and using the waterways to get from one point to another.

- Avoid ridgelines, which are often covered with dense thickets of rattan bamboo and shrub. In addition, cliffs and false floors present a significant threat.

- Keep a steady, slow, pace, and don't get frustrated with the vegetation. When thorns catch your clothing, don't thrash about. Instead, carefully remove each one. If caught by a tendril (stem, leaf, or other part of a climbing plant), slowly turn away from it.

- Protect your skin by wearing a long-sleeved shirt and long pants, along with gloves and a hat.

River Travel

Rivers have been and still are used as a means of travel for many civilizations. Water vessels make travel much faster and require less energy than a hike covering the same distance. In addition, small- to moderate-size boats can accommodate larger loads than a person can carry on their back.

However, river travel is not without risk. Kayaking or rafting a river is an advanced skill, and hands-on training is advised before venturing out on your own.

■ Rivers: Prepare in Advance

Before entering the water, put on your life jacket and other protective gear (wet or dry suit, water shoes, and helmet). Pack your gear in waterproof containers, and stow it away. Make sure to lanyard the gear to your vessel—it would be a shame to survive a capsizing only to lose your gear. If traveling as a team, discuss how you plan to communicate with one another. Finally, all trips require proper planning and an ongoing evaluation as they progress. This means reviewing the river's path, currents, and hazards beforehand and getting out of the raft or kayak at regular intervals to evaluate what is ahead. Don't wait to be surprised by a drop that could be fatal. Avoid all hazards that are beyond your or your team's skill level—walk the vessel around.

■ River Terrain: Things to Consider

A river can present many obstacles that threaten to damage or capsize your vessel. Make sure to review your map (realize that river maps may not reflect new hazards created in the recent past). Understanding these obstacles is the first step to avoiding them.

Obstacles: Logjams and Sweepers

Perhaps the biggest risk posed comes from fallen trees, brush, and boulders that allow water to pass but not a vessel. These obstacles can pin you down or sweep you off your vessel. Try to identify these in advance so that you can walk your vessel around them. Such obstacles are often located at bends in the river.

Suction Holes

The vacuum of a suction hole can separate you from your raft and even pull you down to the bottom of the river, eventually pushing you to the surface and repeating the process over and over. Suction holes usually occur just beyond a drop, where the water crosses over a rock or other object. At these locations the water rapidly descends to the bottom and curls up and back toward the direction it came from. To get out of a suction hole, cut across the current's circular flow until you reach the adjoining water that is rushing by. If the suction hole takes you to the bottom, you can exit the hole by pushing off the river floor, heading downstream below the upward current. Better yet, identify a suction hole in advance and avoid it all together.

Waterfalls

Common sense dictates that you avoid waterfalls at all costs. The powerful suction holes located beneath a fall will make it nearly impossible to resurface.

■ River Hazards: Things to Consider

Staying afloat and avoiding exposure injuries are important considerations related to river travel. There are more! Some basic hazard considerations are listed here.

Water

There is nothing worse than being surrounded by water without a drop to drink. Make sure you bring a means of purifying water.

Drown-Proofing

Don't become a statistic. Wear a Type III or better personal flotation device that fits well and is in good shape. If in a group of ten or more, bring a spare jacket in case one is lost or destroyed.

Keep Your Boat Afloat

Bring a spare paddle, repair kit for the type of vessel being used, bowline, rescue line, and a bailing bucket. Expect the best—but plan for the worst.

Prevent Exposure Injuries

Sitting in water is a great way to get sunburn, hyperthermia, hypothermia, or immersion injuries. Be sure to carry a basic first-aid kit, sunscreen, sunglasses, hat, extra shoes and dry clothes, and waterproof bags or containers. Dress warm, and take the time to dry off whenever you can.

Flood Hazards

Be cautious after rainstorms. Sudden changes in water levels may occur, leading to flooding in low-lying areas. Secondary flash floods and debris flows can occur as a result. During flash flood season, avoid camping in low-lying areas and below gulches.

Bridge Crossings

Be cautious around railroad and road bridges with steel piles. These piles often have sharp edges that can puncture a raft or injure the rafter. If you happen to broadside one, everyone should move to the side nearest the pile to prevent the vessel from flipping over.

◼ River Travel: Key Points

River travel is a great method of getting from one point to another relatively fast. It is also a great journey—allowing spectacular views that might otherwise be missed and sometimes a ride that is better than most roller coasters. A river can be traveled using small to medium-size boats, canoes, kayaks, and rafts. Each method of travel requires a different skill set, but all have similar risks. Learn your sport—and be safe.

Coastline Travel

Traveling on open water is a very complicated journey that requires many of the skills covered in this text. There are many means of open water travel, including ships, sailboats, small motorized boats, and kayaks. Knowledge of how to operate these vessels should be obtained prior to heading into open water. Attend reputable classes in your sport. In addition to compass and chart use and celestial navigation, there are a few key points worth mentioning here. These include how to identify the proximity of land and how to break shore.

■ Identifying the Proximity of a Landmass

- **Cumulus clouds.** Cumulus clouds often hover over or slightly downwind from an island.

- **Greenish sky tint.** The sky will often support a greenish tint close to shallow lagoons or shelves of coral reefs. This tint is best seen on the bottoms of clouds.

- **Light reflection.** The sky will often support a light reflection on the bottoms of clouds when close to snow- or ice-covered land.

- **Light-colored water.** Deep water is often dark, whereas shallow water (perhaps close to land) tends to be a lighter shade.

- **Sounds.** You will probably hear birds and surf long before you see the shore.

- **Smells.** You will probably smell wood smoke, fruits, etc., long before seeing the shore.

- **Sights.** An increase in bird population may indicate land, but don't count on it. Birds often fly toward land and their nesting area at dusk. During day hours their flight pattern is not reliable, since they tend to search for food during this time. In addition, some birds seek shore only during nesting, staying at sea the rest of the year.

- **Winds.** Winds often blow toward land during the day and seaward at night. However, unless land is close, the wind pattern is not a factor.

■ Breaking Shore

Beaching a sea vessel is perhaps the most dangerous part of any coastline trip. Avoid coral reefs and rocky cliffs if possible. Instead try to land on the lee side of the island or at the junction of a stream and the sea. Monitor the wave patterns. Try to identify any pattern that suggests a consistent set of gentler waves, and begin your approach in the calmer waves. To keep control of your vessel, don't surf the waves. Instead, when contact is made with the first wave, paddle backward, preventing the vessel from taking off when the front is lifted by the wave. Begin a forward hard paddle as soon as you feel the front of the vessel dropping. The drop indicates that the wave has passed. As another wave overtakes you, repeat this process. If you capsize in the surf, grab hold and try to ride it in. If you lose the raft and need to swim ashore, use the side or breaststroke. If you're in moderate surf, swim with the wave, diving below the water just before the wave breaks. In high surf, swim toward the shore in the wave's trough and submerge just before the next wave starts to overtake you. If an undertow pulls you down, push off the bottom and swim to the surface. As you get closer to the shore, select a landing spot where the waves run up onto the shore versus violently crash. Once you enter the breakers, move into a sitting body position, with your feet forward and about 2 to 3 feet lower than your head. It's better to absorb the shock of an unexpected reef or rock with your feet than your head.

Chapter Exercises

Evaluate the climate and terrain.

Before venturing out into the wilderness, consider the climate and terrain you are venturing into. Write down obstacles and potential hazards the terrain might present. Next, write down how you plan to avoid these areas of concern, along with contingencies should these concerns become a problem. Use this information to help when creating a trip plan and packing. Expect the best, but prepare for the worst.

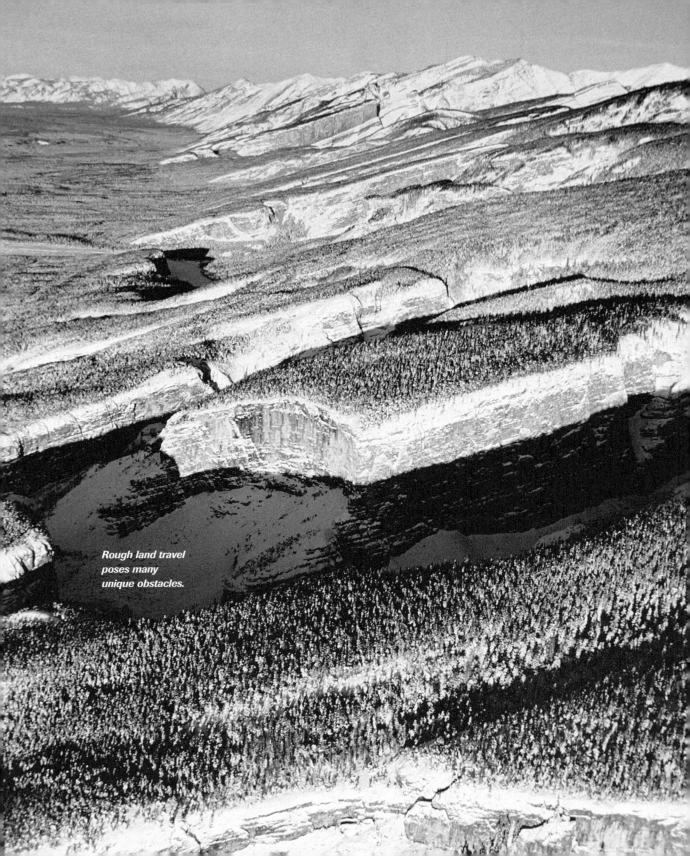

Rough land travel poses many unique obstacles.

SECTION V

Rough Land Travel

For the majority of readers, the preceding basic and advanced navigation skills are all you'll ever need to know. Those who navigate over snow-covered mountains, glaciers, ice, and rock, however, will need additional travel techniques. Some basic concepts and guidelines of rough land travel are covered here. Before venturing into such terrain, however, educate yourself further by taking a reputable class relevant to your venture. Learn from those who have been there and know how to pass on their knowledge.

This section covers details on safety and travel issues unique to rough land travel.

Gear for Rough Land Travel

Rough land travel presents many obstacles that can best be managed by carrying gear specific to the task. Take the time to research this ever-changing market, and make sure you understand how to use each item you carry *before* you need to use it. Some of the various types of gear used in rough land travel are covered here.

Rope

Any rope used for climbing or rough land travel should meet the Union International des Association d'Alpinism (UIAA) approval. Check to make sure the rope you are about to purchase has this approval—if it doesn't, don't buy it. The type of rope you purchase depends on your needs. For steep technical climbs that pose a severe risk of leader falls, use a standard 10 to 11 mm Kernmantle climbing rope (165 feet). This all-around rope can be used for rock or ice climbing and glacier travel. It has a stretch of 6 to 7 percent that reduces the force associated with a fall and abrupt stop. For easy to moderate glacier climbs that pose minimal risk, a 9 mm rope that is 165 feet (50 meters) long will not only meet your needs but will also decrease your pack weight by about three pounds. Use the following general guide to help decide the type of rope needed for your trip.

Table 9-1: The Right Rope for Your Needs

Rope Size	Uses
9 mm	Lightweight rope used for simple glacier travel.
10 mm	Lightweight rope used for rock and ice climbing and for glacier travel.
11 mm	Standard weight rope for rock and ice climbing and glacier travel.

Make sure the rope is up to the task by inspecting it before your trip—and daily during your trek—for potential problems such as a tattered sheath and frayed ends. When in use, don't step on the rope, and pad all sharp corners. Stepping on the rope grinds dirt into the sheath, which can cut the inner filaments and cause damage that is not apparent on the outside. Sharp corners, like rock edges, might cut the rope. Keep a rope journal, listing each time the rope is used and its expected retirement date based on the following rules.

Table 9-2: **Rope Retirement Schedule**	
Retirement Considerations	**When to Retire the Rope**
Ropes used daily	One year
Ropes used during most weekends	Two years
Ropes used only occasionally	Four years
After a severe fall	Retire it now!

When not in use, coil and store the rope so that it can be uncoiled without creating a tangled mess. I prefer the butterfly coil because it is faster and less likely to kink the rope.

Runners

Runners are loops made from tubular webbing or cord that help attach gear, make anchors, create a chest harness, and myriad other uses. Runners are made from 1-inch tubular webbing or 8 mm Perlon accessory cord. Tubular webbing is tied using a water knot, and cord is tied using a double fisherman's knot (see Knots). Burn the ends so that they don't fray. The ideal situation has you carrying six 5½-foot, two 9½-foot, and one 15-foot runner. To help quickly identify the runner size, use a different color for each size.

Seat and Chest Harness

During rough land travel, a seat and chest harness are used to secure your body to the safety rope. The best type of seat harness is one that has adjustable legs and a waist buckle located to the side. These features allow

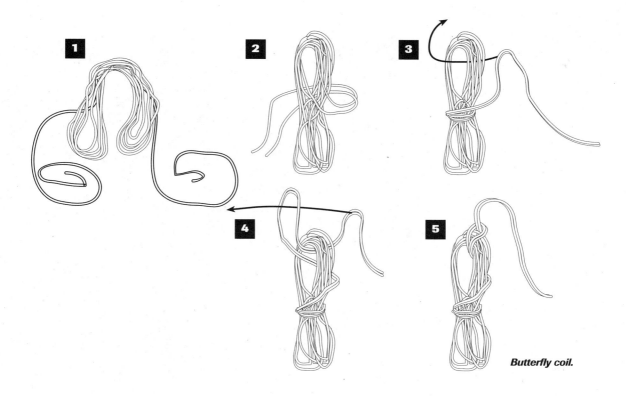

Butterfly coil.

the climber to modify the leg straps when clothing is added or removed, use the toilet while staying on-rope, and keep the waist buckle away from the carabiner. Be sure to consult the manufacturer on how to safely wear your specific harness.

Adding a chest harness is very important during technically challenging trips and glacier travel. It helps keep you upright should you fall. Perhaps the best type of chest harness is the one you make from 1-inch tubular webbing (approximately 10 feet) and a carabiner. Tie the two ends of the webbing together using a water knot (see Knots section) so that at least 2 inches of webbing extend beyond the knot on each side. The resulting loop is twisted to create two loops, and one arm is completely inserted into each loop so that the midpoint of the webbing is located midback. A carabiner is used to bring the two front sides together. For proper fit, you may need to adjust the webbing length. To prevent fraying at the ends, I advise burning them. Make sure the knot is tight before each use.

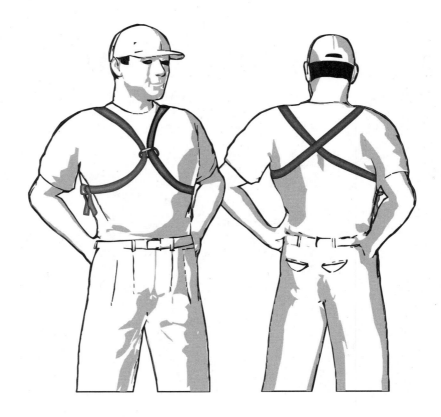

Tubular webbing can be used to make a chest harness.

Prusik Slings

Prusik slings are helpful for ascending a rope after a glacier fall. The most used Prusik sling consists of two slings made of 5 to 7 mm Perlon accessory cord. One sling is for the feet and needs to be long enough for two adjustable foot loops (on each end) and a center upper loop that reaches the climber's waist when he or she is standing with legs straight. The other sling needs to be long enough so that its upper loop reaches eye level when the lower loop is attached to the seat harness (front central carabiner). Making the system requires the use of a figure-eight and a double fisherman's knot (see Knots section). The double fisherman's knot can be used to attach two lines together or as a slipknot by attaching the free end of a single line back to its body. Using a slipknot for the foot loop makes it easier to insert your feet. When doing this, however, an overhand knot is used to control how tight the slipknot can get around your foot, as shown in the illustration on the facing page.

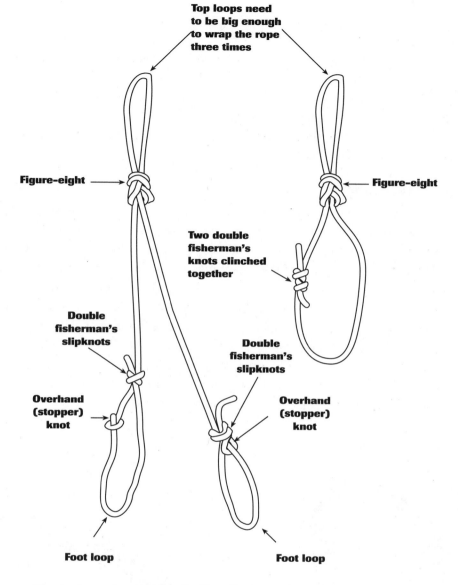

Top loops need to be big enough to wrap the rope three times

The Prusik sling.

Figure-eight

Figure-eight

Two double fisherman's knots clinched together

Double fisherman's slipknots

Double fisherman's slipknots

Overhand (stopper) knot

Overhand (stopper) knot

Foot loop

Foot loop

The last step in creating the Prusik system is to use a friction knot (see Knots) that secures the upper loop of each sling (foot and waist) to the climbing rope. When weight is placed on either sling's lower loop, the friction knots grip the climbing rope and hold the climber in place. When there is no weight on the fixed loops, the friction knots can be moved up the climbing rope with little effort. There are two types of friction methods used to attach cord to the climbing rope—the Prusik and the Bachmann. Webbing is not recommended for either of these knots. If you are short on cord and webbing is all that is available, use a Klemheist friction knot.

The Prusik sling's friction knot should be attached to the climbing rope when the trek begins. The loose line should be secured so that it doesn't get in the way, yet can be easily accessed if it is needed. Stuffing them in your pockets usually does this. Regardless of the type of friction knot used, the Prusik sling is an essential tool for ascending out of a glacier (covered under Glacier Rescue).

Carabiners

The carabiner is a great tool that can be used to attach rope to your seat and chest harness and anchors. There are several types of carabiner designs out there, but I'd recommend the pear-shaped locking carabiner, the bent-gate carabiner, and the straight gate oval carabiner. The pear-shaped locking carabiner is ideal for attaching a rope to your seat harness; the bent-gate carabiner is used with the chest harness where rapid attachment and free rotation are important; and the straight gate oval carabiner is a multiuse item. Regardless of which type is used, make sure the long axis of the carabiner takes the force away from the gate. In addition, keep the carabiners gate clean, and discard all carabiners that fall and hit a hard surface. (Hairline fractures are common and often can't be seen.)

Carabiners.

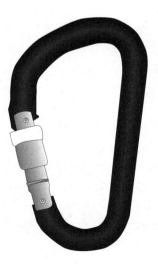

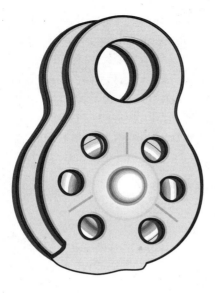

Pulley.

Pulleys

A pulley consists of a mounted rotating wheel with a grooved rim, over which the climbing rope can move to change the direction of force. Pulleys are very helpful during rescues, and several should be carried.

Helmets

A helmet helps protect your head should you fall and adds a buffer against a potential falling rock. It is worth the investment and added weight to carry a helmet. Wear it when you're doing anything technical where there is a risk of head injury. Any helmet used should meet the UIAA standard.

Belay/Rappel Devices

A belay device adds friction to a rope, slowing a person's descent or protecting him or her from a fall. The most common belay systems are a tube-type belay device and a belay plate. A loop of rope is pushed through the device and clipped into a locking carabiner on the other side. The figure-eight descender can be used much like a belay plate by running the rope's loop through its small ring and attaching the loop to a carabiner. When the break side of the rope is pulled backward, the rope pulls the carabiner and plate together, effectively stopping the rope's feed and halting a climber's movement or fall. If you're in a situation where no belay device is available, one can be made using a large pear-shaped locking carabiner and a Munter hitch. When this hitch is applied to the carabiner, it creates a friction system that can be used to belay a climber. This hitch allows you to feed or take up rope through the carabiner, making it useful for belaying someone going up or down. Pulling the brake side of the rope back stops all rope feed and halts the climber in place. The exact methods for using each of these devices are covered in Chapter 11.

Belay Devices

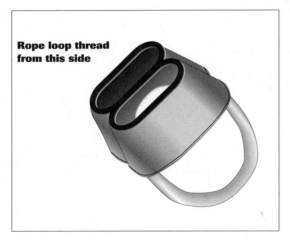

Rope loop thread from this side

The belay tube.

Rope loop thread from this side

The belay plate.

Figure-eight descender.

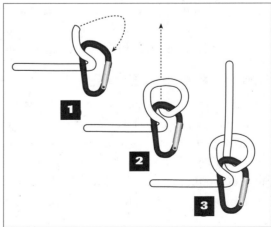

Munter hitch belay system.

The figure-eight descender and tube-type belay devices can be used to rappel. The tube-type belay device is used in the same way for both rappelling and belaying, making it a great multiuse item. The figure-eight descender needs to be attached slightly differently when using it for a rappel (covered in Belay Systems). Another option is using a six-carabiner brake system that threads the rope between four carabiners and connects them to the seat harness with two more. The exact method of using these various devices is covered under Rappelling in Chapter 11.

Rappel Devices

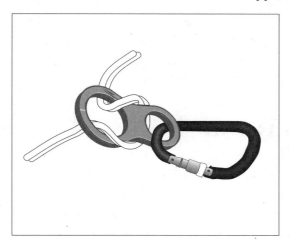

Figure-eight descender.

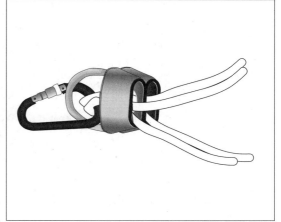

The belay tube.

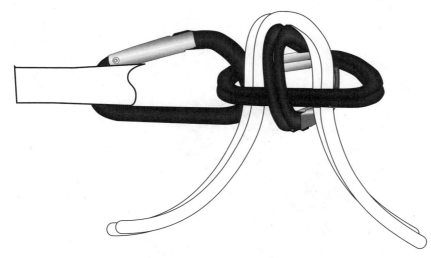

Six-carabiner system.

The market has seen newer belay devices, such as the Petzl's Grigri, which works much like a car's seat belt. This device allows free upward rope movement but jams when a climber falls and tension comes on the rope—perfect for belaying a leader or second on ropes 10 to 11 mm in diameter. Take the time to read the manufacturer's information and practice using the device before departing on your trip (as you should with all your belay devices).

Protection

If your rough land trip has exposure, you will need to bring sufficient protection against it. Protective devices may include wedges and spring-loaded camming devices (cams). Wedges are considered passive protection, unlike the cam, which has moving parts and therefore is considered active protection. The exact type of protection and how much you bring will depend upon the route to be covered.

■ Passive Protection: Wedges

Wedges are aluminum nuts and hexes that have no moving parts; wedges work by being jammed into a crack. Nuts are tapered, with one end larger than the other, making it easy to slide them into a tapering crack and wedge into place. The more surface contact the nut makes, the better it works. Nuts routinely have a convex and concave side. The contact between the concave side and the convex sides make a strong triangular

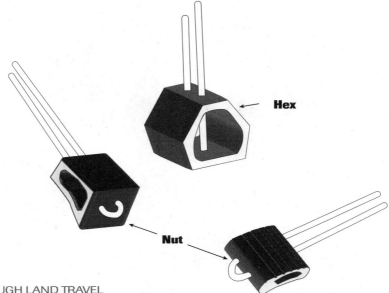

Hex

Nut

Nuts and hexes.

force. Hexes are asymmetrical, six-sided tubes. Hexes can be rotated into cracks that are not as accommodating to a regular nut, making them more useful for cracks with minimal taper. (Try to keep the largest surface upward whenever possible.)

■ Active Protection: Spring-Loaded Camming Devices (Cams)

Cams have moving parts that retract enough to be placed into a crack and then expand to stay in place. A single cam fits into a wide range of crack sizes, decreasing the need to carry as many passive wedges. A cam is made of three or four curved pieces of aluminum attached to a trigger. When the trigger is pulled, the metal retracts, making the device narrower and easier to place into a crack. Releasing the trigger expands the cams firmly into the rock's crack. The cam's teeth/grooves provide added friction, making them even more secure. Used correctly, the cam provides excellent protection for the climber.

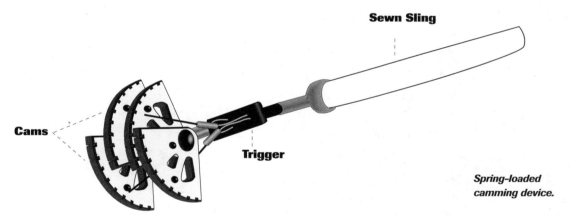

Sewn Sling

Cams

Trigger

Spring-loaded camming device.

Crampons

Traveling on ice or hard snow requires traction beyond that of boots, snowshoes, or cross-country skis. Crampons meet this need—helping you maintain contact with surface ice or snow instead of falling and going for a ride. Crampons are made from strong lightweight steel with twelve support points (five on each side and two pointing forward at the toe). For flat terrain or general-use climbs, crampons with straight points (first row

forward and subsequent rows down) work best. For steep slopes, a crampon that has its first row slightly dropped down and the second row angled toward the boot's toe works best.

Care and Use of Your Gear

Inspect all climbing gear before and after each trip. If you find any cracks, chips, frayed or kinked wires, or other damage—discard the gear. Look closely at your ropes, and follow guidelines on retiring a rope. Store gear in a clean and dry environment, out of direct sunlight, and away from gnawing rodents and pets.

Chapter Exercises

Practice the butterfly coil.

Take out your rope, and tie it into a butterfly coil.

Create a chest harness.

Review knot tying in Chapter 10, and build a chest harness to fit.

Create a Prusik sling.

Review knot tying in Chapter 10, and create Prusik sling. Using a little ingenuity, a solid tree branch, rope, and an anchor provide a great opportunity to try out the system. See how well you can climb the rope.

Build a six-carabiner rappel system.

Put together a six-carabiner rappel system.

C H A P T E R 1 0

Climbing Knots

In the wilderness, knots are the nuts and bolts that hold things together. Knots attach gear to the climber, climber to protection, and belayer to an anchor. Take the time to become proficient in tying knots before departing on your trip.

Knot Basics

The following table illustrates some common knot terms.

Table 10-1: Knot Terminology

Term	Description
Bight	180-degree bend in rope without the rope crossing over itself.
Loop	A bend in the rope where the rope crosses itself.
Running End	The loose working end of the rope.
Standing End	The static nonworking end of the rope.
Dress	Removing all kinks, twists, and slack from the knot.

Backup Knot: Overhand Knot

The overhand is a simple knot that should be used to secure loose rope ends and provide added safety to another knot. A backup overhand knot should be tied to the free ends of all knots.

Overhand knot.

Attaching Two Ropes Together

People frequently use square knots to attach two ropes together. This knot is an inferior one, and I strongly advise against its use—it tends to slip when wet and should only be used on ropes of equal diameter. Instead of a square knot, use one of the following to connect two ropes or ends of webbing together.

■ Double Fisherman's Knot

The fisherman's knot is used to tie two ropes of the same or approximately the same diameter. To make this knot, tie an overhand knot at one end of

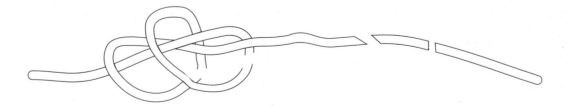

Double fisherman's knot.

the first rope, run the working end of the second rope through the overhand knot, and tie an overhand knot around the first rope with the working end of the second rope. Once done, tighten down the knot ends and tie an overhand knot with the slack. The double fisherman's knot uses a double overhand knot instead of a simple overhand knot and is considered one of the best for attaching two ropes together (see illustration). The ends should come out in opposite directions with a minimum of 4 inches left over. Tie an overhand knot in the excess.

■ Water Knot

The water knot is often used to create runners. This knot needs to be cinched down very tight and should have a backup overhand knot on both tails. To tie this knot, tie an overhand knot in one end of the webbing, and run the other end of the webbing through the knot—following the reverse path that the knot took. Dress the knot. The ends should come out in opposite directions with a minimum of 4 inches left over. Tie an overhand knot in the excess.

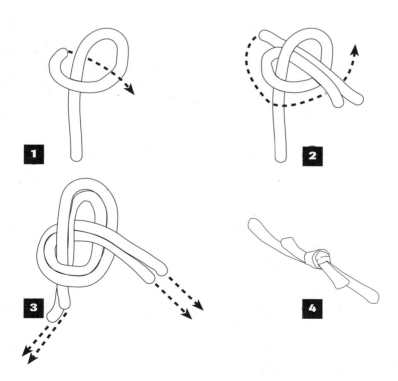

Water knot.

Fixed-Loop Knots

Fixed-loop knots are often used to attach rope to a harness or to an anchor.

■ Figure-Eight Knot

The figure-eight is a very strong load-bearing knot that can be easily untied even after placed under stress. To tie this knot, create a bight in the rope as big as the desired end loop. The bight is now the working end of the rope. Using the bight, create a loop and wrap the working end completely around the standing end (360 degrees). Finally, feed the working end through the loop. Dress the knot so that the ropes in the loop are parallel and don't cross.

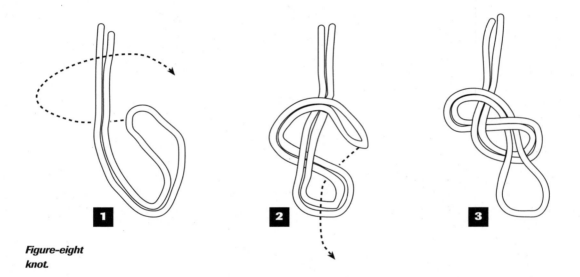

Figure-eight knot.

■ Rewoven Figure-Eight

The rewoven figure-eight knot is most often used to secure end rope climbers (lead and tail person) to the same rope or a rope to an anchor point. Make sure the rope is long enough to reach around the anchor (or harness loop) and tie the knot. To begin, tie a figure-eight knot in the rope's standing part, leaving enough rope to go around the anchor and finish the knot. To tie this portion of the knot, form a loop in the rope, wrap the working end around the standing part, and run the working end through the loop. Dress the knot very loose. Next run the rope's working

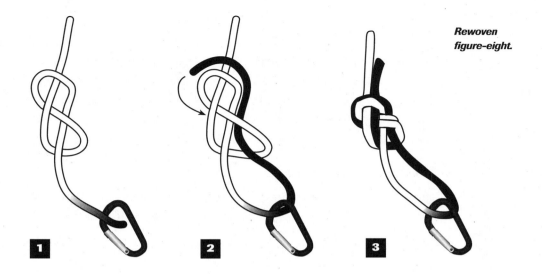

end around the anchor or seat harness loop and back through the knot in the standing part of the rope—following the reverse of the path the first knot took. The rope's running end and body should point in the same direction. Dress the knot so its lines are parallel and don't cross.

■ Single Bowline

The single bowline makes a nonslip loop at the end of a rope that can be attached to an anchor. To tie this knot, bring the working end of the rope around the anchor (from right to left when facing the anchor). Create an

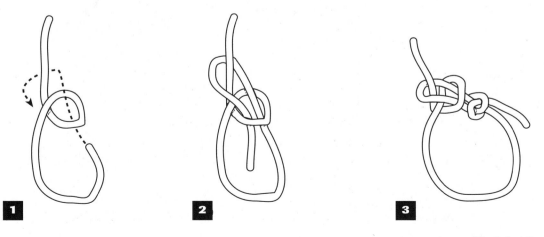

Single bowline.

overhand loop in the standing end, located on the right side of the anchor so that the side of rope closer to the anchor is on the bottom. Reach through the loop and pull up a bight; run the working end of the rope through the bight, bending the end back on itself. Dress the knot so that the working end is inside the loop that circles the anchor. Tie an overhand safety knot on the working end of the line.

■ Double Bowline

The double bowline is most often used to secure midrope climbers to a rope. This knot uses the same technique as the bowline, except that its working end is a bight in the rope.

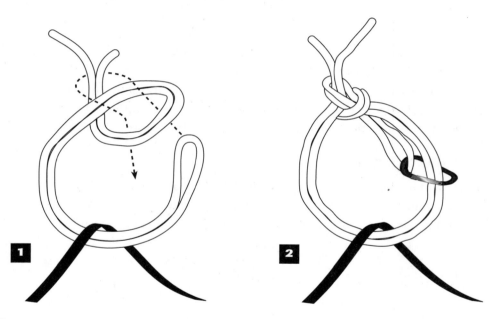

Double bowline.

Friction Knots

Friction knots provide a method of ascending and descending rope by creating friction when weight is applied and moving freely when it isn't.

■ Prusik Knot

The Prusik is prepared from a bight (a loop) in a cord (not webbing) that bends over the climbing rope and allows the two free ends of cord to wrap

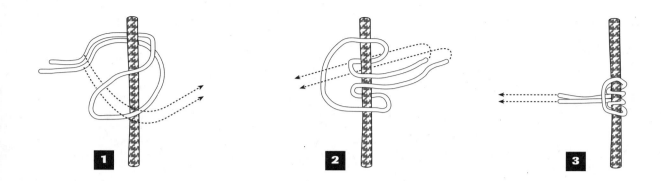

through (the bight) at least twice (see illustration). More wraps create more friction but are harder to move.

Prusik knot.

Bachmann Knot

The Bachmann knot is a friction system similar to the Prusik. This knot, however, ties around the carabiner and climbing rope, providing the climber something to grasp and making it much easier to move. The cord (not webbing) is inserted through the carabiner so that a bight or loop is formed around the long portion of the carabiner. The two free ends are then wrapped around the carabiner and climbing rope as shown in the following illustration.

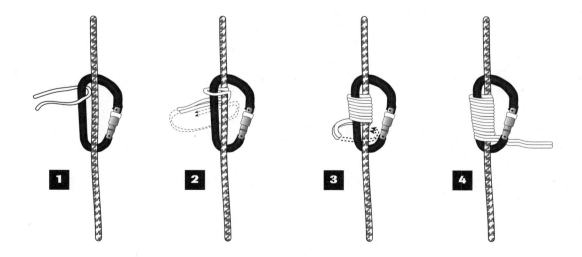

Bachmann knot.

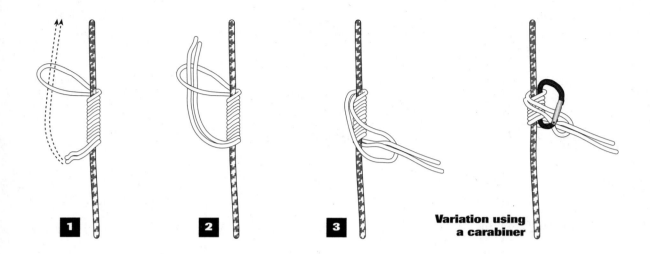

Klemheist knot.

■ Klemheist Knot

The Klemheist knot can be used with either cord or webbing, making it the ideal option when cord is in short supply. To make this knot, place a bight on one side of your climbing rope, and wrap the cord around the climbing rope several times before threading both free ends through the bight. A carabiner can be added simply by doing the same process around both the climbing rope and carabiner.

Chapter Exercises

Practice tying the various knots.

1. Overhand knot

2. Double fisherman's knot

3. Water knot

4. Figure-eight knot

5. Rewoven figure-eight knot

6. Single bowline

7. Double bowline

8. Prusik knot

9. Bachmann knot

10. Klemheist knot

Identify the purpose of each knot.

Teach someone else how to tie each knot.

The best way to learn knot tying is to practice until you're perfect and then teach someone else. Teaching forces you to think through the process and embeds it in your mind.

Traveling Over Rock Surfaces

Traveling up and over rock surfaces requires balance, strength, and forethought. Rough land travel may present exposure risks that could prove fatal if a member of the team falls. If a trip involves such terrain, all members of the team should be well versed and skilled in climbing and the technical aspects of the outing. The time to learn is not during the trek. Although the basics of rough land travel are covered here, you need hands-on training. Take climbing classes, and before every trip hone your skills on local climbing rocks. In addition, make sure all team members bring the necessary climbing and safety gear for the outing.

Climbing: Classifying Rock

The types of surfaces encountered during rough land travel vary greatly and consist of everything from large boulders to steep cliff faces. Tables 11-1 and 11-2 on the following pages reference the types of rock surfaces you might come across and the U.S. rating system for route difficulty.

Table 11-1: Rock Surfaces

Type	Description
Glacis	The rock surface is less than 30 degrees and is considered walking terrain.
Slab	The rock surface is 30 to 75 degrees and requires some technical climbing skills.
Wall	The rock surface is 75 to 90 degrees and requires technical climbing skills.
Overhang	A rock surface has an angle greater than 90 degrees that projects overhead.
Roof	A rock surface has a nearly 180-degree angle that projects outward like a roof.
Cracks	Cracks of all angles can be used for climbing a rock surface.
Chimney	A wide crack that is big enough for a climber to enter and ascend.
Gully	A crack so wide that it actually presents two climbing surfaces independent of each other.
Corner	A corner occurs when two rock walls meet at around 90 degrees.
Groove	A corner where the angle is either greater (shallow groove) or less (V groove) than 90 degrees.
Rib	A small narrow ridge protruding from the rock.
Ledge	A much bigger protrusion that can likely support two to three climbers.

Table 11-2: Route Rating System

Class	Description
1	Hiking on-trail.
2	Hiking off-trail.
3	Scrambling terrain that requires the use of hands and feet to progress, but it is doubtful a fall will kill you.
4	Climbing on steep terrain that requires the use of hands and feet and a rope belay. The maneuvers are relatively easy, but a fall could kill you.
5	Climbing on steep terrain that involves technical moves, protective hardware, and a belay.
5.0–5.4	Beginner level.
5.5–5.7	Intermediate level.
5.8–5.10	Experienced level.
5.11–5.12	Expert level.
5.13–5.14	Elite level.

Safety Considerations

In addition to the accidental fall, a climber faces other problems and risks. These risks include failing to wear protective gear, loose rock, sharp edges, grass and small bushes, wet or icy rock, and communication failure.

■ Protective Gear

Rough land travel is a risky venture! It is better to carry the weight of added safety gear than to find yourself without it when you need it. Proper clothing for unexpected weather, seat and chest harness, helmet, proper footwear, crampons, and gloves are just a few of the items you might need to bring. Evaluate your trip, and be sure to carry gear appropriate for the worst possible conditions.

■ Loose Rock

Loose rock presents many problems for a climber. On the wall it can give way, causing a fall. In addition, the rock may hit the following climbers. Loose rocks that sit on a ledge are another risk for climbers. If these rocks are accidentally pushed off the ledge, they may hit the following climber. Anytime a loose rock is dislodged, communication is very important. The word "rock" should be yelled so that others can protect themselves. If you are climbing and you hear someone yell "rock," don't look up! Instead, seek cover. If there isn't time to find cover, hug the rock face—keeping your helmet between you and the falling rock.

■ Sharp Edges

Sharp edges can break down a rope! Worse yet, they can cut the rope when under extreme stress. Try to pad sharp edges whenever you can.

■ Grass and Small Bushes

The tendency to grab brush or grass for support is hard to suppress. However, the roots of grass and small brush tend to be close to the surface, making it easy for them to come free. Do not use grass and small brush to help support your climb! In addition, wet grass and small brush tend to be very slick and should be avoided.

■ Wet or Icy Rock

Wet and icy rock will make an otherwise easy climb impassable. It also compromises any protection you might have. Look for an alternate route, or take your trip on another day.

Climbing: The Basic Concept

The climbing encountered during rough land travel will often require a lead climber who is belayed by another member of the team. This climber is unprotected until he or she sets some type of anchor (protection) into the rock. The spacing of these anchors will depend on available gear, difficulty of the route, and the skill of each team member. The lead climber must be well versed on establishing good anchors while creating the best route for the team. Using poorly established anchors or anchors too far apart can lead to substantial falls. Lead climbing is a skill that takes a lot of time to master. Don't attempt it until you have first acquired proficiency in top rope belaying and anchor removal (last person up).

In a two-person climbing team, the second person is often the less experienced at setting a route. This person, however, must be well versed on belaying techniques. If the climber slips, the second climber must be able to set the belay's brake and limit the fall to twice the distance between the fallen climber's location and the preceding anchor and rope stretch.

Once the lead climber reaches a ledge he or she can establish a primary and backup anchor and belay the other climbers up. Of course this ledge must be within the rope's length and provide the opportunity for an anchor to be placed. The last climber up removes the protection established by the lead climber.

Belay Systems

A belay system works on friction—any friction, mechanical or not, can stop a fall if applied correctly. The belayer runs the climbing rope around the body (not recommended) or through a belay device (attached to the harness) and feeds the rope out (or takes it in, depending on the situation) as the climber rises. Through a sequence of hand motions, the belayer feeds the rope and takes up slack, all the time ready to apply a brake should the climber fall. If the lead climber falls, the belay person applies the brake, effectively limiting the fall to no more than twice the distance between the fallen climber's location and the preceding anchor, rope slack, and rope stretch. To prevent friction burns and the potential for losing rope control, the belayer should wear gloves. To keep the distance fallen to this minimum, an anchor is attached to the belayer. The effectiveness of a belay depends on many factors, including anchors, stance, and your belay technique.

■ Anchors: Protecting the Belay

Without an anchor, the force of the falling climber may pull the belay person out of position and increase the distance of the fall and potential for injury. Don't rush and forgo an anchor; you might live—or not—to regret it. Anchors are made from webbing or rope attached to a secure point (rock, tree, etc.) and the belayer's seat harness. A belay anchor needs to provide added security, keeping the climber and belayer safe should the climber fall. A well-rooted tree or large unmovable rocks are ideal anchor points. When these anchor points aren't available, it may be necessary to establish an anchor from a crack using nuts or cams. The predicted falling force determines the anchor's attachment point.

If belaying a lead climber, you will probably deal with an upward force if the climber falls. This force is apt to pull a belayer off his or her feet and into the air. To decrease this effect, tie the rope to the anchor at a point slightly below the belayer's waist height (when standing). For a top belay—belaying the second—a falling climber creates a downward force. To optimize an anchor in such instances, tie into the anchor at a point slightly above the waist (adjust for sitting or standing posture). Regardless of what you decide, take the time to evaluate your options and pick the one that provides the most security—and always test the anchor before committing to it.

Single-Anchor Attachment

If belaying from ground level, a single anchor is all you need; but if two can be done—do them. A single anchor needs to incorporate a solid structure such as a well-rooted tree or unmovable rock. The anchor can be attached to the belayer using the rope excess that runs beyond the brake hand or a sling. The sling method takes a little more time and uses resources. Using the climbing rope might not be an option when the distance between belay points is unknown or maximizes the rope's usable length.

If making an anchor from webbing or rope (other than the climbing rope), tie the rope (or runner) around your anchor point and connect it to the belayer with a runner and locking carabiners. When using the climbing rope, a runner is placed around the anchor and attached to the climbing rope with a locking carabiner and figure-eight knot. The end of the rope is attached to the front of the belayer's seat harness using a rewoven figure-eight knot. Locate the knots so that there is no slack between the

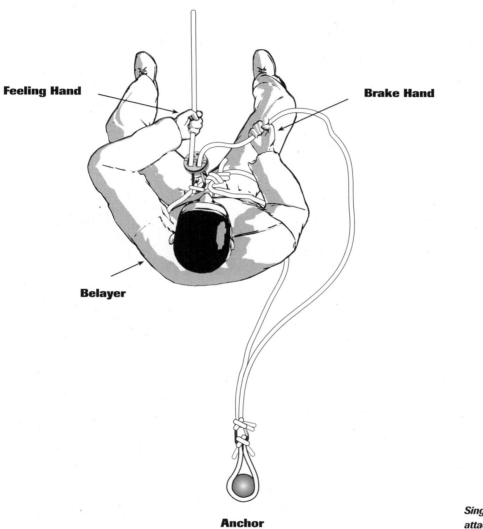

To Climber

Feeling Hand

Brake Hand

Belayer

Anchor

Single-anchor attachment.

anchors and belayer, and tie into the seat harness so that the anchor portion of the rope is on the feeling hand side when used with a body belay. When this type of anchor is used with a mechanical belay, it can be used on either side.

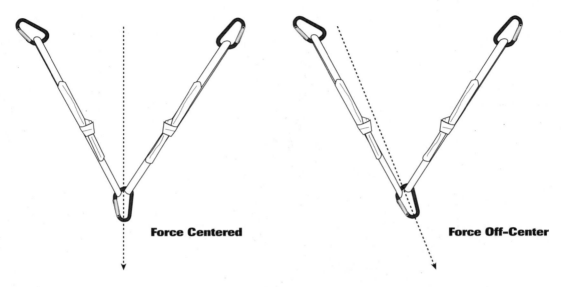

Force Centered   **Force Off-Center**

*Multianchor
attachment.*

Multianchor Attachment

Whenever possible, use multiple anchors, especially when a downward
pull is probable. If you're in an area that provides multiple well-rooted
trees or solid unmovable rocks, use them. Otherwise consider creating
several anchors using nuts and cams. When these anchors are brought
together, using a locking carabiner, the direction of force needs to be
centered—equally divided between each anchor. This may require adjusting the sling lengths by untying and retying the water knot.

The angle between any two anchors and the coming-together point
is important and must be considered. The closer the two anchors, the less
load each bears. As the sling's angles widen, the force on each anchor
increases. At angles beyond 120 degrees, the force on each anchor is
greater than the load weight.

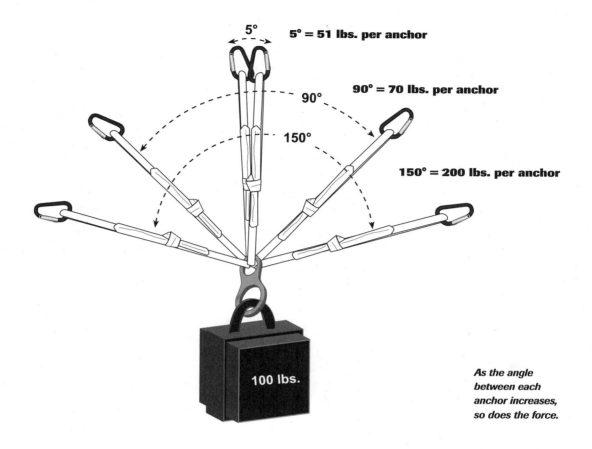

5° = 51 lbs. per anchor

90° = 70 lbs. per anchor

150° = 200 lbs. per anchor

5°

90°

150°

100 lbs.

As the angle between each anchor increases, so does the force.

■ Belaying: The Stance

A belaying site needs to provide an adequate anchor system as well as provide the belayer with a stable stance for doing his job. Besides the anchor, the stance is key to keeping the belayer in control. Whenever possible, establish the belay behind a solid structure such as a rock outcropping. In addition, since a sitting stance is much stronger than standing, try to find a location with enough room for a sitting belay. When sitting, the tripod created between your feet and buttocks is much more supportive, provided the climbing rope runs between your feet and your legs are virtually straight (knee bend between 140 and 180 degrees). A less stable standing stance should be reserved for the first leg of a lead climb, when the belayer can be directly below the climber. This stance places one foot well forward of the other.

To Climber

■ Belaying Technique

For many years the hip belay (nonmechanical) was the only belaying technique used. As the sport of climbing evolved, the addition of mechanical belay devices became available. Both systems are based on a sequence of hand motions that feed and take up rope—always ready to brake should a climber fall. The basics of these hand motions are outlined here.

Feeling Hand

The feeling hand is a simple guide. It is located on the climbing rope between the climber and the friction system. This hand allows the rope to run through it and supports the rope when repositioning the braking hand. For a right-handed belay (right hand is brake hand) the left hand is the feeling hand.

Braking Hand

The brake hand *never* leaves the rope! Never! The braking hand is the hand grasping the rope beyond the friction system (mechanical or not). This hand provides the needed movements to establish the friction that lets rope out, takes it in, or stops all rope movement.

Belaying Hand Placement

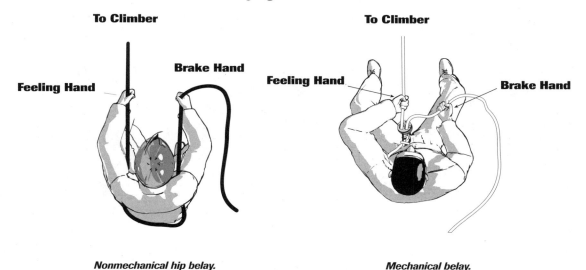

Nonmechanical hip belay.

Mechanical belay.

Sequence of Hand Motions

The sequence of hand motion is a process of letting rope out or taking it in without ever removing the brake hand from the climbing rope.

Belaying a Lead Climber: Feeding the Rope. In this sequence the feeling and brake hands let the rope pass through as the climber ascends the rock. If the climber falls, the brake is applied. If the climber needs rope slack, the belayer uses the brake hand to draw rope toward his or her body. Once the brake hand is within 6 to 12 inches of the body (hip belay)

Belaying a lead climber.

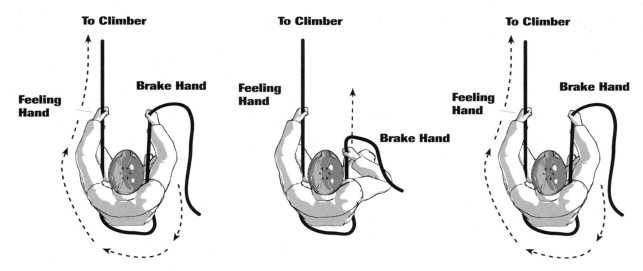

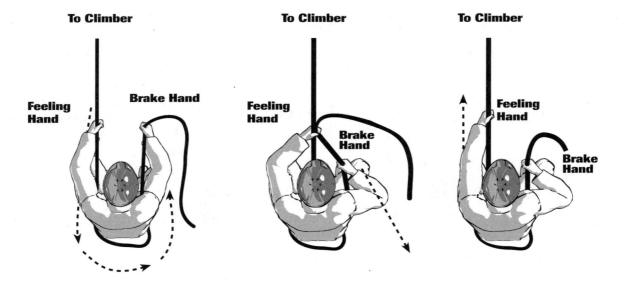

To Climber   **To Climber**   **To Climber**

Feeling Hand   Brake Hand

Feeling Hand   Brake Hand

Feeling Hand   Brake Hand

Belaying a second.

or mechanical belay device, it stops and the brake arm (hand) is extended. During this step, the brake hand must remain closed and in contact with the rope. Once the arm is extended, the process starts over. The guide hand's job is simple—let the rope pass through to the climber.

Belaying the Second Climber: Taking Up Rope. This sequence uses both hands to pull the rope in. With the brake hand close to the body and the feeling hand extended, the rope is pulled toward the body by the feeling hand and pushed away from the body by the brake hand. This movement takes up rope slack between the climber and the belayer's friction system. In order to repeat the process, slide the feeling hand up the rope (just beyond the brake hand) and grasp both ropes with the feeling hand. Without letting the brake hand lose contact with the rope, slide the brake hand down the rope until it is within 6 to 12 inches of the body (hip belay) or mechanical belay device. At this point the feeling hand can release the brake hand side of rope, and the hand sequence can start over.

Braking or Arrest Position

The hip belay uses the friction created between the rope and the belayer's hips and back when the braking arm is extended medially across the body. Mechanical belay devices wrap the climbing rope around a post that creates friction between the post and rope when the braking hand moves laterally away from the body. Although both systems apply friction to the rope, mechanical belay devices are far superior to a hip belay.

Belay Systems Use Friction to Halt a Fall

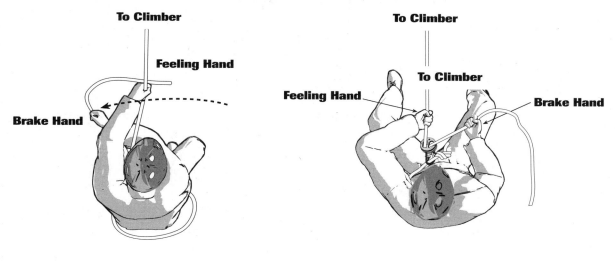

To Climber

Feeling Hand

Brake Hand

Hip belay.

To Climber

To Climber

Feeling Hand

Brake Hand

Mechanical belay.

Holding the Fall

What if someone falls and can't get back on the rock? You may need a method of holding the fall without actually being on the rope. In this instance, a friction knot is the best option. How can you tie a friction knot with just one hand? It is best to wrap the brake side of the rope around

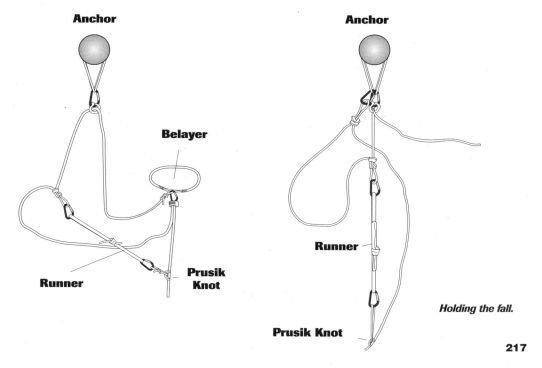

Anchor

Belayer

Runner

Prusik Knot

Anchor

Runner

Prusik Knot

Holding the fall.

your waist (hip belay) or back (mechanical belay) and then around your leg several times. The rope's friction on the leg and waist will hold it in place. Tie a runner to the climbing rope close to where the feeling hand is normally located, and attach the runner to the anchor using a second runner and carabiner. If you can't reach the anchor, tie a fixed loop in the rope as close to the anchor as you can, and attach the runner to it. Before disconnecting, release tension off your belay device and let the setup take it. Make sure it supports the tension before completely coming off belay. In some instances a Prusik knot may be necessary.

■ Hip Belay: Key Points

Hip belay.

A hip belay takes longer to apply the brake, resulting in more slippage and a longer fall. A hip belay is inferior to a mechanical belay but is sometimes the only option. Key points of a hip belay are listed in Table 11-3.

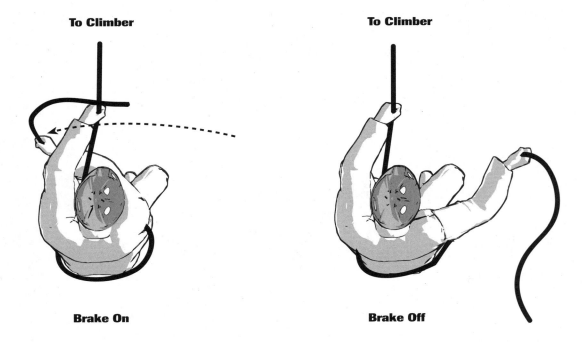

To Climber   **To Climber**

Brake On   **Brake Off**

Table 11-3: Hip Belay

Key Points	Description
How it Works	This belay system uses friction between the rope and the belayer's hips and back.
Anchor Setup	To make the system more effective, the rope attaching the belayer to the anchor should run over the hip opposite the braking hand (same side as the guide hand) and above the rope traversing the hips. This keeps the anchor's tension in line with the climbing rope and helps promote a good braking position should the climber fall. It also prevents the belay rope from riding up the belayer's back during a fall.
Braking	To maximize the body belay wrap and rope friction, the brake arm must be straight and extended medially across the body.
Control Carabiner	For added control, attach a carabiner to the front of the seat harness and clip the rope into it (coming from the climber). This added precaution helps keep the rope and your body in proper position.
Safety	If a carabiner is used, keep your hands clear of it! The rope can pull a finger into the hardware, causing considerable damage to the digit and compromising your ability to belay.

■ Mechanical Belay Devices

A mechanical belay is considered superior to the body belay and in most situations is the belay technique of choice. Several options are shown in Chapter 9. Belay tubes are a modern version of the older belay plate and are perhaps the most-used belay device. The tubes have two equal-size holes, allowing you to switch between single- and double-rope belay effortlessness. During long rappels the tubes disperse heat better and therefore tend to stay cooler than a plate might. However, tube belay devices are not the best choice for rappelling. For wilderness rock climbing the best option for rappelling is perhaps the figure-eight (see Rappelling).

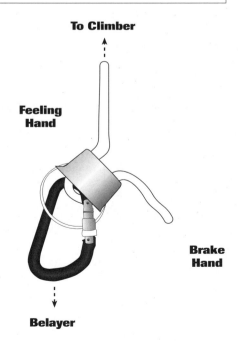

Belay tube.

To Climber

Feeling Hand

Brake Hand

Belayer

For most of these devices a loop of rope is pushed through a central opening and clipped into a locking carabiner on the other side; the carabiner is then attached to the front of the belayer's seat harness. The brake is applied when the brake hand moves laterally away from the body, pulling the carabiner and rope into the device.

Table 11-4: **Mechanical Belay**

Key Points	Description
How it Works	This belay system uses friction between the rope and the belay device.
Anchor Setup	Anchor setup can be done similar to a hip belay, but it isn't as important for the rope to tie in on the feeling hand side of the seat harness.
Braking	Mechanical belay devices wrap the climbing rope around a post that creates friction between the post and rope when the braking hand moves laterally away from the body.
Safety	Keep your hands clear of the belay device! The rope can pull a finger into the hardware, causing considerable damage to the digit and compromising your ability to belay.

■ Communication

Communicating during a climb is very important. The climber must let the belayer know his or her needs—more rope, take up slake, falling rock, etc. The belayer can help the climber by telling the climber what he or she sees—good hold to your right, small ledge just ahead, etc. This communication helps keep the climb safe and helps establish the best route. Some basic meanings are listed in Table 11-5.

Table 11-5: Basic Climbing Communication

Communicator	Statement	Meaning
Belayer	On belay	I am ready to belay the climb.
Climber	Climbing	I am climbing.
Climber	Slack	The rope is too tight; let out some slack.
Climber	Up rope	There is too much slack; take in some rope.
Climber	Tension	Take up all the slack.
Climber	Watch me	I am in a rough spot and may fall.
Climber	Falling	I am falling.
Climber	Protection	I am placing or removing protection.
Belayer	Halfway	About half the rope remains.
Belayer	50 feet (arbitrary figure)	Belayer is letting the climber know how much rope remains.
Climber	Off belay	I no longer need to be belayed (always double-check this command).
Belayer	Again	I want to make sure I heard you right.
Climber	Ready to lower	I want you to belay me down to the ground.
Belayer	Lowering	I am going to start lowering you now.
Belayer	Off belay	I am coming off belay.
Either	Rock, ice, etc.	Falling object—look out.

Attaching the Climbing Rope

Once the route is selected, the belay set up, and communication understood, it is time to attach the climbing rope to the climber's seat harness. At this point the climber and belay person should inspect each other's seat harness to make sure it is worn correctly and the webbing is threaded back over the top of the buckle. For specifics on how to wear the type of harness you are wearing, review and know the manufacturer's suggestions before using the harness. A rewoven figure-eight or bowline on a coil are two types of commonly used knots for attaching the rope directly to the seat harness. A backup knot should also be done. Although most manufactured seat harnesses come with a belay loop, tie the knot around the waist belt and leg loop connecter. Tying in this way provides two points of protection instead of one. Once tied in, go through one final check before the climb begins. Check the harness to make sure it is buckled and worn correctly. Check the knot attaching the harness to the rope to make sure it runs through both loops, is tied correctly, and has a safety knot. Check to make sure the belay person is tied in correctly and ready to begin.

Basic Climbing Movements

The process of climbing is a combination of holds needed to move the climber up the rock. Although each move will be unique, the basic steps are weight, shift, and movement. Most movements begin by shifting the body weight from both feet to one, obtaining balance. Without moving the trunk, the free foot is moved to a new location and the body's weight is shifted to it. Repeat the process on the remaining foot, and then use both legs to lift the body into a stance. At this point, move one hand to a new position (between waist and head high) and then the other. Hand movements should be done in a way that maintains torso balance. At this point the whole process can be repeated. This movement process is established for ideal circumstances and may not always be possible. However, the more you climb the better you'll get at establishing a route where this technique can be used more often than not.

The basic concept is reviewed here; however, climbing is not something you can learn from a book. It is important to attend a reputable climbing school, where you can learn and practice these techniques before venturing into the wilderness.

■ Body Position

Whenever possible, the climber should use his or her legs to push up rough terrain. The larger leg muscles can handle more and don't fatigue as quickly as arm muscles do. The arms and hands are used for balance and positioning. In reality, this will not always be the case. Difficult climbs will require the added strength and endurance of the arms, hands, and fingers. On vertical climbs, at least three of the four body parts (hands and feet) should be in contact with the climbing surface. Proper body position occurs when the body is in a near vertical, with its weight centered over the feet. At times you may be tempted to lean into the rock—don't. Doing this pushes your feet away from the rock and decreases the amount of contact between your shoe and the rock surface—you lose the friction that keeps you from falling. In addition, hip and shoulder position is very important. When using two footholds, center the hip and shoulders over both feet. When using two handholds and one foothold, center the hip and shoulders over the foothold. Keeping the body position balanced makes it much easier to maneuver from one hold to the next. During the climb it is important to conserve leg and arm strength whenever possible. To decrease leg fatigue, keep your legs straight with the heels low. To decrease arm fatigue, keep your hands between waist and shoulder level whenever possible.

■ Footholds

Under ideal climbing circumstances, you climb with your feet and balance with your hands. Some young climbers tend to focus on handholds, failing to see the obvious foothold located below or to the side. This technique often puts the climber out of position and off balance, creates fatigue, and results in an eventual fall. Footholds can be obtained on extremely small irregularities when optimal contact is obtained and the body is centered. Foot contact with the rock results in friction that supports the climber and allows them to push upward. Several methods for increasing the foot's friction with a rock are covered in Table 11-6 on the next page.

Table 11-6: **Climbing Footholds**

Types	Description
Sole Contact	To maximize the friction between the sole of the shoe and the rock, place as much of the shoe's sole on the rock as possible.
Edging	When a rib (very small ledge that can only support a portion of the shoe's sole) is used as a foothold, use the entire side of the shoe. Usually the inside edge of the shoe is used, but not always. The edge of the shoe creates much more friction than might occur if the toe's surface had been used instead.
Smearing	When you're on a rock face and no edge is present, smear the ball of the foot onto the surface. This move is done when the surface angle makes it impossible to use the shoe's edge or entire sole.
Jamming	Jamming the foot inside a wall crack can often provide an excellent foothold. The foot should be positioned in a way that allows as much friction as can safely be obtained.

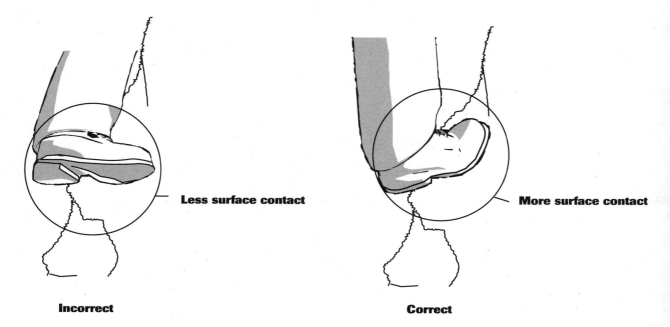

Less surface contact

More surface contact

Incorrect

Correct

Friction is often the key to a good foothold.

■ Handholds

Some young climbers tend to rely on their hands for pulling themselves up a rock wall—don't do this! Handholds are used for balance and the feet for climbing. The ideal handhold—between waist and shoulder—helps preserve good arm and hand circulation while maintaining the climber's balance. Basic handhold options are listed in Table 11-7.

Table 11-7: **Climbing Handholds**	
Types	**Description**
Pushing	Push holds use the friction created between the hand and the rock to balance or move the climber. A push hold can be done using downward, sideways, and even upward pressure.
Pulling	Pull holds occur when a handhold is grasped and pulled on to balance or move a climber. This handhold is used perhaps more than others because grasping the rock creates a sense of security.
Pinching	Pinching a small protrusion may be all it takes to maintain a balanced posture. The pinch usually involves the thumb and fingers. In addition to balance, pinching can also aid push and pull holds.
Jamming	Jamming fingers and hands into cracks can provide resistance to downward or outward forces. This handhold often leads to abrasions and cuts and should be used only when other options aren't available.

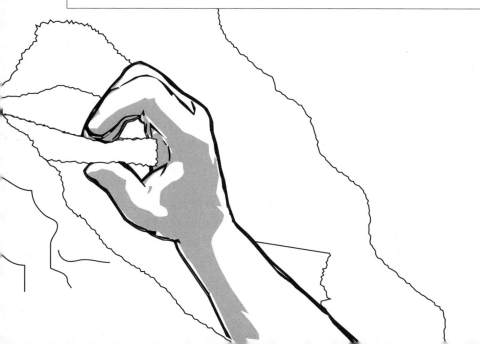

Handholds provide balance.

■ Combination Holds

There are several climbing maneuvers that are very helpful for overcoming certain obstacles. Many of these maneuvers use handholds and footholds that oppose one another. Most of them use the hands for more than balance, and at times these techniques put the climber out of balance. The key to success is planning. Plan your route and each move within it, and then execute those moves with deliberate precision. Four basic combination holds are outlined in Table 11-8 below.

Table 11-8: Combination Holds

Types	Description
Mantling	Mantling is a maneuver that helps the climber scale a ledge or projection. To do this, both palms are placed on the ledge and a downward pushing handhold is used to move the body up until the arms are straight, with elbows locked. At this point, one leg is brought to the top of the ledge and then the other. When the ledge is above head height, the maneuver starts with a pulling handhold and transitions into a pushing handhold when the head is above the hands.
Undercling	An undercling maneuver uses opposing forces between the feet and hands. The hands are placed palms up (on the underside of small outcropping), applying an upward pull. The feet are often against the rock surface, using friction to create a downward force. The upward force of the hands increases the friction to the foothold. For best results, arms and legs should be kept straight.
Lieback	A lieback maneuver uses opposing forces between the hands and feet. This technique works well on dihedral faces, where two walls come together forming a 90-degree angle and a crack at the junction. The crack close to the body is used for handholds, while footholds are created on the opposite wall. With an approximate 90-degree bend (torso to lower extremities), the climber uses pulling handholds and pushing footholds while leaning away from the wall. In order to maximize the foothold friction, the feet need to be relatively high on the rock. While maintaining this posture, movement occurs via alternating hand and foot movements.
Body Jam	Body jam maneuvers are most often used during a chimney climb, where the opposing forces between the feet, torso, and hands help move the climber upward. Perhaps the easiest way to do a body jam is with the back against one wall and the feet on the other. The back provides a significant amount of surface friction. In this process the torso and feet alternate movements up the chimney crack.

Combination Holds

Mantle hold.

Undercling hold.

Lieback hold.

Body jam hold.

Lead Climbing

A trip over rough terrain often requires a lead climber—someone to establish the route and set protection for those who follow. This person needs to be well versed on the process! The route needs to consider rope length, protection placement (good crack), and appropriate locations for belaying the second climber's ascent. The maximum distance the lead should climb before stopping is equal to about half the rope's length. Going higher makes it impossible to lower the climber back to the ground should he or she fall and get injured. The belayer needs to monitor the rope's length and update this information to the climber throughout the climb. Once the lead climber reaches a ledge and establishes an anchored belay, the climbers switch roles and the lead climber belays the second climber's ascent. The second climber removes all protection on the way up to the newly established belay station. The process is repeated until the destination is reached. If both climbers are well versed in leading, time can be saved if the second continues beyond the belay station, taking on the role of lead climber and establishing the second pitch. If this is done, one belay anchor needs to account for an upward force fall and the other for a downward force fall.

Before the climb begins, the route, along with an estimation of needed protection, must be planned thoroughly. The lead climber must carry enough equipment to protect the route and establish anchors for the next belay. It is wise to carry more than you think you will need. This "rack" of gear is carried on a runner draped over one shoulder and across the chest and back, with items in order from smallest in front to largest in the rear.

Typical Leader Rack:
- Gear sling
- Sewn runners (4)
- Tied runners (4)
- Wired nuts (full set of 9 or 10)
- Hexes—midsized (5)
- Camming units (full set)
- Quick draws with carabiners (8)
- Carabiners—oval (25)
- Carabiners—locking (3)
- Nut tool
- Belay/rappel device
- Added gear dictated by route

◼ Placing Protection

During the climb the lead climber provides protection by placing passive and active protection between stable positions. The protection should be placed so that if any climber falls, the fall will not be long enough or hard enough to cause an injury. As a climb's difficulty increases, more protection should be placed. To decrease the distance of a potential fall, protection should be placed as high as a climber's balance allows. In situations where the climb traverses the rock face, the lead climber can reduce the risk of a severe pendulum fall by placing protection prior, during, and at the end of the traverse. In addition, the lead climber must set protection that minimizes friction between the protection and rope. This friction problem is referred to as "rope drag." Routes that zigzag through carabiners have significant rope drag. Ropes that follow a direct path between climber and belayer have minimal rope drag.

Since protection doesn't always allow a direct path, sometimes you will need to extend the protection. An appropriate length of sling (runner) can be used to extend the distance between the protection and the desired

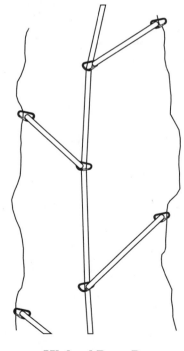

Minimal Rope Drag

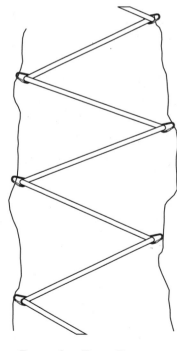

Excessive Rope Drag

Whenever possible, use runners to minimize rope drag.

rope line. Simply attach one end of the sling to the carabiner (attached to the protection) and use another carabiner to attach the other end to the rope. This allows the climber to adjust a route while keeping the rope line relatively straight. Since the runner will increase the potential fall distance, use the shortest runner needed to get the desired result. Rope drag is also known to cause correctly set protection to wiggle or pop free.

There are several types of removable protection made by various manufacturers. All, however, fit into either a passive or active classification and work by holding the stress of a falling climber. Basic aspects of passive and active protection are covered here. Learning this art, however, requires hands-on training that can only be obtained by attending a reputable climbing school. In addition, take the time to read manufacturers' literature on the types of devices you are using.

Passive Protection Placement

Wedges (nuts and hexes) are classified as passive protection. These anchors should be used instead of camming devices whenever the option is available. An appropriately placed wedge can hold up to ten times as much as a camming device. Before and during the climb, look for a crack that has a solid surface with unparallel sides. Cracks with crumbling walls and near-parallel sides may not hold the wedge. Select a wedge that provides the best fit, and slide it deep inside the crack. The more surface contact between the nut and the crack, the better it works. Pull the wedge's wire in the direction of your anticipated load, and see if it holds. After this is done, you should not be able to wiggle the nut. Provided the wedge is seated well the first time, give it a harder second tug to set it firmly in place. Clip a carabiner into the wedge's wire sling. If webbing is used, attach it to the carabiner. Do not run the webbing directly through the wire—under certain circumstances, the wire could cut through the webbing.

Places Where Wedges Should Not Be Used:
- Crumbling, soft, or hollow rock
- Parallel-sided cracks (use spring-loaded camming devices)
- Where the wire is loaded over a surface edge
- Loose or rattling placements
- Where only the corners of the wedge make contact with the rock

Active Protection Placement

Spring-loaded camming devices placement is a skill you need to master before leading a climb. These spring-loaded devices work by generating friction on a crack's walls. Cams are least effective on smooth, hard rocks that don't allow them to dig in. However, rock that is too soft may allow the cam to track through it. A cam placed in a parallel-sided crack may move with the rope's back-and-forth sway and eventually walk out of the crack. In an ideal situation, a cam is placed so that it is in line with a potential load. In other words, it will be in line with the force created from a fall. Usually this is perpendicular to the ground. If a cam were placed with its wire parallel to the ground, a fall would put tremendous stress on the device—rotating it out of position or, worse yet, causing it to fail. Take the time to learn the technique and the gear you intend to use. This skill needs to be practiced—over and over again—before leading a climb.

Regardless of the type of protection used, the carabiner is attached to the climbing rope with its gate facing *away* from the rock or crack. (A gate facing the rock may be forced open by a protrusion or edge.) To attach the rope, place a bight (a loop) into the carabiner in such a way that the carabiner doesn't twist when the rope is released. Before moving forward, check to make sure that the pull created from your intended direction of travel doesn't twist the carabiner. Adjust the carabiner based on the direction you came from and the direction you are going. The rope should run against the spine of the carabiner (not the gate), entering from the rear (between rock and carabiner) and exiting the front (carabiner between the rope and the rock). Once the lead climber reaches a new belay site and establishes an appropriate anchor, he or she can belay the second person up. With a proper belay, the second climber can fall only as far as the rope can stretch.

The Second Climber

The second climber can climb the route using Prusik knots (see Chapter 10) or commercial ascenders or by climbing it. No matter which method is used, the protection needs to be removed so that it can be used again. In some instances removing the protection may require the use of a nut tool. Communication between the second and the lead climbers is important—especially when removing the protection requires the climber to place his or her whole body weight on the rope. The command "tension" should be given in such instances. Retrieved protection should be placed on a sling, in order from smallest to largest, so that it is ready to use once the second climber reaches the new belay site. When both the second and lead climbers are equal at leading, the second may continue past the belay person and assume the lead for the second pitch. In such instances, make sure the belay anchors are set to protect a potential downward or upward pull.

Rappelling

The greatest risk during rough land travel isn't going up—it's coming down. If there are other alternatives, use them. If other alternatives aren't available, a rappel may be your only option. Since setting up a rappel may put you close to the edge of the rock face, attach a safety rope to your harness before you begin. Next establish an appropriate anchor that is above the rappelling departure point. The best anchor is a well-rooted stout tree trunk, and two anchors are always better than one. Try to give the sling enough length to keep the rope from rubbing on the rock edge. If you decide to use a rappel ring, run the webbing through it prior to tying it to the anchor. A rappel ring is an inexpensive metal ring, measuring about 1½ inches in diameter that makes rope retrieval easier. Before the rappel begins, run the length of the climbing rope to make sure it hasn't sustained any damage. All rappels should be done using a double rope that can be created in one of the following methods. If the rappel is less than half the rope's length, a single rope can be used. Simply run the rope through the anchor (webbing) or rappel ring until it reaches the halfway point. If using two ropes, put one end of one rope through the sling and tie the two ropes together using a double fisherman's knot backed up with an overhand knot.

Throwing the rappel rope may seem like an easy task—and it is, provided you take a couple of minutes to prepare the rope. Simply throwing the rope off the surface often results in a tangled mess that requires retrieval and time to untangle. Coil the rope into four equal-size butterfly coils—two on each half of the anchor—and throw the coils out and over the edge one at a time. Start on one side, throwing the coil closest to the anchor first and the free end second. Repeat the process on the other side. At this point you're just about ready to clip in and have your seat harness and hookup checked before taking off. But what type of hookup will you use? Depending on the circumstances, you might use a nonmechanical rappel (hasty and body rappel) or a mechanical rappel (figure-eight descender, belay tube, or six-carabiner system).

■ Nonmechanical Rappel

Nonmechanical rappels are used on mild to moderate slopes when no other options exist. These rappels use friction between the body and the rope to control the rate of descent.

Hasty Rappel

The hasty rappel is used only on low angle pitches where no other options exist. Its main advantage is that it is easier and faster than other methods. If wearing a pack, position the rope so it runs over the back surface of the pack.

Table 11-9: **Hasty Rappel**

Key Points	Description
Hookup	Facing slightly toward the anchor, place the rope across your back and under your armpits, and then wrap it once around each arm. The downhill hand is the brake hand; the uphill hand is the guide.
Gear	Gloves and added clothing should be used to pad areas of high friction (arms, armpits, and back).
Rappel	Face slightly sideways, with the brake hand on the downhill side. With straight back and relatively straight legs, take a wide stance and lean your body perpendicular to the rock surface. During the descent, the foot on the brake hand side is always in front of the guide hand.
Brake	To brake, turn your body toward the anchor point and bring the brake hand across the front of your body.

Hasty rappel.

Body Rappel

This rappel uses the friction between various body surfaces and the rope to control the rate of descent. Once the rope is attached to the anchor and deployed, a body rappel can be used. This technique is limited to mild slopes that allow the feet to maintain surface contact. If you are wearing a pack, position the rope so that it runs over the back surface of the pack.

Table 11-10: Body Rappel

Key Points	Description
Hookup	Face the anchor and straddle the rope. Pull the rope up from behind and run it around one hip, diagonally across the chest, across the opposite shoulder, and to the brake hand (located on same side as the hip used).
Gear	Use gloves and added clothing to pad areas of high friction (neck, thigh, chest, and back).
Rappel	Face slightly sideways with the brake hand on the downhill side. With straight back and relatively straight legs, take a wide stance and lean your body perpendicular to the rock surface. During the descent, the foot on the brake hand side is always in front of the guide hand.
Brake	To brake, lean back and face directly toward the rock area so that your feet are horizontal to the ground.

Body rappel.

■ Mechanical Rappel

A mechanical rappel uses hardware instead of the body to absorb the rope's friction and control the rappel. Although there are several options available, my advice is to carry a rappel device that can also be used for other purposes, such as a figure-eight descender, a belay tube, or carabiners. A locking carabiner should be used to attach the rappel device to the seat harness. Whenever a locking carabiner is not available, use two carabiners with the gates opposed and reversed.

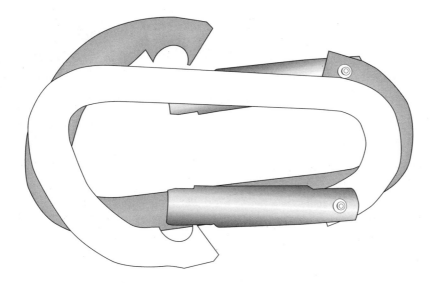

Doubled carabiner with gates opposed and reversed.

The three types of mechanical rappelling systems discussed here are the figure-eight descender, the belay tube, and a six-carabiner system. Of the three, the figure-eight is perhaps the most popular for rappelling. The figure-eight, however, requires a locking carabiner—a double carabiner setup will not fit. To hook the rope to the figure-eight, pass a bight through the large eye and then over the small eye onto the neck. Place the small eye into a locking carabiner so that the working end of the rope is on the brake hand side (see illustration, next page). The setup for a belay tube is exactly the same as done for belaying (see illustration, next page). A carabiner brake system uses a series of carabiners attached to create friction on the rope. Oval-shaped carabiners are ideal for this setup. To create this system,

Mechanical Belay Devices

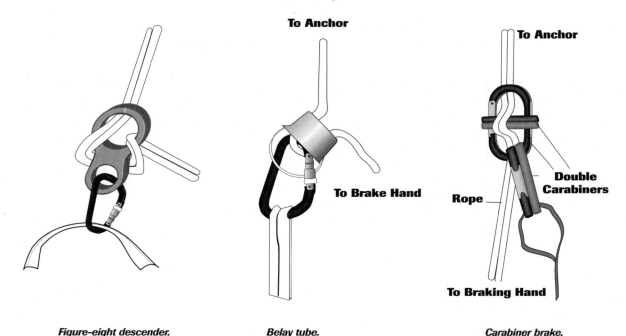

To Anchor

To Anchor

To Brake Hand

Rope

Double Carabiners

To Braking Hand

Figure-eight descender.   *Belay tube.*   *Carabiner brake.*

attach a locking carabiner or two regular carabiners (correctly positioned) to the seat harness. Clip two carabiners to the first carabiner with the gates opposed and reversed. While facing the anchor, lift a bight of rope through the bottom of the outer two carabiners and clip another pair of carabiners over the outer two so that the rope runs over them. The carabiners need to be clipped in so they open on the opposite side of the rope's path. In other words, the rope crosses the carabiners' back spine (see illustration above).

All mechanical devices are used with a simple seat-hip rappel technique. As you rappel, the rope slides through the device, allowing you to move down the slope. The brake hand controls descent by adjusting the amount of friction between the rope and the piece of equipment. These devices hook to the rappeller's seat harness so that the hand on the same side of the body as the descending rope is the brake hand. The other uphill hand is the guide hand. Any shirttails, belts, hair, or other items that might get caught in the brake system need to be tucked in or removed.

After the rope has been inspected, anchors established, friction system created, and harness and hookup check by several members of the team, it is time to review communication procedures and begin the rappel.

Rappel Checklist:

- During setup, attach safety rope to your harness.
- Inspect the rope.
- Set up rappel anchor system.
- Attach friction device to harness and rope.
- Check harness and hookup. Are gates correctly aligned or locked? Are the harness belts run back over the buckle?
- Tuck in shirttails, loose straps, hair, or anything else that might get caught in the brake system. Put on leather gloves.
- Review communication.
- Begin rappel.

The hardest part of a rappel is often the first few steps. This often requires standing on the ledge and letting your buttocks drop while bending at the waist to form an L-shaped body position. To do this the rope is allowed to move through the brake system at the speed comfortable to the rappeller. If all goes well, once in the L-shaped position, the rappeller simply walks down the slope—torso and feet parallel to the wall's surface. The crux of the rappel is perhaps the first couple of feet. During this time the rope drops from waist high to the rock edge, often creating a moment of instability. If unable to counterbalance this effect, simply sit down and gently rotate your body off-ledge while turning inward so that you are facing the wall. At this point, bring your feet to the wall's surface and assume an L-shaped posture.

During descent, keep your feet shoulder width apart, knees slightly bent, body in an L shape, and look over the brake hand shoulder to see where you are going. Never remove the brake hand from the rope. If you find yourself out of position, don't panic. Take the time to maneuver your body back into place and evaluate what went wrong. In most instances, your feet were too close together or you failed to commit—lean back far enough. The rappel should be done in a slow, methodical manner without jerking or bounding on the rope. At times you may find yourself dangling away from the rock wall. Don't worry—stay in position and continue your descent, using the brake hand to control your speed. Let the rope slide freely through the guide hand while keeping the guide arm extended and elbow locked. The guide hand simply helps with balance during the rappel. The brake hand moves the rope out away from the body when slowing or stopping descent and inward when increasing descent. The brake hand never releases the rope until the rappel is done.

The crux of a rappel is often the first move.

As a safety measure, the first rappeller may opt to use a friction knot for added safety. In this case, the sling is attached to the rope (above the brake system) using a friction knot and to the seat harness with a carabiner. As the rappel progresses, the knot will need to be walked down the rope. If the rappeller falls, the fall forces the knot to grip the rope and stop the fall. The first person down belays all other rappellers. A simple belay for rappelling is to pull the rope tight or walk the rope out and away from the rock wall. The increased tension or angle between the rope and the rappeller is all the friction needed to stop a fall. It may be necessary to stop during the rappel. If this occurs, run the brake hand–side of the rope around your waist, and then wrap it three to four times around the guide hand–side leg before tying it off using an appropriate knot.

Chapter Exercises

Practice anchor setup for belaying.

In your backyard or a nearby forest (without disturbing the environment or breaking any laws), practice your anchor placement. Practice using both the climbing rope and a sling.

Practice belaying.

With a friend, set up an anchor and belay site on flat ground, and assume a good sitting belay posture. Attach your friend to the free end of the rope and have him or her provide a variable degree of tension on the rope. The mock climber's (your friend) tension allows you to practice taking in and letting out rope. The key here is to become accustomed to the proper hand movements while keeping the brake hand on the rope at all times.

Practice holding the fall.

Practice tying off the belay rope so that the mock climber is supported while you come off belay.

Practice climbing and rappelling.

Find a local well-known and respected climbing gym; take lessons and practice.

Practice hasty and body rappels.

Find a mild slope that provides an adequate anchor, and practice the hasty and the body rappel.

Snow & Glacier Travel

Travel on snow and ice can provide some of the most exhilarating moments! The view, which is often not done justice in photographs, leaves a lasting impression. However, as with all other rough land ventures, snow and glacier travel is not without risk, including avalanches, crevasses, and slips and falls on icy surfaces. On such trips you need to prepare by attending a reputable school that teaches technique and safety related to this terrain. You don't want to be caught in a blizzard without knowing what to do.

In addition to your routine climbing, backpacking, and safety gear, consider carrying a few safety items specific to cold weather environments. These include an avalanche transceiver, probes, snow shovels, an inclinometer, and the AvaLung. Don't just carry these items, learn how they work and review how to use them before each trip.

Avalanche Safety

Before you begin an exciting snow adventure, be sure to check the avalanche and weather conditions. Contact the ranger station or other wilderness authorities for the area you intend to travel into. They should be able to provide you with relevant safety information. In addition, check the *United States Avalanche Danger Descriptors* level for the area. The color-coded guide is a great augment to a ranger's advice, your experience level, and your knowledge of the area you plan to visit. If conditions are questionable, it is better to postpone a trip than to risk your life.

Table 12-1: United States Avalanche Danger Descriptors

Danger Level (& Color)	Avalanche Probability and Avalanche Trigger	Degree and Distribution of Avalanche Danger	Recommended Action in the Backcountry
What	*Why*	*Where*	*What to Do*
Low (green)	Natural avalanches very unlikely. Human-triggered avalanches unlikely.	Generally stable snow. Isolated areas of instability.	Travel is generally safe. Normal caution is advised.
Moderate (yellow)	Natural avalanches unlikely. Human-triggered avalanches possible.	Unstable slabs possible on steep terrain.	Use caution in steeper terrain on certain aspects (defined in accompanying statement).
Considerable (orange)	Natural avalanches possible. Human-triggered avalanches probable.	Unstable slabs probable on steep terrain.	Be increasingly cautious in steeper terrain.
High (red)	Natural and human-triggered avalanches likely.	Unstable slabs likely on a variety of aspects and slope angles.	Travel in avalanche terrain is not recommended. Safest travel on windward ridges of lower angle slopes without steeper terrain above.
Extreme (black)	Widespread natural or human-triggered avalanches certain.	Extremely unstable slabs certain on most aspects and slope angles. Large, destructive avalanches possible.	Travel in avalanche terrain should be avoided and travel confined to low-angle terrain well away from avalanche path run-outs.

Avalanche Safety Basics

Avalanches don't happen by accident, and most human involvement is a matter of choice, not chance. Most avalanche accidents are caused by slab avalanches, which are triggered by the victim or a member of the victim's party. However, any avalanche may cause injury or death, and even small slides may be dangerous. Always practice safe route-finding skills, be aware of changing conditions, and carry avalanche rescue gear. Learn and apply avalanche terrain analysis and snow stability evaluation techniques to help minimize your risk. Remember that avalanche danger rating levels are only general guidelines. Distinctions between geographic areas, elevations, slope aspects, and slope angles are approximate, and transition zones between dangers exist. No matter what the current avalanche danger, there are avalanche-safe areas in the mountains.

■ Avalanche Risk Factors

If you find yourself in the outback and pondering the avalanche threat, take the time to evaluate the terrain, snowpack, and weather. A thorough consideration of these three areas, along with some common sense, will help you identify your risk and decide whether you should start or continue your journey.

Terrain

The slope angle, character, and shape all play a role in determining avalanche risk.

Slope Angle. Slopes with an angle between 25 and 60 degrees are considered high risk for avalanches. The greatest risk, however, is found on slopes with angles between 30 and 45 degrees. Snow rarely sticks to a steep slope, and shallow slopes don't have enough momentum to slide.

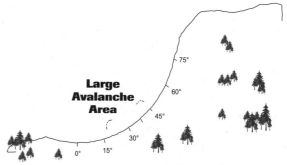

Slope angle.

Slope Position. A slope's position relative to the sun and wind play a huge role in its potential for avalanche. In winter, slopes with sun exposure tend to be more stable than those without. In spring and summer the opposite is true. Slopes facing the wind are more stable than those that don't, since wind packs down or carries the snow away. Slopes opposite the wind tend to build cornices, deep unconsolidated snow, and wind slabs from snow blown off the other side.

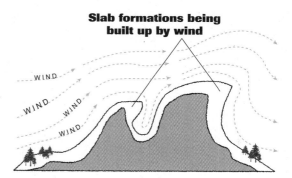

Slope position.

Slope Character. Does the slope have a convex or concave appearance? Snow located in a convex slope is under a great deal of tension and is more prone to release than snow covering a concave slope. A straight, open, and steep slope is an obvious hazard. Trees that are bent down and away from the upward slope and missing limbs on the uphill side are signs that a major avalanche has traveled through that area.

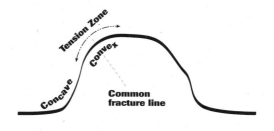

Slope character.

Snowpack

A snowpack is multiple layers of consolidated snow—one on top of the other. If the new layers do not adhere to the layers below, the snowpack is unstable and presents an avalanche risk. Mother Nature provides clues about the snowpack's stability. Paying close attention to them will provide additional information about the relative risk associated with your current location. These clues, however, are not a precise measurement of the snowpack and should be used only in conjunction with other relevant information for the area you are in.

Mother Nature's Clues to Avalanches:

- Signs of recent avalanches on similar slopes.
- Whumping noises are heard; these sounds are produced when a weak layer collapses and indicate instability between the layers of snow.
- Shooting cracks may indicate an impending slab avalanche.
- A sudden warming trend often weakens the bond between snowpack layers and can lead to a slab avalanche.
- Hollow drum sounds radiating up from the snowpack may indicate a weak layer that could lead to a slab avalanche.

Weather

Snowfall, rain, wind, and the temperature can increase the risk for avalanche.

- New snow increases the risk of avalanche, especially when as much as 10 to 12 inches fall or when more than 1 inch per hour is falling.
- Rain penetrates the snow layers and weakens the bond between them, making it easier for a slab to break free.
- Recent wind loading on the nonwind side of a hill may set the stage for a slab avalanche.
- Temperature differences between the snow's surface and the ground or layers of snow can create an unstable layer of snow and increase the risk of a slab avalanche.

■ Decreasing Avalanche Risk

Although you may try your best to avoid avalanche risk, at times it may be unavoidable. In such instances avoid large, steep lee bowls, gullies, and cornices. Instead look for routes that take you on ridgetops, valley floors, low-angle slopes, and through dense forest. Before crossing a risky area, remove ski pole straps, undo pack buckles, secure all gear and clothing, check your beacon to make sure it is on transmit mode, and identify escape routes. To decrease risk, try to cross at the top or bottom of a threatening area, and let only one person go at a time.

■ What to Do If Caught in an Avalanche

Hopefully you are prepared and have appropriate gear and have selected a route that allows escape. This includes checking reviewing beacon use, inserting new batteries, and making sure the beacon is on before departing. In addition, the AvaLung should be carried so that its mouthpiece is only inches from your mouth, making it easy to access should the need arise. In the event of an avalanche, follow these steps:

- Shout to let everyone else know about the avalanche.
- Insert the AvaLung mouthpiece.
- If able to ski to the side, out of danger, do so. If you cannot, discard any gear that might tangle you up (skis and poles).
- If a safe area is accessible, try to get to it.
- If you're knocked down, use a swimming motion that keeps you on the snow's surface and takes you toward the side of the avalanche.
- If you're unable to stay above the surface, do everything you can to provide adequate air and promote rescue. This includes trying to get a hand above the snow's surface so that it can be seen and using the other arm to make an air space in front of your face.
- If you have an AvaLung, relax, conserve your energy, and wait for your friends to find you. Hopefully they are current on avalanche rescue techniques.

Anchors and the Ice Ax

Traveling in snow is not without risk. In order to reduce this risk, it is wise to know how to tie a few knots, use an ice ax, and create safety anchors.

■ Anchors

The type of anchor you use will depend on snow conditions and what is available. All require proper placement and knowledge of use. Take the time to practice *before* you need to put your life in the hands of these devices.

Snow fluke deadman.

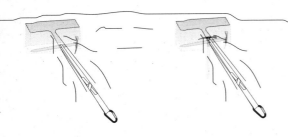

Ice ax deadman.

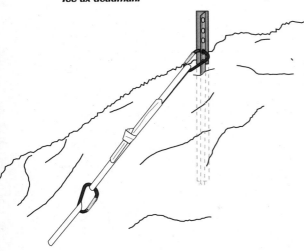

A picket is an aluminum stake that functions as a snow anchor.

Deadman

This anchor is created when a rope is attached to something buried in the snow. Deadman anchors work best in snow that is moist and heayy and worst in dry, fluffy snow. A snow fluke is made specifically for this purpose and consists of a metal plate with a steel cable. These commercial anchors come in various sizes and shapes, but in general they all function the same. The plate should be buried in the snow so that its forward plate is approximately 45 degrees to the slope with its top pointed away from the cable's direction of pull.

In a pinch, the ice ax can be used for deadman-type snow anchors. Bury the ax in the snow, with its shaft horizontal to the snow's surface, and attach a runner to its midsection. For best results tip the head back so that the pick (or adze) forms a 45-degree angle between it and the snow's surface. If added support is needed, place a second ax perpendicular to the first one (spike 45 degrees to snow's surface), and attach the runner line to the second ax above the first.

Picket

A picket is an aluminum stake (18 to 36 inches long) that can be driven into the snow and used as an anchor. This anchor works best in snow that is too hard for a deadman. Like a deadman anchor, it needs to establish a 45-degree angle between it and the slope, with its top angled back. Attach a runner or carabiner to the picket as close to the snowline as possible. Higher attachments might leave the picket vulnerable to being pulled out.

Bollard

A bollard is an anchor made from snow and webbing (not cord or rope) when hard snow conditions exist. This horseshoe trench (open end downhill) should be 1 to 1½ feet deep, 8 inches wide, and 3 to 10 feet in diameter. The firmer the snow, the smaller the diameter will need to be. Make sure to leave a wide-open end that is level with the snow's surface. Bringing the ends close together will weaken the anchor. If weak layers are noticed during digging, use another anchor system or choose a different, uncompromised site. If able, back up the bollard with another anchor and pad its back (decreases the threat of your webbing cutting through it).

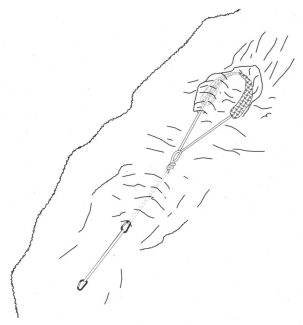

Bollard anchor.

■ The Ice Ax

An ice ax can be used to stabilize the snow hiker (third point of contact), self-belay (anchor) in harsh terrain, and self-arrest a fall. When conditions are right an ice ax is a great tool for a rapid descent, through a process known as glissading.

Sizing an Ice Ax

Several types of ice axes are made for the winter adventurous. The type you choose depends on your sport and your body size. To determine the right size for you, hold the head of the ice ax (fingers draped down the shaft's side) so that the ax and your arm are perpendicular to the ground, and use the following guidelines:

- **Basic climbing (general use).** The ax tip should be just shy of touching the ground.

- **Intermediate climbing (high-angle use).** The ax tip should be 2 to 4 inches (5 to 10 cm) shy of the ground.

- **Snowshoeing.** The ax tip should extend 2 to 4 inches (5 to 10 cm) beyond the ground.

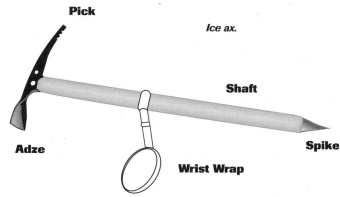

Ice ax.

Pick

Shaft

Spike

Adze

Wrist Wrap

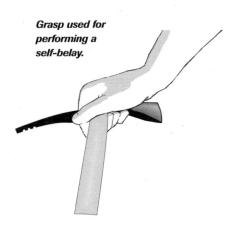

Walking with an ice ax.

Grasp used for performing a self-belay.

Walking with an Ice Ax

The ice ax is a great tool for snowshoeing or glacier hiking with crampons. It provides a third point of contact that stabilizes the hiker, especially when on a slope. In this scenario, the ice ax is carried on the uphill side as an anchor and support. When not in use, secure the ice ax to your pack, or carry it by grasping the center of the shaft so that it is parallel to the ground with the spike forward and the pick toward the ground. Regardless of how it is being used, a lanyard that extends 6 inches beyond your arm's reach should be attached to the ice ax.

Self-Belay

In addition to helping balance a climber, the ice ax can be used to prevent or stop a fall—a process referred to as a self-belay. Several methods of belaying with an ice ax are listed here. Although there are several types of self-belay, the way you grasp the ice ax is the same for each: The ice ax is held with your palm on top of the adze, thumb and index finger hanging over opposite sides of the pick, and the spike pointing toward the ground.

Going Up Gradual Grades. When using a diagonal or traversing pattern on gradual grades, hold the ax like a cane, using the self-belay grasp (uphill side). In this position it can be used for balance or as a self-belay by setting its spick into the snow with each move.

Going Diagonally Up Steep Grades. When using a diagonal path to travel up a steep grade, hold the ax in a cross-body position: Hold the ax by grasping its head with the downhill side hand and the shaft with the other, and jam it 90 degrees into the uphill side of the snow slope. Since the ice ax will cross in front of you, make sure the pick doesn't point toward your body. Using the belay for support and balance, take a step forward. This process is repeated until the top is

Using an ice ax on a diagonal climb.

reached or a different method appears to be a better choice.

Going Directly Up a Steep Slope. Using a kick step, jam the spike end of the ice ax deep into the snow's uphill surface; use it to belay your next step. This technique has both hands on the ice ax head and is repeated until the top is reached or a different method appears to be a better choice.

Going Downhill. When a plunge step is used to go straight down a hill, hold the ice ax so that its spike is on the downhill side—pointing toward the snow surface—ready to be jammed into the snow if you lose your balance. On moderately steep slopes, use the ax as a belay by planting it into the snow (down-hill side) every two steps (one with each foot). On really steep slopes, face into the slope and use a kick step to climb down the hill. For this technique, use the ax as a belay by planting it into the snow (uphill side) every two steps (one with each foot).

Self-Arrest

A self-arrest is used when you fall or your self-belay has failed. It will need to be implemented quickly once you have fallen and have begun your rapid, out-of-control downward descent.

Self-Arrest Basics. If you are lucky, you'll fall on your belly with your head uphill and your feet facing downhill. In this ideal textbook example, use the following technique to self-arrest your fall.

■ **Proper ax control.** The ax should be held using the self-arrest grasp—your palm on the pick, your fingers draped over it on one side, and your thumb going under the adze next to the shaft. If using the belay grasp when you fall, you'll need to switch to the self-arrest grasp quickly. The other hand should be placed as close to the spike as possible.

Using an ice ax for going straight uphill.

Using an ice ax for going downhill.

Grasp used for performing a self-arrest.

Pick

Adze

- **Pick placement.** Once you fall, the pick should be forced into the snow so that the adze is located between your ear and shoulder. This placement is key to providing enough force to slow your descent.
- **Shaft placement.** The shaft should cross your chest on a diagonal plane, with the tip close to your hip (opposite side of the adze and pick).
- **Using your body weight.** Press your chest down hard on the shaft of the ice ax. Your weight will have a greater impact on forcing the pick into the snow than you can create using your arms. Keep your head down, and slightly arch your lower back away from the snow. These two maneuvers will increase the downward chest force on the ax shaft.
- **Leg position.** Spread your legs apart, and dig your knees and toes into the snow's surface.

Should you fall, a properly executed self-arrest will stop your descent.

Self-Arresting a Nontextbook Fall. The odds are that if you fall, it will not be on your belly with your head uphill. Instead, you may find yourself in a position that requires digging the pick of the ice ax into the snow and rotating your body until you obtain this position. Some possible scenarios are listed here.

■ **On your back with your head uphill.** Roll toward the ax head, plant the pick into the snow once you're on your side, and assume the basic self-arrest posture once on your belly. Do not roll toward the spike of the ice ax. Doing this may result in the spike digging into the snow, which may pull the shaft from under your chest.

*Self-arrest—
on your back with
your head uphill.*

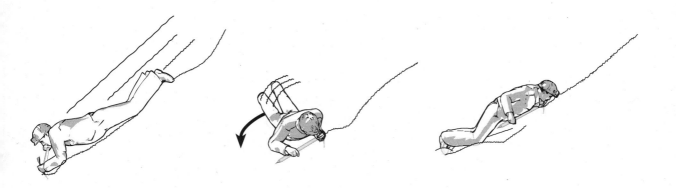

■ **On your chest with your head downhill.** The first step in this position is to get your body turned so that you're on your belly, with your feet facing downhill. With the ax out front (downhill side), dig the pick into the snow and use it to pivot your body around into a textbook position (on belly with head uphill). It is important to pivot (rotate) toward the spike side of the ax. Rotating the other way fails to put your chest over the ax shaft and may lead to an injury when your head rotates around the ax head.

*Self-arrest—
on your chest
with your head
downhill.*

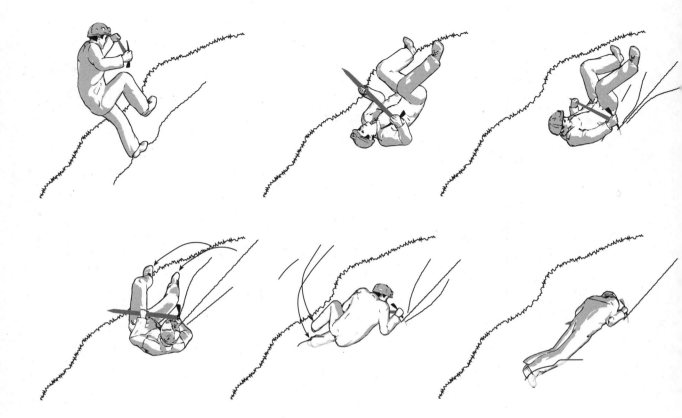

*Self-arrest—
on your back
with your head
downhill.*

■ **On your back with your head downhill.** This position requires rotating onto your chest and pivoting your body so that your feet are downhill. With the ax shaft crossing the abdomen, drive the ax pick into the snow and twist and roll your body so that it rotates from under the ax shaft and onto your chest with your head uphill.

Glissading

Glissading not only saves a lot of time—it is fun. Glissading, however, is not without risk and should be done only when the terrain is well known and poses no avalanche hazard. Don't risk an exposure injury—wear appropriate clothing that protects you from the cold, wet snow. Perhaps the easiest glissading technique is a sitting glissade. Make sure to remove crampons and secure your gear so that you won't lose it. To begin, sit down so that your torso is upright, your knees are bent, and your feet are flat on the snow-covered surface. Begin sliding down the slope, with the ice ax held in the self-arrest position. Let the ice ax spike scrape the snow— varying the amount of pressure needed to control your rate of descent.

Sitting glissade.

Travel in Snow

Learn to travel in the snow and you will wonder why you hadn't done it before. The experience is well worth the effort. Short of a snowmobile or other motorized vehicle, snowshoes and cross-country skis are perhaps the best methods of getting from one point to another in a snow environment.

■ Snowshoes

I like snowshoes! I can get just about anywhere I want, regardless of the terrain, snows depth, or type of snow (provided safety is not an issue). They help disperse my weight over a greater surface area, which keeps me on top of the snow. Compared with cross-country skis, they are superior in snow-covered areas that have brush or rock obstacles.

Snowshoe Design

The western-style mountaineering snowshoe is a great all-purpose design that performs well when ascending or descending slopes. This type of shoe is made with an oval-shaped, lightweight tubular frame that supports a durable decking material. It comes with bindings that attach to your boot and cramponlike metal plates at the toe and heel to aid in traction. The exact type of snowshoe you use will depend on its purpose and your weight. Most western designs range in size from 8 by 22 inches to 9 by 38 inches. As a rule, pick the smallest snowshoe that will support your weight plus the weight of your backpack and gear.

Snowshoe Travel

The type of terrain and climate conditions play a role in deciding what type of snowshoe to wear and how you attack your trek. Some basics of snowshoe travel are covered here. In each technique, use an ice ax as a self-belay (see the Ice Ax section of this chapter for details) to help anchor and balance your movement.

Uphill Travel. The toe hole of the western-style snowshoe makes it possible to use a kick step (covered in Chapter 7) when traveling up a steep slope. The kick step is done wearing a snowshoe the same way as previously outlined. Using the kick step on steep slopes makes the ascent easier for the lead person and those who follow.

Downhill Travel. Traveling down a mild slope in a western snowshoe is a simple process, provided the snowshoe is equipped with toe and heel crampons. The crampons help dig into the snow surface, making the downhill trek much easier. On such slopes, slightly bend your knees, lean back, and point your toes down so that the snowshoes crampons make full contact with the snow surface. On steeper slopes it may be best to traverse down the hill or to carry the snowshoes and descend using a plunge step.

Traversing. Traversing a steep slope is often easier than a direct ascent and can be done in a western snowshoe using the same method as discussed earlier.

Getting Up. If you should fall while snowshoeing, the easiest way to get back up is to roll your body and snowshoes toward the downhill side of the terrain. This position will make it much easier to get your snowshoes and feet underneath you and back into an upright position.

■ Cross-Country Skis

The modern day cross-country ski is a versatile tool for snow travel. Perhaps its only downfall is when you're traveling with a heavy backpack in areas of dense forest or heavy underbrush.

Cross-Country Ski Designs

Nordic-style cross-country skis use a boot binding that attaches to your toe but leaves the heel free. The mountaineering-style cross-country ski is slightly wider and heavier then the Nordic style, and unlike the Nordic ski it allows you to secure the heel in place for downhill travel (skiing). Both styles require skins for uphill grades greater than about 15 degrees (depending on personal skills). Skins attach to the bottom of the ski, providing the traction needed for uphill travel. Cross-country skis work though a process of gliding and kicking. The gliding ski makes contact at the toe and heel (not at the center), while the kicking ski is in full contact with the snow. The kicking ski is aided by the traction located at the bottom center of the ski. The gliding ski glides when the central traction is off the snow's surface. In addition to the traction, skis come in wax and waxless designs.

Waxed Cross-Country Skis. These skis use a wax to aid in glide and traction. A glide wax is used at the ends, and a kick wax (sticky) is used in the center. Provided you are skilled at applying the wax and keep up with it, these skis are fast.

Waxless Cross-Country Skis. These skis are designed for low-maintenance use. The ends have very little or no pattern, and the centers have a tread (kick) pattern for traction. The trade-off for low maintenance is a ski that's much slower than a properly prepared waxed ski.

The type of cross-country ski and accessory you choose will depend on its use: Do you intend to use groomed trails or go off-trail? As a rule, however, use the following guidelines:

General Use Cross-Country Skis. Select a ski that reaches your wrists when it is perpendicular to the ground and your arms are raised high over your head.

Backcountry Use Cross-Country Skis. Select a ski that reaches to about the top of your head when it is perpendicular to the ground. The shorter ski will provide greater ease of turning and maneuverability between various obstacles.

Accessories. In addition to skis, you will need boots, bindings, and poles.

- **Boots.** The boot you choose needs to have a toe bar for attaching bindings in addition to enough protection to keep your feet warm and dry. It's best to buy your boots first and then find bindings that work with them versus the other way around.
- **Bindings.** Bindings come as either a step-in or manual style. A step-in binding works much like a downhill ski binding (no heel attachment). You simply insert the toe into the forward bar and press down until it snaps into place. A manual binding requires just a little more effort, but not much. This binding requires you to secure a latch over the top of the boots toe bar. Regardless of which type of binding you use, have them professionally mounted.

- **Poles.** General-use poles should be as long as the distance between the ground and halfway between your armpit and shoulder. Touring poles should be slightly longer. Both types of poles should have a round basket at the bottom.

Cross-Country Ski Travel

I advise taking classes on cross-country skiing and, until you are certain this sport is for you, renting your gear. The type of terrain and climatic conditions play a role in deciding what type of cross-country ski to wear and how you attack your trek. There are, however, some basics of cross-country skiing techniques that can be easily mastered. These include the diagonal stride or double pole technique (used on level ground) and traverse, forward sidestep, or herringbone technique (used for uphill travel). Downhill travel is not as easy and is actually an advanced skill that uses a downhill ski or telemarking technique.

Level Ground. The most often used techniques for cross-country skiing on level ground are the diagonal stride and double pole technique.

- **Diagonal stride.** The diagonal stride is used on level terrain where its movement mimics a body's walking motion. When one leg moves forward, so does the opposite arm. Unlike walking, however, the feet are not picked up. Instead, they glide across the surface. In addition, there is a slight pause when each foot reaches its forward extreme. This pause is followed by a down-and-back kick that allows the ski's sticky center to make full contact with the snow. The kicking leg is slightly bent when the backward push begins and straightens as the kick nears its end. A weight transfer to the kicking ski in conjunction with continued downward force is needed for best results. The non-weight-bearing ski simply slides forward—opposite of the kicking foot. Repeating this process from one foot to the other promotes a gliding motion that moves you forward with the least amount of energy expansion.

  With each glide of the ski, the opposite pole arm should move in the same direction. The pole is grasped when brought to its forward point, which is located just behind the heel. As the pole begins its backward journey, the grip is loosened once it crosses the hip's plane. Doing this allows the pole to maintain contact with the snow at all times. To hold the pole, insert your hand from the strap's underside and lightly grip the handle (your pressure should focus primarily on the strap).

- **Double pole.** The double pole technique is used on level terrain when diagonal stride is too slow or difficult. This method of travel keeps the skis in contact with the snow while using the poles to propel the skier forward. With your legs relaxed and fairly straight, both poles are planted in front as far forward as comfort allows and then a down-and-backward push is used to promote a gliding motion and forward movement. During the process no kick is used, and both skis are kept in full contact with the snow.

Going Uphill. When going uphill, the best option may be to take off your skis and use a kick step (see preceding). Other options include using an uphill traverse or forward-sidestep technique. If you have skins, they can be used to add traction to the bottom of the ski

- **Uphill traverse.** The uphill traverse is simply traversing the hill using a diagonal stride. The stride is slightly shortened, but the same rhythm is used. This same technique can be used to come down a hill.
- **Forward sidestep.** In tight spaces and on firm snow, sidestepping up the hill is both easy and quick. Use a sidestepping pattern that digs the uphill side of the ski into the slope. This same technique can be used when coming down a hill.
- **Skins.** Skins are strips of nylon or similar material that can be attached to the bottom of skis when ascents or descents require more traction than the ski alone can produce. The skin's one-way nap lets the skier slide in one direction but not in another. The skin should cover the ski's bottom but leave the edges free.

Going Downhill. When going downhill you can traverse, forward sidestep, or use skins. Other options include telemarking and downhill skiing. Regardless of which method you use, when going downhill it is best to keep your knees slightly bent (enough to feel a bend in your ankles) and your hands out in front of you, with poles angled behind.

Getting Up. If on the side of a hill, rotate your body and skis until the skis are on the downhill side. Next squirm, kick, and roll until your skis are under your knees and your toes are pointing forward. Raise a knee, plant your poles into the ground, and push down on the poles while moving into a standing position.

Travel on Glaciers

Glaciers are basically rivers of snow and ice that form when the existing snow doesn't completely melt before the next year's snowfall. The glacier's lower layers melt, only to be replaced by a new top layer. Crevasses, cracks in a glacier, are perhaps the greatest risk for glacier travelers. These cracks are formed when the glacier stretches or bends too fast and are often 100 feet deep. When crossing a glacier, it is best to avoid crevasses (unless you are well versed and trained in crevasse crossings and rescue). Glacier travel is an advanced skill that requires hands-on training. Basic skills required for glacier travel are covered here, but in no way should they replace hands on training.

■ Roping Up the Team

The position you take on a rope depends on how many climbers are in your party and the length of your rope. The ideal climbing party consists of two roped teams of three, each using a 120-foot rope (36.576 meters). The rope's attachment points should occur at both ends and the center. Roping up this way allows enough stability for the roped team should one member fall and provides an additional rescue team if needed. For a four-person rope team, a 165-foot rope should be used, and climbers should be attached at both ends and at the one-third and two-third points of the rope.

Although a locking carabiner can be used to attach the rope to your seat harness, it is better to tie the rope directly to the harness. End climbers should tie in using a rewoven figure-eight, and midrope climbers should use a double bowline (see Chapter 10). Those using a double bowline need to secure the resulting end loop using an overhand knot or carabiner.

Depending on your preference, the rope can run from the seat harness through the chest harness carabiner or not. If you're not clipped to the chest harness, make sure to do so anytime you cross a snow bridge or other apparent threat. Having the rope attached to the chest harness plays a big role in your staying upright should you fall. Finally, before you depart don't forget to attach the Prusik slings to the climbing rope (see preceeding for details on how to make these slings).

The rope team should maintain a distance that keeps the rope fully extended but not to the point of being tight. Maintaining this distance helps keep team members upright should one member fall. Too much rope slack puts the falling climber at greater risk for injury (falls farther before caught) and may pull the standing climber off his or her feet when the rope tightens (sudden snap).

■ Crossing the Crevasse

If on a glacier, be sure to wear crampons, carry an ice ax (for self-belay and arrest), rope up, and try to identify potential crevasses in advance.

Detecting a Crevasse

Detecting a crevasse should begin before you depart on your trip. Reference field books, look at maps, and discuss the trek with guides who know the route. Plan a primary and an alternative route, and change as needed before and during each trek. Once there, look over your plan and try to identify potential crevasses using the following suggestions. Realize that nothing in Mother Nature is a given, and be prepared for the unexpected snow bridge or crevasse.

- **Trenchlike lines in the snow.** This pattern often suggests a hidden crevasse.
- **Areas of increased tension.** Crevasses often form at areas of higher tension, such as glaciers outside curves or where its angle increases.
- **Cracks in the snow.** Cracks in the snow are often an indication that an underlying crevasse is present.

Crossing a Crevasse

The ideal course avoids a crevasse by crossing above its upper lip while keeping the rope path at 90 degrees to the crevasse path (rope straight— not in an S pattern). Doing this prevents a climber from taking a pendulum ride should he or she fall into the crevasse. During late summer, you will most likely be able to identify a crevasse and its upper lip, making it easy to circumnavigate. At other times it may be difficult to identify the presence of a crevasse or where its upper lip is located. In such instances, use your ice ax as a probe to identify a crevasse, and make every attempt to find its upward lip. A probe with a uniform resistance most likely indicates the presence of snow to ice ax depth. A probe that produces a sudden drop in resistance may indicate the presence of an underlying crevasse covered by a snow bridge. Although jumping a crevasse may seem a viable option, avoid the temptation. It is better to take the time to find the upper lip than spend all day getting pulled out of a crevasse—or worse.

Crossing a Snow Bridge

If you cannot find the crevass's upper lip, the next best option is a solid snow bridge. Identifying one of these, however, may present a challenge. In addition, be cautious when crossing a snow bridge, even if you have done it before. A snow bridge that is solid during cold times or in early morning may be unsafe during the midafternoon thaw. If the crossing is questionable, look for a better option. If none is available, the leader should try to find a safe passage by using an ice ax probe. During the probe, the rope should be kept taut; the other two climbers should brace themselves in case the lead climber breaks through the bridge. All team members should cross the snow bridge in the exact footsteps of those before them, while braced by others and keeping a taut rope.

■ Crevasse Rescue

If a member of your team disappears below the snow's surface, immediate action is critical, both to protect the person who fell and to prevent harm to others on the rope. The following steps are a general guideline on what should be done if a member of your team falls into a crevasse.

Prepare for Success

If traveling into an area of crevasse risk, all members of your team should attach their Prusik slings to the climbing rope. End climbers need to attach their slings to the body side of the rope. The middle person cannot predict which way the fall might take him or her and therefore should tie one sling to each side of the climbing rope. This requires moving one sling after a fall, but it's better to move one than two.

Arrest the Fall

The two standing team members should immediately fall into a self-arrest position (using the ice ax), facing the opposite direction of the rope's pull (the fallen individual).

Establish an Anchor

The other rope team establishes an initial anchor. If this isn't an option, the lead climber establishes an anchor while the middle climber maintains a self-arrest posture (see the Anchors and Ice Ax section of Chapter 12). This anchor should be placed on the lip side of the crevasse, approximately 10 feet down rope from the middle climber. The exact type of anchor used

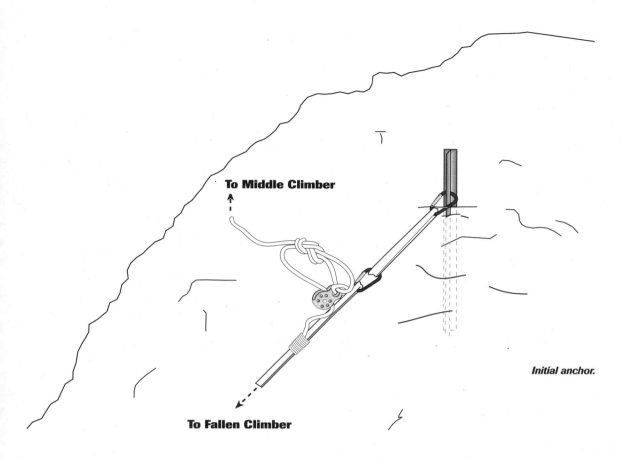

To Middle Climber

To Fallen Climber

Initial anchor.

will depend on your gear and conditions. The most often used anchors are the deadman, pickets, and bollards (see Anchors and Ice Ax section). Attach one end of a short sling to the anchor and the other end to a locking carabiner. A second, short sling attaches to the carabiner at one end and to the climbing rope—using a Prusik or Bachmann knot (see Chapter 10)—at the other end. The friction knot should be tied so that it can be moved toward the fallen climber. Finally, push the friction knot toward the crevasse until the slings are tight. At this point the climber in the self-arrest position can ease off—not come off—tension, transferring it to the new anchor. This should be done slow enough to evaluate the new anchor. Next add a locking carabiner to the one already on the sling, tie a figure-eight in the climbing rope (1 foot above the friction knot), and attach the figure-eight to the second carabiner. Finally, run the rope that lies between the friction knot and the figure-eight onto a pulley, and connect the pulley to the new carabiner. This setup provides a backup knot and establishes a rescue pulley system should it be needed.

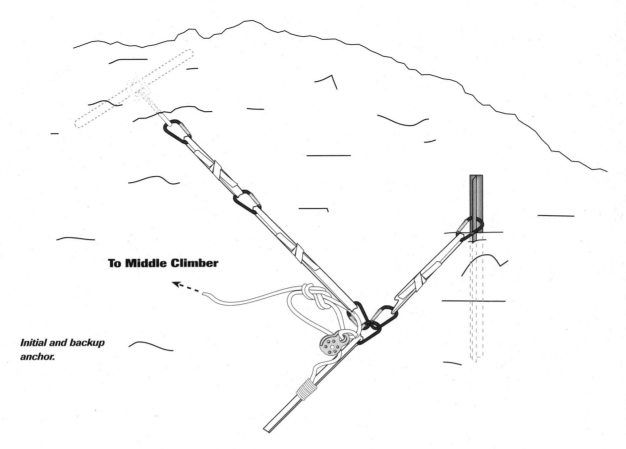

To Middle Climber

Initial and backup anchor.

Establish a Backup Anchor

Before the middle climber comes off the self-arrest position, set up a second anchor to the carabiner that is holding the pulley. This will probably require several slings held together with additional carabiners. Once this is done, the middle climber can come off the self-arrest position.

Evaluate Status of Fallen Climber

After the climbing rope is anchored, the lead climber needs to evaluate the fallen climber. The lead should approach the crevasse with much caution —using the ice ax to probe the snow and a sling self-belay in case of a fall. The sling self-belay is created from a sling attached to the climbing rope using a friction knot (Prusik or other) and the climber's seat harness. Once the crevasse edge has been reached, call out to the fallen climber and try to establish his or her status. Can the person perform a self-rescue using the Prusik sling, or is assistance required? Does the fallen climber need medical help? Clothing? The answers to these types of questions will determine the type of rescue performed.

Rescue

Depending on the situation, a self-rescue or team-rescue should be performed. Both methods warrant padding the rope at the crevasse's edge, as close as you can safely go. If this isn't done, the rope will dig into the snow and make it very difficult for the fallen climber to Prusik over the crevasse lip. Padding can be made from a pack, sleeping pad, or even the shaft of an ice ax. Regardless of what is used, the padding needs to be anchored so that it doesn't fall into the crevasse.

Self-Rescue. The uninjured climber can perform a self-rescue using the Texas Prusik technique:

- Remove the foot loops from your pocket; slip one loop over each foot, and cinch them down.
- Stand up in the foot loops. Doing this should take the tension off your climbing rope–seat harness attachment and transfer it to the climbing rope–Prusik sling.
- Unclip the rope from your chest harness.
- Remove slack from the Prusik sling that is attached to the climbing rope and your seat harness by sliding the friction knot up the climbing rope.
- Sit in the seat harness. This removes tension from the friction knot supporting the foot loops.
- Remove the slack from the Prusik sling that is attached to the climbing rope and your foot loops by sliding the friction knot up the climbing rope. This step requires bending the knees into the chest.
- Stand up on the foot loops. This removes tension on the friction knot supporting the seat harness.
- Repeat these steps until out of the crevasse.

Team Rescue. The type of team rescue used will depend on the fallen climber's status and number of members in your team. The rescue options most often used include rope pull, single pulley, and a Z pulley rescue.

- **Rope pull rescue.** Like a tug-of-war, this technique pits the rescue team's strength against the gravitational pull and rope drag of the fallen climber. The rescuers should position themselves beyond the friction knot holding the anchors to the climbing rope. The friction knot on the climbing rope is slid down the rope as it advances. This prevents the fallen climber from another fall should the rescuers lose their grip on the rope. Before the pulling begins, unclip the backup figure-eight from the carabiner. At this point the process is simple: Rescuers grab the rope and pull as hard as they can—one hand over the other—while another person makes sure the friction knot advances toward the fallen climber. This technique can be done with a conscious or unconscious subject.

- **Single pulley rescue.** The single pulley technique uses a second rope (or unused end of the climbing rope) and is a good option when the climbing rope is heavily entrenched into the crevasse's edge. The rope must be twice as long as the distance from the anchor to the climber. If a second rope is used, establish a primary and backup anchor away from the crevasse lip, and pad the lip at the point where the rope crosses it. Be sure to anchor the pad so that it doesn't fall into the crevasse. Place a pulley at the rope's midpoint and an unlocked locking carabiner on the pulley. Lower the pulley to the fallen climber and have the person attach and lock the carabiner to his or her seat harness. To keep the person upright, have him or her run the pulling side of the rope through the chest harness carabiner. At this point, the rescuers can pull on the unanchored end of the rescue rope using a hand-over-hand technique. Be sure to assign one rescuer to the initial climbing rope and have that person keep slack out of the climbing rope by constantly moving the friction knot toward the climber. This prevents the climber from another fall should the rescuers lose their grip on the rope. This technique works only when the climber is conscious.

- **Z pulley rescue.** The Z pulley uses two pulleys, giving rescuers an added mechanical advantage. This advantage is ideal when the rescue party is small and other, quicker options seem inappropriate for the situation. The rope takes on a Z appearance after the two pulleys are attached, giving this technique its name. The first pulley in the Z was established when the initial anchor was built (review establishing an anchor). The second pulley is established at the bend in the Z located between the rescue end of the rope, the crevasse, and the first pulley system. This pulley is attached to a carabiner that supports a sling running to the rope between the first pulley and the climber. The sling is tied to the rope using a friction knot. Use the following steps to pull the fallen climber to safety.

  - Unclip and untie the backup figure-eight (so that the rope can run through the pulley).
  - Place a rescuer at both friction knot locations so that they can take up slack as needed during the rope's advancement. This prevents the climber

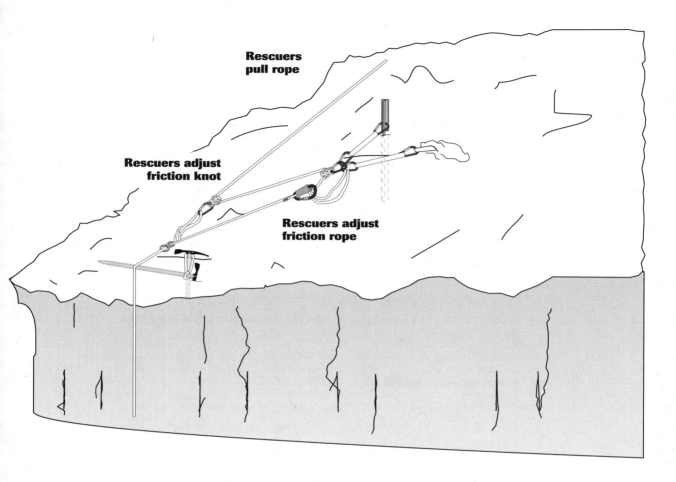

Rescuers pull rope

Rescuers adjust friction knot

Rescuers adjust friction rope

The Z pulley system.

from another fall should the rescuers lose their grip on the rope.

■ The remaining rescuers are placed at the far end of the rope (away from the climber) and begin a steady pull using a hand-over-hand technique. During this process the friction knot on the rope closer to the crevasse will pull the second pulley close to the first pulley. Stop pulling when this distance is about 2 feet, and allow the anchor's friction knot to take the weight of the fallen climber.

■ Move the friction knot located at the second pulley down the climbing rope (toward the climber) until it is taut.

■ Repeat this process until the climber is out of the crevasse.

The Z pulley system takes more time to set up but may be the only option when the fallen climber is unconscious and you are traveling in a small team where the mechanical advantage is needed.

Chapter Exercises

Practice how to hold an ice ax.

Practice self-belay and self-arrest handholds, and become familiar with both.

Practice ice ax use.

Practice the various ways in which you might use an ice ax to aid you during a trek. How would you hold and use it going uphill, downhill, or during a traverse? If you have snow, practice on a small slope. No snow? Practice on a grassy slope. It is important to feel the pull of the slope when learning how to hold the ax.

Practice glissading.

Now it is time to have some fun. Find a nonthreatening small snow-covered slope, and practice your glissading techniques. Develop a feel for how well the ice ax works as a brake and rudder. Be sure to dress for the conditions.

Practice ice ax self-arrests.

On the same hill you glissaded on, practice various self-arrest recoveries. Practice using different starting positions (head uphill, head downhill, chest up, chest down, etc.) so that you can develop a sense of what it takes to twist into a proper arrest posture.

Practice anchor placement.

Once the snow hits, pull out those anchors and ropes and head to the nearest snowdrift. If you don't have any drifts, look for safe areas where a snowplow has created a packed drift. Practice anchor placement to include making a Z pulley. It is a lot easier to fumble through this at a snow park than when a friend is dangling inside a crevasse.

*A twelve-channel
GPS unit.*

SECTION VI

Electronic Navigation

The Global Positioning System (GPS) and a handheld GPS receiver are tools that can augment solid navigation skills, but they should NEVER replace those skills. Learn how to use a map and compass before ever laying hands on a GPS unit. Remember that search-and-rescue team you met in the beginning of this book—the ones who ended up needing rescue themselves when the batteries in their GPS units died? They relied too much on technology without first learning basic navigation techniques. Once you've mastered those skills, however, a GPS receiver can be a great adjunct to your wilderness travel—pinpointing your position with greater accuracy and in less time than with traditional methods.

This section covers the nomenclature and use of the Global Positioning System and the GPS receiver.

Global Positioning System (GPS)

A GPS receiver is a great tool that you should consider adding to your gear to supplement your map and compass. The Global Positioning System is a worldwide radio-navigation system that uses satellites to help individuals, cars, boats, ship, and aircraft identify their locations. The system uses satellites that orbit the earth while sending a signal to a ground unit that includes the exact time it was sent. The signal travels at the speed of light. The ground stations use this information to calculate a satellite's location by applying it to the dead-reckoning formula: Rate X Time = Distance.

Velocity (Speed of Light) X Amount of Time It Took to Receive the Signal = Distance

GPS Makeup

Navigation Satellite Timing and Ranging (NAVSTAR) is the official U.S. Department of Defense name for the GPS. The system consists of a control segment (ground stations), space segment (satellites), and a user segment (GPS receiver) that allow the system to measure distance, velocity, and time.

■ Control Segment

The GPS control segment consists of one master ground station and four unmanned receiving stations. The four receiving stations constantly receive information from the satellites and then forward the information to the master control station. The master control station corrects the satellite information and, with the help of two antenna sites, sends updated information to the GPS satellites. Simply put, the control segment tracks each satellite—keeping them in proper orbit and telling them their exact location and time (each satellite has four atomic clocks).

■ Space Segment

The space segment consists of twenty-four satellites orbiting approximately 12,000 miles above the earth surface. All satellites follow one of six orbit paths and complete one orbit every twelve hours. This pattern makes it possible for all GPS users to receive at least six signals at any given point on earth. The satellites continuously send radio signals that the GPS receiver uses to identify its location. The signal travels at the speed of light and within line-of-sight limits. In other words, it can pass through clouds, glass, and plastic but not through tall buildings and mountains. The travel time multiplied by the speed of light equals the distance from the satellite to the GPS receiver.

■ User Segment

A GPS receiver is often a handheld device not much bigger than a small cell phone. These receivers consist of a radio receiver, a quartz clock, memory, and central processing unit (CPU). The receiver determines position by measuring the amount of time it takes the radio signal to arrive.

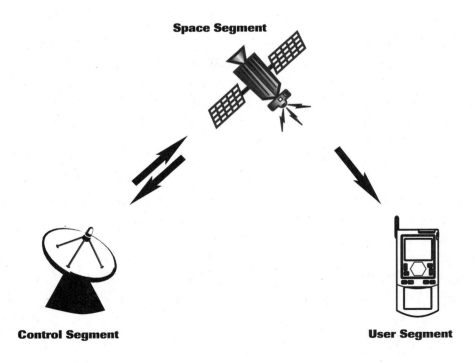

Space Segment

The GPS system.

Control Segment

User Segment

How the GPS Works

In order for the GPS receiver to work, it has to know the satellite **location** and **distance**. The ground station is constantly monitoring the satellite's location (orbit, altitude, and speed) and forwarding this information to the master control station. In turn, the master control station sends this updated information to the satellite and the satellite relays it to the GPS receiver. The GPS receiver knows the satellite's distance (how far away it is) by using the dead-reckoning formula.

Once the system locks into three satellites, it can use the three imaginary lines (from known satellite location in line with where it would meet the earth—distance) to triangulate and identify our approximate location (latitude and longitude). Using three satellites produces a potential error similar to what is experienced when triangulating with a compass. To better pinpoint location and identify latitude, longitude, and altitude requires locking into four satellites. Using a fourth satellites creates three additional triangulations, making it much more accurate.

GPS receivers equipped with a differential beacon receiver and beacon antenna are often accurate to within 3 meters. This feature allows the system to receive differential GPS correction signals transmitted from a network of towers. Simply put, the towers receive GPS satellite signals, correct small errors, and then transmit the corrected signal by beacon transmitters. Without this feature, the accuracy of the GPS is perhaps to within 15 meters. Once the GPS receiver's position is known, it can calculate other information such as bearings and distances.

Basic GPS Nomenclature

Although the GPS receiver design can vary from one manufacturer to another, it is pretty basic.

- **Batteries and antenna.** The type of power source or antenna your GPS has will probably depend on its intended use. For outdoor use I recommend a NiCad or lithium battery and an internal antenna. These types of batteries can handle cold weather, and an internal antenna removes the risk of breaking it.

- **Memory.** The amount of memory a GPS has may not seem important at first, but play it safe—the more the better. Think about the last time you purchased a computer and how quickly it filled up.

- **Channel.** Most modern-day GPS receivers come with twelve parallel multichannel designs. Three channels lock on a satellite for triangulation (latitude and longitude) and a fourth for altitude. These four channels continuously and simultaneously track the four satellites in the best geometrical positions relative to you. That leaves eight channels to track all other visible satellites, ensuring reliable, continuous, and uninterrupted navigation even if the unit drops one of the original four satellites.
- **Screen.** The GPS screen varies from one receiver to another; the one you choose will most likely depend on your budget.
- **Buttons.** Depending on the type of GPS you get, you will have an assortment of user buttons that guide you through the various options and functions. Read the user manual and become familiar with what each button does. The Garmin GPS 12 CX that I use has nine buttons, as noted in Table 13-1 below.

Table 13-1: Garmin GPS 12 CX Buttons

Button	Function
POWER	The POWER button turns the machine on and off.
PAGE	The PAGE button scrolls through the main data pages in succession and returns from a submenu page to a main page.
MARK	The MARK button captures a location and displays the mark position page.
GOTO	The GOTO button displays the GOTO page, where the waypoint can be highlighted for the GOTO operation. Pressing the GOTO button twice activates MOB (man overboard).
ENTER	The ENTER button confirms data entry and activates highlighted fields to allow data entry.
QUIT	The QUIT button returns the display to a previous page, or restores a data field's previous value.
IN and OUT	The IN and OUT buttons either increase or decrease the map scale.
Rocker Key	The rocker key controls the movement of the cursor and is used to select options and positions and to enter data.

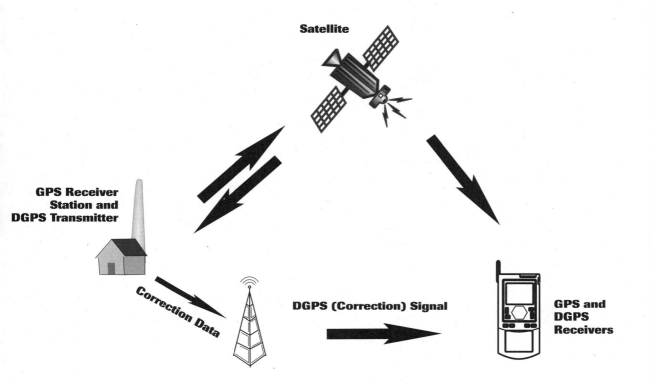

Satellite

GPS Receiver
Station and
DGPS Transmitter

Correction Data

DGPS (Correction) Signal

GPS and
DGPS
Receivers

■ **DGPS.** Differential GPS (DGPS) corrects errors in the satellite signal. To do this, a GPS receiver (reference station) is placed at a known location, allowing it to determine if there are errors in the satellite's signal. The error—difference between the measured and calculated range—for each satellite becomes the differential correction. This correction is sent to DGPS receivers and is applied to the GPS receiver calculation.

DGPS corrects for signal error.

A GPS, like a car, can come with the basic standard features or with all the bells and whistles. Take the time to decide what you need and whether the cost of the added features is worth it.

GPS Receivers: Main Pages

Most GPS receivers have main pages that support the receiver's functions. My system has five pages, which include satellite status, position page, map page, navigation page, and a menu page. Your system may have more or fewer functions. To get from one page to another, I just press the PAGE button. Thoroughly review the various pages your system uses. Don't fumble through them while in the wilderness. A simple review of pages your system may have is provided here.

■ Satellite Status Page

The Satellite Status page allows you to watch as the receiver locks in the satellites. Once my system has locked four satellites (giving me latitude/longitude and elevation), it automatically goes to the position page.

■ Position Page

The Position page provides the latitude and longitude of my current location along with time, track, speed, distance, and altitude. This page allows me to pinpoint my map location by applying the latitude, longitude, and altitude to the map I am using.

■ Map Page

The Map page displays all logged waypoints and major cities. The type of display you have will depend on your receiver unit. The display can be as simple as dots and names or as detailed as an actual map might appear. This page allows you to see the relationship between known points.

■ Navigation Page

The Navigation page provides a compass and bearing arrow. In addition, this page has several data fields that track time, distance, speed, and heading information.

■ Menu Page

The Menu page allows you to input waypoints, review waypoint lists, establish the closest waypoint to your location, create and review routes of travel, and set up the receiver so that it can relate to the map being used. Simply put, this page helps with GPS setup and information storage.

Table 13-2: **The Five Main Pages That Support the Author's Garmin GPS**	
Page	**Function**
Satellite Status	Displays satellite acquisition.
Position	Provides elevation and position.
Map	Shows logged waypoints, such as car and camp locations.
Navigation	Provides a compass that can be used for navigation.
Menu	Helps with GPS setup and information storage.

GPS and Map: Working Together

Using a GPS with a map implies that the receiver and map understand each other. This isn't always the case. In most instances you will need to adjust the GPS settings to match those used to create and interpret the map you are using. These settings include such things as the location format, map datum, unit measurement, direction display, and magnetic variation. These settings usually can be adjusted from the "Setup Menu," located on the Menu page.

■ Location Format

There are many coordinate systems used in the mapping world, but for all practical purposes you will probably use either latitude/longitude or Universal Transverse Mercator (UTM) coordinates. Although either coordinate system can be used with the GPS, if the datum isn't known, use latitude and longitude. Using the wrong datum for UTM coordinates results in a much larger error than with latitude/longitude. For details on how to identify and read these coordinates, refer to Chapter 3. When providing these coordinates to another person, don't forget to give the datum.

Latitude/longitude: 47° 22' 30" North, 115° 37' 30" East Datum NAD27
UTM: Zone 11 603750 Easting, 5247650 Northing Datum NAD27

■ Map Datum

The earth is not a perfect sphere, and its shape is not perfectly uniform. To compensate for this, mathematical models (datums) were created. These datums closely approximate the earth's shape for a given region, making the map more accurate. Every couple of decades, a new improved datum is created and put into use. In the United States, there are three datums that you may come across and use with your GPS:

- NAD27 (North American Datum 1927)
- NAD83 (North American Datum 1983)
- WGS84 (World Geodetic System 1984)

Although NAD27 is an old datum, it was used to create many topographic maps that are still in use. NAD83 is the datum that replaced it and that has been used to generate more recent maps. WGS84 is the default standard used in the United States for GPS operations. WGS84 is almost identical to NAD83, creating only small errors when interchanged. However, if the same were done between WGS84 and NAD27, the error would be noticeable. USGS topographic maps are either NAD27 or NAD83.

Knowing the map's datum is important if you intend to exchange information between the map and GPS. If this is the case, the GPS datum needs to be set to the map's datum. In addition, if you're relaying information such as your position to another GPS user, the datum needs to be included.

■ Unit Measurement

Metric, statute miles, and nautical miles are the options for measuring distance. The one you choose will depend on your situation, map, and life experiences. I prefer metric, since it is a universal measurement and the one I learned to use when reading maps.

■ Direction Display

Directions can be done in degrees or mils. For all practical purposes, degrees will be the choice in almost all outdoor navigation ventures.

■ Magnetic Variation

The magnetic variation can be set to true north, auto (GPS receiver sets it), user (you input the desired deviation), or grid (deviation set based on grid to true north deviation for the map in use). When user input is done, the east or west declination value must be given.

How to Use a GPS Receiver

The basic uses of a GPS are covered here. However, GPS technology is rapidly changing, and your device may do more. Take the time to read the owner's manual thoroughly. Learn your GPS and how to interpret its information. Learn how to input information such as waypoints, routes, and treks. Personally, I keep the "owner's quick reference guide" with my GPS wherever it goes on a trip with me. Regardless of which GPS you purchase, it will provide you with information about your position, waypoints, headings, distances, and progress.

■ Identifying Position and Waypoint Coordinates

The GPS uses the Satellite Status page to track and lock three to four satellites to determine your angular (latitude and longitude) or rectangular (UTM or other similar grid system) coordinates. These locations can be given a name and stored as waypoints for later reference. For all waypoints obtained using this method, the GPS uses the WGS84 datum. When a user manually changes the receiver's datum, the system adjusts the coordinates appropriately.

Waypoint coordinates can also be manually entered. When this is done, the GPS automatically converts the coordinates to fit with its internal WGS84 datum. For the converted coordinates to be correct, the GPS receiver must be set to the same datum the coordinates originated from before the coordinates are entered. Since the coordinates are stored at the internal WGS84 datum, they can be used with any map, provided the user's datum is changed prior to viewing them. In other words, all datum conversions are based on coordinates stored using the WGS84 datum.

Waypoints can be given names and icons that help identify them. The GPS's map screen can show waypoint locations and how they relate to other waypoints using name, icon, or both. In addition, the map screen will allow you to see your current location in relationship to the various waypoints.

■ Identifying Headings and Distance

Creating a route or using the GOTO button are the two GPS methods for identifying headings and distances. Regardless of which method is used, make sure the GPS, map, and compass parameters are in synch. This is especially true if you intend to switch between a GPS and a map and compass. Make sure the GPS is set to the coordinate and measurement system used by the map and is providing a heading that is similar to the compass heading for the same location. For me this means the GPS setup parameters provide latitude and longitude coordinates, metric measurements, and a magnetic compass heading.

GOTO Button

Pushing the GOTO button takes you to the GOTO waypoint page, allowing you to choose the desired waypoint. Once you select a waypoint, most GPS units change the screen to the Navigation page, where the waypoint is listed along with a heading and distance from your current location.

Creating Routes

The GPS allows you to create a route of travel using a series of sequenced waypoints. My Garmin GPS 12 CX allows me to do this in the ROUTES option, located on the Menu page. Once the waypoints are entered (in order of travel from starting point to final point), this page will display the heading and distance from one waypoint to another, along with the total distance from the first point to the last. The route is given a name, and once this name is activated the receiver guides you from point to point, letting you know when each one has been reached and what the heading and distance is to the next.

■ Monitoring Trip Progress

As long as the GPS is left on, it will monitor and record your movement. This track log allows you to reverse course and retrace the path that you came in on. Most GPS map screens will provide a line denoting the track of your travel, along with an icon showing your current location. The big downfall of monitoring trip progress is the drain it places on your battery.

Potential GPS Errors and Problems

Some basic problems associated with GPS receivers include operator error, system errors affecting position, and electronic failures.

■ Operator Errors

Operator error usually occurs when the GPS is not in synch with the map or compass being used. The best way to avoid this problem is to set up the GPS prior to each trip. Take the time to enter the correct coordinate system (UTM, latitude/longitude, etc.), hemisphere if using latitude and longitude, datum, measurement units, and compass declination setting.

■ System Errors Affecting Position

System errors can occur as a result of signal delays, clock errors, and satellite related problems (orbit, geometry, and visibility).

Signal Delays

Any delay in the satellite signal makes the satellite appear to be farther away than it actually is. As a result in of the delay, GPS errors can occur. There are two main causes of these delays—the atmosphere and objects such as large rocks or tall buildings. The atmosphere increases signal time by slowing it down. With large objects, the signal time increases when the signal bounces off the object before reaching the receiver. The GPS has a built-in model that estimates signal errors created by the atmosphere. Large objects, however, cannot be predicted, and no built-in adjustments are available.

Clock Errors

The satellite has four atomic clocks that are constantly monitored and adjusted by the control system. The GPS receiver, however, does not have an atomic clock. The receiver's built-in clock can create very small timing errors.

Satellite-Related Problems

A satellite's orbit, geometry, and visibility have been known to cause small errors in the GPS. Satellite orbital errors can cause inaccuracies in reported satellite locations. Satellite geometry refers to the relative position of the satellites at any given time. Optimal geometry occurs when the satellites are located at wide angles to one another. Sound familiar? This is also true when triangulating with a map and compass. Bad geometry occurs when the satellites are located in a line or a tight grouping. The wider the angles, the more precise the triangulation process is. Buildings, terrain, and electronic interference directly affect satellite visibility. Poor visibility causes position errors or no reading at all.

■ Electronic Failures

Like all other electronic devices, a GPS is vulnerable to cold, moisture, sand, and heat. All battery-operated devices are prone to cold, soaking, and corrosion. If you intend to use your GPS, take care of it. Protect it from harsh environment and climatic conditions by using a protective carrying case. You might even consider placing it inside a heavy, zippered freezer bag. In addition, in cold environments, keep the batteries between layers of clothing, and when not in use turn the GPS off.

GPS and the Six-Point Navigation Checklist

The GPS can be used to create your six-point checklist, but it should be done in conjunction with a map and compass. This is especially true when creating waypoints, which should be part of your detailed terrain evaluation. Just because you have a GPS, don't think you can skip this very important part of planning your trek! In addition, never rely solely on a GPS—always carry a map and compass. You never know when the batteries might fail or when your GPS unit won't be able to lock in enough satellites.

Table 13-3: Route-Finding: The Six-Point Checklist

Point	Description
1. Heading	Compass heading from point A to point B.
2. Distance	Distance measured from point A to point B.
3. Pace Count	Number of paces between each terrain feature and total paces from point A to point B.
4. Terrain Evaluation	Be aware of and document each prominent land feature between point A and point B.
5. Point Description	Understanding how the final point should look is key to knowing your destination has been reached.
6. ETA	Estimated time of arrival may be altered by terrain and other features.

Chapter Exercises

Get out that GPS and owner's manual.

Although there are many similarities between GPS receivers, get out your owner's manual and walk through how yours functions. Format it for the map you will be using.

1. Latitude and longitude, UTM, etc.

2. Datum

3. Units of measurement (kilometers, miles, etc.)

4. Magnetic variation

Create a six-point checklist.

Use the GPS to establish a six-point checklist. Perhaps this can be done at the same time you are creating a checklist using a map and compass and you can compare your results (make sure the datum is the same). Do this several times, working through the various methods of finding a route. Have fun.

Index

About the Author

Greg Davenport is the founding member of Simply Survival, a wilderness education program based out of Stevenson, Washington, and the author of numerous books related to outdoor survival. He has been conducting wilderness trips for more than twenty years and has students from around the world follow him into the mountains and deserts to learn both basic and advanced wilderness navigation and survival skills. As a former U.S. Air Force Survival Instructor, he is considered one of the best global survival experts in the world and has consulted or appeared on such shows as *48 Hours, BBC, NBC Nightly News, CBS News, ABC PrimeTime Thursday, NBC Today, MSNBC,* and *Fox and Friends.* Greg is the host of *Risk Takers/History Makers,* which appears on the History Channel. This show re-creates the incredible journeys of past explorers such as John Wesley Powell and Ernest Shackleton.